LIFEBLOOD OF THE PARISH

T0385495

NORTH AMERICAN RELIGIONS

Series Editors: Tracy Fessenden (Religious Studies, Arizona State University), Laura Levitt (Religious Studies, Temple University), and David Harrington Watt (History, Haverford College)

In recent years a cadre of industrious, imaginative, and theoretically sophisticated scholars of religion have focused their attention on North America. As a result the field is far more subtle, expansive, and interdisciplinary than it was just two decades ago. The North American Religions series builds on this transformative momentum. Books in the series move among the discourses of ethnography, cultural analysis, and historical study to shed new light on a wide range of religious experiences, practices, and institutions. They explore topics such as lived religion, popular religious movements, religion and social power, religion and cultural reproduction, and the relationship between secular and religious institutions and practices. The series focuses primarily, but not exclusively, on religion in the United States in the twentieth and twenty-first centuries.

Books in the series:

Ava Chamberlain, *The Notorious Elizabeth Tuttle: Marriage, Murder, and Madness in the Family of Jonathan Edwards*

Terry Rey and Alex Stepick, *Crossing the Water and Keeping the Faith: Haitian Religion in Miami*

Jodi Eichler-Levine, *Suffer the Little Children: Uses of the Past in Jewish and African American Children's Literature*

Isaac Weiner, *Religion Out Loud: Religious Sound, Public Space, and American Pluralism*

Hillary Kaell, *Walking Where Jesus Walked: American Christians and Holy Land Pilgrimage*

Brett Hendrickson, *Border Medicine: A Transcultural History of Mexican American Curanderismo*

Annie Blazer, *Playing for God: Evangelical Women and the Unintended Consequences of Sports Ministry*

Elizabeth Pérez, *Religion in the Kitchen: Cooking, Talking, and the Making of Black Atlantic Traditions*

Kerry Mitchell, *Spirituality and the State: Managing Nature and Experience in America's National Parks*

Finbarr Curtis, *The Production of American Religious Freedom*

M. Cooper Harriss, *Ralph Ellison's Invisible Theology*

Shari Rabin, *Jews on the Frontier: Religion and Mobility in Nineteenth-Century America*

Ari Y. Kelman, *Shout to the Lord: Making Worship Music in Evangelical America*

Joshua Dubler and Isaac Weiner, *Religion, Law, USA*

Elizabeth Fenton, *Old Canaan in a New World: Native Americans and the Lost Tribes of Israel*

Alyssa Maldonado-Estrada, *Lifeblood of the Parish: Men and Catholic Devotion in Williamsburg, Brooklyn*

Lifeblood of the Parish

Men and Catholic Devotion in
Williamsburg, Brooklyn

Alyssa Maldonado-Estrada

NEW YORK UNIVERSITY PRESS

New York

NEW YORK UNIVERSITY PRESS
New York
www.nyupress.org

References to Internet websites (URLs) were accurate at the time of writing. Neither the author nor New York University Press is responsible for URLs that may have expired or changed since the manuscript was prepared.

Library of Congress Cataloging-in-Publication Data
Names: Maldonado-Estrada, Alyssa, author.
Title: Lifeblood of the parish : men and Catholic devotion in Williamsburg, Brooklyn /
Alyssa Maldonado-Estrada.
Description: New York : New York University Press, [2020] | Series: North American
religions | Outgrowth of the author's thesis (Ph.D.)—Princeton University, 2018. |
Includes bibliographical references and index.
Identifiers: LCCN 2020004693 | ISBN 9781479872244 (cloth) |
ISBN 9781479830497 (paperback) | ISBN 9781479868346 (ebook) |
ISBN 9781479887941 (ebook)
Subjects: LCSH: Shrine Church of Our Lady of Mount Carmel (Brooklyn, New York, N.Y) |
Brooklyn (New York, N.Y.)—Church history. | Brooklyn (New York, N.Y.)—Religious life
and customs. | Williamsburg (New York, N.Y)—Religious life and customs. | Masculinity—
Religious aspects—Catholic Church. | Catholic men—New York (State)—Brooklyn—
Religious life. | Catholic men—New York (State)—Brooklyn—Social life and customs. |
Italian American Catholics—New York (State)—Brooklyn—Religious life. |
Paulinus, of Nola, Saint, approximately 353–431—Cult—New York (State)—Brooklyn. |
Catholic Church—New York (State)—Brooklyn—Customs and practices.
Classification: LCC BX4603.B8 M35 2020 | DDC 282/.74723—dc23
LC record available at https://lccn.loc.gov/2020004693

New York University Press books are printed on acid-free paper, and their binding materials are chosen for strength and durability. We strive to use environmentally responsible suppliers and materials to the greatest extent possible in publishing our books.

Manufactured in the United States of America

10 9 8 7 6 5 4 3 2 1

Also available as an ebook

For James, my one

CONTENTS

FIGURES

Introduction

The way into Catholic masculinity in Brooklyn is through an unlikely door—the door to the basement of the Shrine Church of Our Lady of Mount Carmel (OLMC). The basement is the hiding place and workshop for devotional objects. If the sanctuary, with its marble walls and stained glass and its chapel full of bright-eyed saints, is the most obviously sacred part of the church, the basement is its foil, a graveyard of defunct statues. Dusty angels lie tipped over on shelves. Saints recline injured on tables like in nineteenth-century operating theaters. Figures of Jesus with broken benediction fingers are surrounded by stacks of decades-old paint cans. In the basement there seem to be no hierarchies of objects sacred and profane. Everything is equally coated in a layer of grime. Through the concrete ceiling, organ music often bleeds into room, interrupted by the grating sounds of a table saw. It smells like paint and glue, not wax and incense. Dim, like a dungeon, and full of nooks and cavities for religious refuse, the basement is where a lot of men spend their time. While it might not seem so on first glance, the basement, just as much as the sanctuary above, is a site of religious practice.

Every Saturday, and sometimes on weekday evenings, a group of men in cruddy clothes can be found there. Some smooth thick glue over strips of paper to make papier-mâché molds of saints like Francis, Rita, and Anthony. From so many strips, saints' bodies are formed and their iconographic attributes carved. Paper and glue turn into lilies, rosaries, and Bibles. Others prime the saints' bodies with thick white coats of paint, readying them for colors—brown for Saint Anthony, dark gray and black for Saint Rita's habit, deep red for the Sacred Heart of Jesus, and brown and gold for Our Lady of Mount Carmel. Often while the solemn ritual of Mass takes place above, the basement is full of laughter as men joke about whether angels have penises and play doctor as they patch up the broken bodies of the saints. They do all this work to prepare for the crowning event of the church's calendar: the Feast of Our Lady of Mount Carmel and the Dance of the Giglio, which have been celebrated in Williamsburg since 1887 and 1903, respectively.

This book examines how religious men come to understand themselves and be recognized as men. At this church men walk on processions, are devoted to saints, and see themselves as sustainers of their church. For the Catholic men with whom I spent six years, religion does not always look like seriousness, piety, and interiority. Religion can be raucous and playful. Religion can be about revelry and friendship. In this corner of North Brooklyn, the stuff of Catholic devotion may not always be rosary beads, prayerful petitions, and pews, but might include table saws and spectacular displays of strength. In this book I trouble what it means to be devoted and argue that devotion can be found in tattooed skin, in wearing costumes and reenacting the lives of saints, and in mundane acts like painting and woodworking. Devotion is not simply about intimate connections to the saints but contributes to the very construction of masculinity and authority in religious communities. Angry, disaffected men, empty pews, and shuttering parishes define this contemporary moment in discussions of American men and discussions of the Catholic Church. In a time when scholars and journalists alike agree that there is a growing malaise among men and that the Catholic Church is in crisis, I argue that churches continue to be vital sites for the making of masculinity. This book centers on the OLMC in Williamsburg, Brooklyn, an ethnic parish established in 1887 and built in a neighborhood of industry and manufacturing. It now exists in a neighborhood that is a brand, a concentrated site of capital and development, and a destination for tourists and young New Yorkers alike. By all reasoning, OLMC seems to be a holdover from both an earlier time in Brooklyn and an earlier time in American Catholic history, yet it endures. It may be but one parish, but it demonstrates how churches provide men with spaces to gather, to build and maintain networks of mentorship and friendship, and continue to offer appealing and enduring models of manhood. This book explores how men imagine and construct themselves and their rituals as the lifeblood of the parish. It is about scotch, swords, inked skin, and stacks of money: the adornment and kinetics of the Catholic male body.

On a walk through Williamsburg in July, one might run into the Feast of Our Lady of Mount Carmel. During the feast the streets are electrified by the sounds of a brass band, a turning Technicolor Ferris wheel, and all the olfactory markers of Italian Americanness: the heat around the zeppole tent, the simmering fat and acid of sausage and peppers. Temporarily, the church and its surrounding streets become a terrain to eat street food, process with saint statues, pay respects to the Blessed Mother, light candles, drink beer, smoke cigars, gamble, and play carnival games. At the corner of North Ninth and Havemeyer streets, unmissable because of its sheer scale, is a massive seven-story tower. Piercing the sky, it stands in stark contrast to the glass of the surrounding condominiums. It is quite baroque. Made of steel, wood, and papier-mâché and studded with saints, arches, and columns, it blends ecclesiastical architecture and craft. In 2019 it was even adorned with bells, a Risen Christ, and flying *putti* and wrapped in a larger-than-life rosary. Like an exclamation point, it punctuates the block of the church. This tower is the giglio. It dwarfs the surrounding condominiums and the holdover buildings, those brick structures and old homes from the early twentieth century that have not yet been knocked down for new luxury developments. During the feast the giglio becomes a devotional machine.[1] During the Dance of the Giglio over one hundred men lift all four tons of the structure down the streets in front of the parish under the brutal July sun. The aluminum poles dig into their shoulders. They become an orderly tangle of limbs, tanned arms and legs clad in cargo shorts. They do this all in honor of San Paolino (Saint Paulinus), the patron saint of Nola, a small town outside of Naples in the Campania region of southern Italy. They do this for the love of the parish, each other, the saints, and Italian American tradition. In this twenty-first-century neighborhood, revelry, play, power, and devotion are entangled.

Beginning in late February or March, the men who organize the Feast of Our Lady of Mount Carmel and the Dance of the Giglio meet in the church's lower hall—a multipurpose room with a gray floor, large folding tables, bright fluorescent lighting, and subway-tiled walls. The room used to be the church's bowling alley but now has a stage in the back for theater performances. Each Wednesday evening in the spring men stand around outside the church, catching up and smoking cigarettes before descending into the lower hall. Some live nearby and others travel

Figure 1.1. The giglio surrounded by new construction, 2014. Photo by the author.

Figure 1.2. Lifters, 2014. Photo by the author.

in from Queens, Staten Island, and Long Island for the meetings. They often wear T-shirts from feasts past or other garments that speak to their various affiliations, like the fraternal order of the Sons of Italy or the Knights of Columbus. At the start of the meeting the pastor always leads the men in prayer, often the Our Father and the Hail Mary. To conclude the prayers he says "Our Lady of Mount Carmel," and the men respond "Pray for us" in unison, their gruff voices filling the large space. "San Paolino"—"Pray for us."

Gender and Devotion

What do a Catholic community and devotional culture offer contemporary men? How do men see themselves as central to the vitality of embattled Catholic communities? Broadly, this is a study of Catholic masculinities: masculinity as an ongoing process and shifting formations of values, performances, and practices produced and reproduced (in this case) by men, but also as affective, embodied experiences. Masculinity and religious identity are produced in and through the body. Religious masculinities are composed not just of values or traits, but also of ways of feeling and moving individually and collectively through the world. This book is an ethnography of Catholic men, not those in vestments or those who can act as *alter Christus*, but laymen.[2] In exploring networks of laymen, I argue that churches, and devotional culture in particular, offer enduring sites of homosociality, places for men to socialize and be socialized into Catholicism. Men enact their Catholicism *together*. They do their devotion together. They spend time in church together, often in peripheral spaces that fall outside of the scope of the ethnographic gaze or the archive. Stories about their religious lives prominently feature their relationships with male kin, mentors, and friends.[3]

The history of Catholicism has been a history of men wielding religious, worldly, and relational power. Catholicism is a tradition in which male power has often been spectacular and sacramental, so the hierarchy occupies public discussions and imaginings of the relationship between gender and religious authority. Many scholars have turned to women's devotion, which had been invisible in the public history of the Church before feminist historiography and religious studies scholarship decentered the clergy. This scholarship did the crucial work of highlighting women's practices and the creative ways they have dwelled within the disciplines and structures of Catholicism. Focusing on domestic piety, prayer lives, and material culture introduced new ways of thinking about lived religion and enriched our understanding of the many contexts in which people live and practice their religious identities.[4] But this turn has created a binary that codes devotionalism as an especially female domain of practice. It has been almost doxa that devotion is what women do: how they petition, honor, and love the saints in and outside of church and how the saints structure their relationships to those on earth and those in heaven. I question and complicate this scholarly and popular assumption about devotion and argue for a more capacious definition of devotion that thinks about how religious practice shapes and is shaped by gender and power but also refuses to put the practices, objects, and affects of devotionalism in a box as the purview of women.

What we find at this church and its feast is an intergenerational community of men dedicated to transmitting traditions and keeping their parish afloat by contributing their bodies, time, and labor. In this community men are bearers of devotion and feel themselves responsible for its reproduction. Whenever I have formally and informally talked about this project, I have heard common responses: "What's Catholic about this?" or "Does the Vatican know about this?" Men and their revelry are not seen as the real stuff of religion. Some presume that "men do all this, but surely behind the scenes there are women planning all of it, right?" or "There must be some matriarchal core to this?" or "Women must be raising the money, right?," assuming that where there are men doing religion there are women working the gears and making things run, doing the invisible and underappreciated labor. While that is often true, this ritual and community asks us to look for where and how men *do* religion. In this devotional community, men are both its public face and its machinery.

Devotion is sustaining work. According to the Church, devotions are the many forms of piety that surround and "extend" the liturgical and sacramental life of Catholics. The catechism categorizes venerating relics, walking on processions, going on pilgrimages, and performing object-centered actions like wearing medals and rosaries and praying as devotions.[5] From this definition it is clear: devotion is what Catholics *do* to connect with the divine, often outside of the contexts of Mass or the sacraments. Praying to a saint for the well-being of one's family, install-ing an image of the Sacred Heart of Jesus in one's home, adoring the Eucharist, and visiting a shrine all do the work of sustaining and nour-ishing earthly and heavenly relationships. Devotion maintains those networks and the very presence and vitality of the divine in everyday life. Devotion sustains communities. Identities accrue and are enacted through devotional actions. Acts such as walking on a procession, wear-ing a brown scapular, and lighting candles go beyond individual piety; they construct communities both visible and invisible, past and pres-ent.[6] Devotion is composed of all the actions that sustain relationships, communities, and institutions—actions that exceed the bounds of the liturgy, that exceed the bounds of religious authority, that exceed overtly religious spaces and times.

Devotion is also about service. For these Catholics in Brooklyn, de-votion to the parish matters over all. While they seldom talk of God, what they do say is that above all else they are devoted to their parish, to keeping it a vital community. This does not necessarily mean show-ing up at Mass every Sunday. Devotion to the parish means using their skills to benefit and support the community: whether that be coding a website, constructing the giglio, or fundraising and accounting to ensure the feast is a financial success. Devotion means building and mobilizing one's expertise to serve the church and the saints.

Devotion is about time, training, and giving. Mundane activities like painting, posting, and working long hours are all understood within a broader framework as the dedication required to keep the community cohesive and to keep traditions stable. While the Church has historically understood devotions and nonliturgical practices as "popular piety" that is supplemental to the liturgy, in Brooklyn devotion is not just ancil-lary to Catholic life. The stakes are much higher: devotion is under-stood as the very work of keeping the parish alive. Devotion—broadly conceived as the many ways Catholics demonstrate their love for the saints and their parish—does the work of sustaining the institution in Williamsburg.

Joe Mascia, the social media manager for the parish and feast, cap-tured this devotional ethic and practice. At the end of the feast, after twelve days of walking on processions, videoing Masses, and counting collections, he was "spent: mentally, physically, everything." Reflecting on all those actions, he explained, "You've gotta give your time . . . you've just gotta be here for the right reasons, doing the stuff to make this feast happen, to keep this parish alive." While Joe does not live in Williamsburg, he commutes for meetings, Masses, and events. Facing a long drive back home that night and explaining what motivates him, he said, "You've got to have a love for this feast. And traveling back and forth from Staten Island every day is rough. It's devotion."

Scholar of American Catholicism Robert Orsi has argued that "Catholic devotionalism is a woman's world," that "the qualification of a popular devotion as a 'women's devotion' is redundant."[7] In ways both spectacular and mundane, women have borne devotional burdens and worked behind the scenes to secure the spiritual and material stability of their families and their religious institutions. The most sensational and memorable image from Orsi's groundbreaking study of Italian Catholic immigrants in early twentieth-century East Harlem, *The Madonna of 115th Street*, is of a woman "crawling on her hands and knees from the back of the church toward the main altar, dragging her tongue along the pavement." When she tired, her family members helped drag her, a literal display of how devotion has fallen on the shoulders—and knees—of women.[8] The dragged, hurting woman has been a dominant figure of the field's imagining of devotion, her body a metaphor for its intensity. From the literature on gender and devotion, we know of Catholics, often women, desperate, crawling, crying, bleeding, or gazing upon images of the bloodied, open corpus of Christ and/or the warm visages of the saints.[9] Men may have power in the Church, but women feel its dictums, disciplines, and devotions in their bodies, perhaps more abundantly than those men.

Since *Madonna*, scholars have understood devotion as what women do in the privacy of their homes, in the streets, and with each other. Many have done the important work of shifting the lens away from institutional histories, away from those who wield traditional sorts of authority and power, and have challenged the very spaces in which scholars look for religion.[10] This has meant a shift away from men: as priests, pastors, preachers—those who called the shots, whose voices dominate the archive, who surfaced all too often in studies of religion and obscured all of those laypeople, largely women, who contributed to their communities and had complex religious lives. Many have argued that when Catholic devotional traditions thrive, it is because of women's participation; when they whither, it is because they are becoming irrel-evant to women.[11] Devotional traditions are passed on through matri-lineal networks. Some have come up with formulas in which women are the transmitters of devotion and children are receivers of devotion as their female relatives instill in them emotional attachments to saints.[12] Whether presented in mathematical or poetic terms, Catholic devo-tion has been gendered feminine. The binary of clerical men / women devout persists.[13] Men are priests, they are soldiers, they are fathers, they are employees, they are husbands, but seldom are they devotees. It seems clear: men are not bearers of devotion, and they have a mini-mal role in its transmission.[14] When men peek through the pages in the feminine sphere of devotion, it is as husbands dragged on processions, under threat of no dinner, or "roped into" devotions by their more pious wives.[15] It is odd to say it, but laymen are largely invisible in histories of Catholic devotional life. Or they are foils, by contrast heightening the piety of women.[16]

Unfortunately, these kinds of gendered frameworks limit who counts as a religious subject and whom we deem worthy of study. The idea that women are more religious or more prevalent in church and men's sub-sequent hand-wringing over it have shaped histories and historiogra-phies of religion (particularly Christianity) and masculinity in America. In books, polls, and pulpits men may be the leaders, but women are the sustainers of institutions. This binary often occludes the everyday religious lives of laymen. Scholarship and survey data alike firmly cat-egorize women in the United States as more "devout" than men. Pew Research Center, in an analysis of a worldwide survey, found that Chris-tian women were largely more religious than men and that the gender difference was most prominent in the Americas. They measured religi-osity according to a few factors: women were more likely to be affiliated with a particular religion, were more likely to believe in hell, heaven, and angels, had higher rates of weekly attendance at religious services, and prayed more frequently.[17] While these survey data are recent, they reflect the more pervasive idea that women are more devout, an idea that inflamed men's religious movements in the nineteenth and twenti-eth centuries.

When it is studied, men's religion, especially Christian men's religion, has been conceived of as revivalistic and reactionary. The well-known

Muscular Christianity movement from 1890 to 1920 has become para-digmatic in this regard. Men's religion was a reaction against a perceived feminization of Christian identity. Throughout the United States, white men hardened their bodies, imagined and emulated a more virile Christ, and took to the gym and the outdoors to forcefully supplant introspec-tion and sentimentality with athleticism. This trend in scholarship con-tinues, and masculinity is often explored on a national scale rather than approached in its local forms. Men's religion is consistently used to think through ideas and structures of nation and power, and women's religion is consistently used to think through intimacy and relationality. Most recently the Promise Keepers, a 1990s revival, captured the imagination of scholars and the public. Christian men who gathered by the tens of thousands in stadiums, the Promise Keepers seemed to be reacting to the global economic changes and rights movements of the previous de-cades. Downward mobility was more common than upward mobility for young Americans in the 1990s.[18] Deindustrialization and the rise of the service economy and a more global corporate order destabilized tradi-tional routes to manhood for white men, like being the financial head of household. The feminist movement and rising rates of divorce and abortion worried Christian men throughout the nation and destabilized the traditional roles of husband, homeowner, breadwinner, and father as routes to manhood. Overwhelmingly lonely, and perhaps feeling so-cially, economically, and spiritually impotent, they turned to religion.[19] This reactionary impulse continues to frame the appeal of religion to men. Promise Keepers' return in 2020, with its "new era of men's minis-try," responds to the social and religious needs of politically disaffected Christian men, reacting to what they see as a culture of political correct-ness, "misguided" ideas about gender fluidity, and a "culture increasingly toxic to masculinity."[20]

Yet revivalism is not the only way that men engage with religious identity and devotion. Masculinity should be visible to the scholarly gaze or part of conversation not just when it is seemingly in peril or remaking, or when national movements crystallize to restore or retrieve a masculinity lost or make masculinity anew. Those who proclaim a (pe-rennial) "crisis of masculinity" most loudly have dominated discussions of masculinity and religion.[21] Masculinity should be approached in its enduring and local forms, as always being promised by and constructed in religious communities. This parish provides a window into a men's world of devotion that has endured for over a century and demonstrates how devotional practices confer authority and bolster men's reputations. How does Catholicism provide venues for the performance and naturalization of gender? How do Catholic rituals and practices *make* men?

Masculinity is not inherently tied to or emergent from male bodies. Bodies, objects, and practices are *masculinized*. They are made and imagined as the domain and natural expressions of those with male bodies. Here I am interested in those processes by which subjects come to understand themselves and act in the world as Catholic men, through religious practice and individual and communal action. I agree with scholars R. W. Connell and Sarah Imhoff that masculinities "are configurations of practice that are accomplished in social action," and assemblages of the "values, rituals, and ideas" available in a culture that are performed in routine, processual, relational, and material ways.[22] As sociologist Shannon Davis put it, "Gender is not a thing that is done, that is, a noun. Instead, masculinity is a process." Judith Butler declared that gender is "an identity instituted through a stylized repetition of acts"; it is not natural, but accomplished, a verb as much as an identity.[23] We can look at many of the public rituals of the feast as "doing gender," the acts through which values of masculinity and manhood congeal and are repeated, broadcast, and emulated. Because hierarchy is central to the feast and there are men who wield more power than others, men "elicit deference" from those below them in rank with embodied acts and props that signify that authority. They command the respect of spectators and signify "with or without conscious awareness—that [they] possesses the capacities to make things happen."[24]

Through this study of a Catholic parish and those men who are institutionally visible and valued, I trace the processes through which men become respected public figures in their community, and those most visible here are white, heterosexual men. They are eligible to be lauded by and included within a Catholicism that over and again asserts a divinely given gender binary and warns of the separation of biological sex from gender.[25] The Church's rejection of gender theory and its theology of essentialism and complementarity define those who do not conform out of existence, except as aberrations. That is not to say there are not queer or gay Catholics generally, but here, in a community that so publicly and loudly proclaims a certain kind of masculinity, these Catholics are much less visible and less welcome.[26] Those few (that I know of) who are gay are less visible in the feast and deliberately confined to the margins of space and history. I explore the process through which they are excluded from performances that enshrine a certain kind of heterosexual manhood.

While discussions of hegemonic masculinity—the privileged, rewarded masculinity in any given society—have seen emotional detachment, competition, and objectifying women as the glue of relationships between men, the religious community at the parish complicates that. The relationships between men are also built on real affections and shared religious practice.[27] Costumes, money, cigars, liquor, and fun are all part of this men's world of Catholic ritual. If we bracket these activities off as simply social or camaraderie, an entire world of consequential practices that tether people to their religious communities falls out of view. Catholic tradition allows men revelry, dress-up, and fun in ways it does not necessarily allow women. Play is a male privilege, the dividend for men's work.[28]

Men are allowed to be "irreverently" devoted because they are also imagined to be uniquely productive: they *work*, they *produce*, their bodies are imagined as uniquely capable of bearing the literal weight of tradition. Men and women might both be devoted to the saints, but men reap different benefits from their devotional labor.[29] While work and productivity do not actually correlate to male bodies, these values are charged as masculine in the community. Men's work is more valued and thus more visible than that of women, even when it occurs backstage. Their work is semantically charged as the labor of survival and longevity. Whether work is seen as consequential or is considered frivolous is a gendered and gendering process.

Ethnography and Religion Backstage

This book is a methodological provocation on how and where to find religion. I trouble what practices fit under its analytical umbrella and how to study the often inaccessible, invisible, and unmarked construction of masculinity in action. Churches and devotional communities are as much arenas for the making of masculinity as boxing rings, stadiums, workplaces, and fraternities. Architecturally, churches are much more than sanctuaries; to understand Catholic masculinity is to fully explore the interiors of church buildings—places like meeting rooms, rectories, and basements—and the practices that take place there.

The streets in Williamsburg are alive as sites of religious negotiation and ritual only temporarily. This is not simply a study of religion in public. While the giglio is a show of muscles, strength, sweat, and struggle, it is but a piece of the whole picture. This book offers a view not only of the foreground of ritual, where men's authority is performed in public, but also of the background, where it is constructed, contested, and reproduced.[30] I consider peripheral sites of practice, like the basement and the rectory, and argue that through the mechanics of ritual production we can discern the mechanics of gender.

I began this story not on the streets but in the basement. The basement is where the giglio hibernates for the rest of the year, dismembered. From the streets, the Dance of the Giglio might look like a brute and uncomplicated display of masculinity, another Catholic tradition in which men lift heavy things (there are many of these, which may or may not be surprising).[31] Before the ritual, men take celebratory shots of limoncello and moonshine, and some of them break for beers between lifts. From the street the giglio looks like all brawn. But this view is not enough to understand the complexities of gender and religious identity at work here and in Catholic devotional traditions more broadly.

This study privileges the spaces where men spend their time, where they move with ease, where they hang out with friends, where they conceive of themselves as contributing to their church. Spending time with men like Neil brought those peripheral spaces into view. When he was a little boy, Neil would watch the giglio in awe from behind the gate of his house. He lived on North Ninth Street, right around the corner from the church, in a house that has since been demolished for the construction of new condominiums. While no one in his family was involved in the feast, Neil has always been a parishioner of OLMC. He went to Catholic school there and completed all of his sacraments within the walls of the orange-brick church. As a kid he would watch the older men lift the giglio, dreaming of being a lifter. In Neil's words, "I could see it, the giglio right down the block at the corner from the front of the house. When I was six I wasn't allowed to go past the fence, so I would stand there and watch. Each year I would sneak a little farther down the block, a little more. . . ." Neil was entranced by the giglio and by the men who animated it, so much so that when he was ten his father approached one of the feast organizers and said his son wanted to help out. "That's how I started, I would help them carry the pieces, get them water. You do whatever you can to help." He was a tall, husky kid and fulfilled the dream of lifting when he was twelve years old, "as soon as I was able to reach without standing on my tippy toes."

"You do whatever you can do to help." When I first heard Neil say these words, I did not understand their magnitude, the way they anchor the philosophy of work and dedication in this community and the way they would soon come to define my own relationship with the parish and the feast. Neil told me this story in the summer of 2014, right after my first few months of research. It was August and we were sitting in Sal's Pizzeria, an old neighborhood joint on Lorimer Street that all the men swore by. The walls were wood paneled and the slices were thick and greasy, perfectly New York (this place has since changed management, to the chagrin of the neighborhood men). As we ate our folded slices, Neil flashed his calf, baring a tattoo of the giglio in single-needle fine black line work. His next sentence was, "I can do papier-mâché with my eyes closed." That was when I first understood that the feast is so much more than the dance. His tattoo depicted the 2005 giglio, the very first that Neil helped build when he was a teenager. He would spend his Saturday mornings that year holed up in the basement with a crew of guys. He told me about how elements of the giglio were made of hand-carved Styrofoam and how the saints were created from decades-old concrete molds. I had not much thought about the construction, but it was important enough that Neil inscribed on his body the first giglio he helped create. His tattoo captured months of hard work and the relationships (and structures) he built in the basement. What I did not know, and probably would never have guessed that day, was that I too would have my own stories to tell about the basement and that I too would help make the giglio.

Ethnographic access is not an event but a process: an evolving constellation of relationships, knowledge, and sites, like a funhouse in which one discovers new doors and mirrors. But for me it was a process not of wandering and discovery but of being invited to open those new doors.

At the beginning in 2014 I routinely attended feast planning meetings and sat in the lower hall of the church, a big room that looked more like a hospital or a lunchroom than a church space. At those meetings I first met the men who will appear in the following pages. They gathered here for weekly meetings to discuss processional routes, T-shirt colors, and raffle ticket sales. Mostly mundane but sometimes explosive, the meetings were the first behind-the-scenes spaces that emerged as important.

During the 2014 feast I worked the shrine. Women at the feast work in the shrine, in booths selling ride tickets, and in the "beer trap" slinging cans of Stella and Brooklyn Brewery. In the shrine I carried heavy boxes of candles out of storage closets in the church and sold faux-crystal rosaries and prayer cards. Alongside older women who were feast volunteers, I tossed dollar bills into plastic yellow boxes and watched as people lit candles and kneeled before the statue of Our Lady of Mount Carmel nestled in the back of the outdoor space. I watched as the ribbon draped around her carved body was filled with dollar bills, securely pinned by a shrine worker. These were the obvious devotions in the shrine: prayers and supplication to Our Lady of Mount Carmel. But in the shrine volunteers also talked about how hard they worked, how exhausted they were from sitting there every night of the feast, how they did all this work because they were devoted to the Blessed Mother. The hours spent in there matter just as much as the prayers uttered in front of the statue, or the petitions folded up and put in the box stationed next to her. Work, measurable in hours, days, months, and years, was central to belonging in this Catholic community.

Over the next four years, I was enlisted to do whatever I could to help. I learned that to do fieldwork in this community I could not be an idle ethnographer.[32] My volunteer work begot more work, begot more legitimacy, more trust, and more access; all of this meant that the more time I spent with the men of this community, the more I became an "observant participant" rather than a participant observer.[33] My time in the meetings and in the shrine mattered, and the next year I was recruited by one of the feast organizers to help out in the "money room." Circuits of money are generated at the feast: from raffles, beer sales, and ride tickets to Mass collections. Stacks on stacks of money and obscure and specific methods of accounting for all of it are central to devotion's success. Success is partly measured in the number of people who walk on processions or show up for novenas, or the number of new lifters re-cruited each year. But ultimately it is calculated in how much money the feast raises. Money, literally and symbolically, means keeping the doors of the parish open as surrounding churches struggle and shutter.

Men at the feast understand themselves as productive and dedicated members of the community; they work for the church with their bodies. Eventually, they welcomed me into the masculine world of the base-ment, but I had to work alongside them. I found that embodied engage-ment in the form of painting was a type of ethnographic apprenticeship and that without it spaces of masculine practice would have remained closed to me. My embodied method of engagement is of course not without ethical dilemmas but lays bare my routes of access in the field and raises questions about the rigidity, liminality, and flexibility of gen-der in fieldwork. To paint the giglio I learned how to maneuver around the basement, how to see in "giglio dimensions," how to identify spoiled paint, tolerate heavy fumes in the nonventilated space, and use proper colors and iconographic markers for the saints. With unprecedented ac-cess as a woman ethnographer, I became a competent practitioner of masculine devotional labor.[34] It was only when I became dedicated to producing the feast and able to quantify my time and point to my labor that I was invited into other homosocial spaces of the parish. That work gave me a sort of "masculine capital."[35]

But my femininity was also being mentioned and relationally made in our interactions. It was made every time I had to decide what to wear in the grueling July heat. For the first few years I chose jeans, summery pants, and clothing that would not in any way be considered revealing. I was conscious of and always navigating a real and imagined suspicion about my role in the community and my sexuality. It was marked in the dance of female modesty that was part of being in the field but also part of the writing process. Other scholars wondered about how my own body, my feminism, my sexuality, my ethnically marked body, and my gender performance shaped my entry into this community, insisting I make decisions about talking about my looks, my feminine presenta-tion, and how exactly all these men accepted me, however provisional or tenuous that acceptance was at times. These are choices that male ethnographers or historians never have to make. Remember, white male ethnographers have not marked details about their bodies or gender presentation, even when studying across gender and ethnic lines. Gendered expectations not only shape fieldwork but shape expectations of how we are to write about it.

Being a female ethnographer in the field, as much as on the page, means I had to and have to perform for my interlocutors and for my readers. Doing this research was an act of ethnographic and real empathy, but also an act of studying how power and piety are intertwined. From the very beginning the men in Brooklyn knew I was coming from elite academic circles, but they also knew I was a New Yorker. From my very first meetings with them they said they had to be careful about what they said, lest they offend me, but as we got to know each other those barriers (while likely never completely gone) came down. As relationships and friendships developed, sometimes we disagreed about politics or argued about white privilege, and there were tears and anger. But that is not for this book. Feminine subjects are often expected to share their stories, to make their pains public, to justify and qualify. It was my place as an ethnographer not to be consistently contrary but to learn about them and to learn from them.

Ethnographers study humans who always talk back, who are always multidimensional, who can never simply fit the easily indictable or stock character of patriarch or villain. As the late Karen McCarthy Brown, foundational feminist scholar of lived religion, put it, ethnographic research "is a form of human relationship," a "social art form." Theory can be embedded in "rich, textured stories" that enliven the religion of our interlocutors on the page.[36] That aliveness means that often real lives exceed academic jargon or theoretical language. I forgo some of that here in order to tell the stories of these men, to fully represent them in all their seriousness and levity—when they are sympathetic *and* unsympathetic—and to spark fresh conversations about power, masculinity, and lived religion.

Orsi wrote a powerful, enduring piece about the racial logics of Italians in Harlem and the way they guarded their spaces from Puerto Rican others who threatened the imagined cohesion of their neighborhood. Orsi declared that Italians in the 1940s hated Puerto Ricans, a too "proximate other," something fierce. Spatial competition always intertwines with racism and ethnic boundary making in New York. I was a Puerto Rican woman studying Italian American men. These identities might have marked me and these men as irreconcilably different, but we were not wholly other to each other. We shared a New York demeanor, we shared the proclivity to narrate and mourn changing neighborhoods, we shared the impulse to show affection through insults. Personality mediates ethnographic access too. This research, at its heart, was about engaging difference—the kind of difference that renders the making of gender brighter and more discernible—but also about exploring the powerful pull of religious communities, the incredible social bonds and enduring gendered identities created there, and the impetus and fierce desire to protect and perpetuate them.

The perpetuation of gendered identities takes work: building the giglio, running the feast finances, and lifting for hours. While some men say the feast is "in their blood," they maintain and achieve their belonging and masculinity in embodied, sensuous, and kinesthetic ways. As one man told me, "I have been coming here since I was a baby in the carriage. You don't understand unless it's in your blood. My great grandfather and my grandfather lifted . . . since the carriage it's in my blood." This discourse is interesting for understanding the way participation in this community is seen as wholly natural, "inscribed in a particular biological individual," and thus a product of ethnicity, family, and upbringing.[37] At the very same time, belonging in this community is contingent on labor and bodily knowledge honed and sharpened over a lifetime of practice.[38] Men, often as boys, have to learn that lifting is an honorable act and learn the kinesthetics that go along with it. They have to learn the craft of giglio-building and learn the money work that is understood as central to parish survival. To be masculine or to be Catholic (and to be both) is to share techniques of the body.[39] These are material and bodily processes that are not easily expressed through language and not easily accessible in an interview.[40] It is not easy to ask about masculinity or discern the practices through which it is constructed through a conversation. Masculinity, much like religious identity, is contingent on embodied pedagogy. It is a product and process of engagements with material objects, social networks, and relational exchanges. Masculinity is often about having a certain set of skills that are publicly valued and recognized. Gender often determines who has access to those arenas in which one can learn those skills and those bodily ways of knowing.

I recount my routes of access here and throughout the book to propose new ways of studying religion and masculinities. Anthropologists and sociologists of "bodily arts" and "kinesthetic cultures," like dance, military culture, and modeling, to name a few, have argued for the importance of conducting research "not only of the body, in the sense of the object, but also *from* the body, that is, deploying the body as a tool of inquiry and vector of knowledge."[41] Devotion too is a kinesthetic culture. Scholars of religion have explored how devotion and religious subjectivity are made and felt through sharing kneeling knees, nimble fingers, and blistered feet with devotees and practitioners.[42] Often the way into this kind of ethnographic practice is not deliberate. Just as I did not know I would work in the basement or in the money room, this kind of practice is often cultivated in the field, contingent on invitations and relations of reciprocity and obligation to those we are studying.[43]

To do this kind of work means to render that firsthand experience on the page and to reflexively narrate (gendered) embodied processes of knowledge. As Loïc Wacquant, a sociologist and ethnographer of boxing, put it, bodily engagement "enables us to pry into practice in the making."[44] For religious studies this means not assuming what practices matter to our subjects but exploring how practices come to matter. For the purposes of this study, this method illuminates how the "ordinary knowledge" central to Catholic and masculine identity is "incarnate, sensuous, situated 'knowing-how-to'" and how it has little to do with circumscribed definitions of religious practice or narrow notions of Catholic devotionalism.[45]

This learned and shared feeling is an ideal but not always a reality in the field, and there are surely limits to this method. Gender, as much as religious identity, determines how and when ethnographers can cultivate a "visceral knowledge of social life."[46] Women ethnographers have rightfully critiqued this model because gender norms and stereotypes often prevent women from observing the social worlds of men.[47] Accounting for the salience and liminality of gender in fieldwork is central to understanding routes of access. Women researchers have been able to access male worlds, like that of the police force, by taking on a "masculine spatial orientation," as Jennifer Hunt did when she moved through the worlds of pistol practice, ride-alongs, crime scenes, and bars.[48] She argued that access and rapport are contingent not only on gender but also on achieved *status*, which points to how skills are central to gender identity and competency. She used her judo skills to protect others on the job, rebelled against management cops, and partook in informal joking and violent talk and thus performed as a "competent 'man.'"[49]

While Italian American men before me who have studied this community have lifted the giglio, I was unable to access that arena of practice.[50] Their research has largely focused on the music, the folklore of the ritual, the "macho" nature of the giglio lift itself, and the feast as a site of evangelization and the maintenance of the Italian American ethnicity they largely share with their subjects.[51] Closeness and shared identity may illuminate some perspectives, while rendering others opaque. My alterity made the taken-for-granted nature of masculinity, pedagogical processes, and logistics of ritual production visible and most interesting. Through my labor in the basement and the rectory I was able to achieve status and demonstrate competence in valued modes of practice. I could paint, work with money, and take photos. I could not apprehend the feeling of the metal pushing on bone that so many of the men shared (although lifting was not at the center of all of their practice, as we will see in the following chapters). Because of this competence, I was invited into spaces women typically do not occupy.

After noting the spaces I did access and the richness of those spaces for understanding the complexities of religion, gender, and embodiment, it is also important to note the spaces I did not venture into. As this is a study of the parish as a public institution and men as the faces and public representatives of the parish, I did not delve into the domestic lives of these Catholic men and the gender dynamics of their homes, their sexual histories, or their intimate lives. It is easy to forget when reading the end products of ethnographic work that these pages are contingent on interpersonal relationships and trust. Because this community and its central rituals are so public, it is impossible to ensure the anonymity of my interlocutors, and it is important to protect their privacy as well as their families.[52] The feast community does not exactly correlate with a residential or territorial parish community. The community is both enduring and ephemeral; men travel to the church for meetings, Masses, and volunteer work. Their relationships are bound by consistently renewed and imagined neighborhood ties, despite the fragmentation of residential ethnic communities. In privileging the relationships *between* men, those developed in church spaces, the domestic is not central to this study. Despite that, this book very much deals with how men imagine and publicly present themselves as fathers, grandfathers, husbands, and upstanding men in the community and what those relational duties have to do with religious duties. Domestic relations are performed on the public stage of ritual, and that is important to understanding the values and embodiment of masculinity.

Williamsburg

The Shrine Church of Our Lady of Mount Carmel sits on the corner of North Eighth and Havemeyer streets. The stretch of North Eighth between Havemeyer and Union Avenue, where an elevated portion of the Brooklyn-Queens Expressway (BQE) begins, was renamed Padre Pio Way for the southern Italian stigmatic saint.[53] This corner of Williamsburg is one of jarring architectural contrasts, a place where the past and the future—in glass, plaster, and brick—uncomfortably collide. For those unfamiliar with the history of Italian immigration and Catholicism in Brooklyn, the trendy streets of contemporary Williamsburg may seem an unlikely place for a feast of these proportions. The giglio is framed on either side by buildings that speak to the transformation of the neighborhood over the past fifteen years, as Williamsburg became a premier site for new construction. Behind the giglio sits an aquarium of a building, with windows framed by algae-green panels. On the left side is a three-story home composed of sand-colored brick, its face crisscrossed with the black bars of a fire escape. This little building is the holdout. It had been floating for years in a sea of scaffolding, dwarfed by the concrete skeleton of a new building that was set to span the entire block. The generic architecture of rapid development now surrounds the giglio, the adjacent church, and this brick building from the turn of the twentieth century. I have heard rumors that men carrying suitcases full of a million dollars knock on doors to proposition the holdout homeowners in the neighborhood, hoping to secure their lots for development.[54] Intransigence, capital, and tradition collide on these streets.

New Yorkers are always mourning—be it a closed store, a shuttered church, a dead dive bar, or an empty lot. Being from the Lower East Side, right across the bridge, myself, I shared this affect, this impetus to grieve. That perennial urban genre is very much a part of the way people talk about changes in Williamsburg. They can move through razed blocks and old businesses in their memory, an archive of past architecture. Carlo Rotella, in his study of urban literature and postwar and postindustrial cities, argues that city dwellers are always caught up in "logics of decline": "Any city at any time is always going to hell in one sense or the other."[55]

In 2015 I stood on the corner of Havemeyer with a man named Danny as he took a break from helping other men tote huge pieces of the giglio's face out of the church basement. He shared, "The day I leave is the day I die. Plus I have friends here. You see all these guys? We are the holdouts, the die-hards. When people hear I live in Williamsburg they are like 'Oh my god, how?' I've lived here all my life," he said as he mimed directions to his childhood home just a few blocks away. "This neighborhood went from an industrial park—the only reason you came to Williamsburg was for prostitutes or heroin—to the chicest zip code in New York. Back in the 'good old days' the feast used to run for three weeks. I couldn't imagine a summer without the feast. This is my whole life, I grew up here." He looked down the block of Havemeyer and as if dredging up or 3D modeling the past, he pointed to each lot and building and said, "I could tell you, that used to be an iron scrap yard, [and] before [that] it was a parking lot, there was a candy store on the corner, and a funeral home down the block." This narrative about the Williamsburg of the past marks it not only as industrial and seedy, but as a particularly masculine landscape—of work, sex, and drugs. The contrast between that description and the choice descriptor "chic" to describe Williamsburg now speaks to its feminized gentrified landscape, built for shopping, leisure, and consumption.

Williamsburg and this parish are a microcosm of broader social change. Once an immigrant enclave and industrial district with a reputation for crime—a place where people were ashamed to say they lived—Williamsburg is now one of the most expensive and coveted neighborhoods in New York City. It seems permanently clad in the orange mesh of construction sites and in a constant state of upgrading. In what was once a manufacturing district, streets once occupied by longshoremen are now lined with an Apple Store, a Sephora, a Whole Foods market, bank branches, and numerous upscale boutiques. The smokestacks of factories are now deliberate backdrops to the manicured lawns of waterfront parks. The syrup tanks from the Domino Sugar refinery building stand in one of those parks, aestheticized archives of the district's past.[56] The landscape of manual labor and manufacturing is now staged, dissected, dressed up as artifacts and mobilized to sell real estate. Williamsburg is a series of photo ops, as much a hashtag as a place—a neoliberal dreamscape. In this urban context money, survival, and devotion are, and have been, inherently linked to sustaining religious institutions.

On July 5, 1957, the *Tonight Show* filmed a segment in Williamsburg, capturing hazy footage of the streets during the Feast of Our Lady of Mount Carmel and San Paolino di Nola. Like the dotted illuminated outlines of a Lite-Brite, flowers made of small lights curve over the sidewalks, creating a seemingly infinite canopy of light. The host announces, "That's a giant wooden statue of Saint Paulinus that you see in the distance. And it is giant!," as the camera zooms in on the giglio: a large tapered white tower. In the recording it is the only structure visible in the dark of night. The camera follows the men as they gather under the poles of the giglio in uniforms of white T-shirts and slacks. The men march to the staccato music of a brass band, a disciplined ensemble coming together to lift the colossal weight of the giglio. The camera pans over the dense tangle of onlookers on the ground and people hanging out of tenement windows. The lifters loop their arms around the poles of the giglio, and some loop their arms around the waists of the lifters in front of them for extra support. Later on during the show cameras capture the statue of Our Lady of Mount Carmel being carried into the shrine by men in short-sleeve button-downs. She carries a Christ Child and wears a shiny crown on her head and long robes, their colors obscured by the black-and-white television clip. They carefully detach her from her rolling float and support her body, two men flanking her sides, two supporting her back.[57] The large brown felt scapulars affixed to the statue sway with their steps. Because of the grainy footage and the dark of night, the feast is decontextualized.

Figure 1.3. The statue of Our Lady of Mount Carmel. Photo by the author.

We cannot see the orange brick of the church, the surrounding buildings, or the businesses that line the streets. Watching this footage, with its focus on the efforts of the men and the statuary of the feast, it is uncanny how little seems to have changed. Swap slacks for cargo shorts and crisp white tees for new colorful screen-printed T-shirts and matching bandanas, and the lifters in 1957 look much like those more than six decades later. They hold each other's bodies and cock their necks under the weight of the poles in the same way. The same statue of Our Lady of Mount Carmel is hoisted tenderly by a group of feast organizers and deposited in the shrine at the start of the feast, although in color one could see her mustard and brown robes, her dark brown eyes that look like they have been smudged with eyeliner, and the stones dotting her brass crown. The lifters in their matching outfits, the giglio, and Our Lady of Mount Carmel are the consistencies in the history of this Italian American community. With the neighborhood context smudged out by the darkness and the opening ceremonies boiled down to kinesthetics, it all seems the same, but the darkness of night obscures changes in architecture, economy, and community cohesion.

Context is invisible in the darkness, in the blur of this aged footage—at this time the Italian American community on North Eighth street was settling in to its third church building. Also obscured in this footage are the modest structures that surrounded the church: brick tenement buildings, vinyl-clad homes, empty lots, and brick industrial buildings.[58] In a neighborhood that has undergone a building boom since the mid-2000s, many of these structures have disappeared. If there is one constant in New York City, it is change. Architectural writers remind us that New York is a city "constantly renewing itself." It is a city of layers, a "city of see-through pentimenti."[59] This is true in Williamsburg and at OLMC. Here change and looming decline are about not just losing parishioners or being cash-strapped, but rather the looming specter of architecture, development, newcomers, and private capital. The specter of development has haunted the church throughout the twentieth century. Neighborhood change has been a spectral presence but also a destructive reality in this community, which has seen its church buildings knocked down in the name of urban renewal, and the architectural boom of today likely dredges up those collective memories.[60] While the movements may look the same, today the giglio dances in a very different Williamsburg.

What is also obscured in the parity between 1957 and the contemporary feast is a very different institutional context. Because of the sex abuse crisis and the decades of violence perpetrated by priests and perpetuated by bishops' cover-ups, Catholics have been losing trust in the Church.[61] While disaffiliation and declining rates of Mass attendance and Catholic school enrollment have been quantitative measures of distrust, it is important to note that the sex abuse crisis also has had broad financial effects, in both payouts and declines in giving. The *National Catholic Reporter* estimates that the crisis has cost the Church in the United States nearly four billion dollars.[62] According to the Diocese of Brooklyn, there have been 108 abuse claims. The diocese has paid tens of millions to victims in lawsuits and also set up an Independent Reconciliation and Compensation Program for survivors and cases that might fall outside of the statute of limitations, on the condition they do not seek further legal action.[63] Money is central to thinking about the state of contemporary Catholicism nationally and locally. Financial security is always on the minds of the people and leadership at OLMC. In this gentrified neighborhood, private investment and development surround the parish as real threats, attracting young, non-Catholic newcomers to the area. Other parishes in the neighborhood have closed or merged. All of this heightens the stakes of the feast as the financial engine of the parish.

Chapter Outline

In this community the impetus to survive in a changed and changing neighborhood is made to be a distinctly masculine responsibility and obligation. This book challenges what we think about piety and masculinity and the intersection between these two forces often imagined to be at odds. In this community men, and young men in particular, are not indifferent to religion; rather the parish and devotion to the saints are potent forces in their lives, structuring their interpersonal relationships and their very pursuit and achievement of manhood. This book explores how they come into being as Catholic men in spaces and through practices largely unseen by the public or by scholars. In these pages a story of devotion cultivated between men unfolds. In this community devotion is imagined to be a productive pursuit integral to securing a healthy future for the parish. The problems of gentrification bring into relief this community's ethic of survival and how it is masculinized and imagined to be the burden of male bodies. This book is about how devotional tradition has offered the promise of greatness to generations of men.

Chapter 1 is about tattoos, costumes, and play; it introduces the feast through the narratives of men who spectacularly dress up to perform Saint Paulinus's hagiography and who have images of the giglio tattooed on their bodies. Through material culture—costumes, jewelry, tattoos, and structures—it explores how materiality and the cultivation of embodied know-how are central to the making of masculine Catholic bodies at the feast. It especially reflects on the stuff and rituals through which children learn to love the feast. Chapter 2, on the church basement, examines how artistic and manual labor is devotional labor and describes the masculine valence that practices of construction and production carry in this community. I look at the basement as a backstage and subterranean space where men learn to embody masculine values and skills and how they learn Catholic iconography and craft and negotiate questions of sacred presence. It also examines the methodological mechanics of studying male spaces as a woman ethnographer. Chapter 3 explores how devotion and money go hand in hand at the feast. It demonstrates that money is symbolically linked to the futurity of the parish and endowed with moral qualities. By considering logistical and financial labor, and the backstage space dubbed the "money room," it explores how men construct masculine authority in the community by imagining themselves as the sustainers of a financially needy and threatened parish.

While the first three chapters are dedicated to the behind-the-scenes practices of men, chapter 4 fleshes out how they perform authority and make claims to the neighborhood in public spaces during the feast. The chapter follows processions through the neighborhood where men contend with gentrifiers, present themselves as fathers, grandfathers, and producers of future generations, and bask in the glory that a lifetime of involvement in the community promises them. Processions and rituals like the Dance of the Giglio are gender performances, and I explore how heterosexuality, a command of the neighborhood, and a commanding physical presence are all central to these public performances of masculinity and how men who do not fit those standards are marginalized. Across these chapters I demonstrate how devotional acts coexist with joking, drinking, play, and friendship.[64] Religion need not always look serious, pious, and solemn. This constellation of practices physically as well as narratively sustains institutions like the parish in Williamsburg.

The feast offers spectacular displays of Italian American Catholic community cohesion, but it is important to note how the parish and feast have struggled with urban policy and demographic change. The success of the feast is in part contingent on Haitian devotees who visit from other parts of Brooklyn. Chapter 5 explores how Italian Americans contend with diversity. In everyday conversation at the feast Italian Americans construct Haitian devotion as different from their own: admirably emotional but also excessive, superstitious, and foreign, revealing the logics of gender and productivity that undergird their definitions of devotion. I explore the construction and enactment of what I call *Catholic propriety* and argue that public devotional rituals are sites where Catholics evaluate each other and articulate norms of practice and expressions of Catholic identity. Italian Americans create boundaries between themselves and Haitian devotees by mobilizing discourses that once set them and their devotional practices outside the bounds of "good" American Catholicism. Chapter 6 demonstrates the importance of religion in understanding urbanism and how communities contend with gentrification.

OLMC, an ethnic parish constructed for Italian immigrants, thrived in an industrial district that experienced the drastic architectural and demographic changes of urban renewal and deindustrialization. The neighborhood underwent various stages of abandonment, gentrification, and renaissance. From the nineteenth century to the twenty-first it transformed from a neighborhood of factories and ethnic enclaves to an alternative artsy haven and then to a hub of state-led gentrification and a premier site of investment and real estate development. Despite these transformations and persistent upheavals, devotion to the saints buttresses persistent practices of male power, leadership, strength, and skill. Models of masculinity and the routes to achieve them are lasting at OLMC, despite a Church and city that are changing around it. That is not to say that protecting and reproducing those models does not take work. This book is about the work, the labor, the discursive moves, the ritual movements, and the performances that make up an enduring public manhood. For this community everything has changed, and at the same time nothing has changed.

1

Turks, Tattoos, and the Masculine Body of the Feast

Loving the feast begins not when a man is old enough or tall enough to lift the giglio, to understand the pain of lifting as penance, or to comprehend the sacrificial logics of Saint Paulinus's hagiography. A love for the feast often begins much earlier, when he is a child. I have always loved the way Joe Mascia put it: he had been coming to the feast since he was in the carriage. Some men remember getting wheeled around through processions before they could even string together sentences. Others recall being in elementary school and admiring the lifters of the giglio so much that they emulated them, lifting chairs and milk crates on their shoulders. As children some even traveled to Nola, the southern Italian town and origin of the giglio, where Saint Paulinus was a bishop in the fifth century. Through the sweet haziness of childhood memory they remember seeing the *gigli* (plural of *giglio*) in Nola. Some remember being terrified of the giglio, its massiveness and mobility making it seem peculiarly alive as it moved down Havemeyer Street.

Men are not born loving the feast—even though many liken that love to something that is inborn; young men are very much trained to love, lift, and make the giglio and to see themselves as central to the future of their parish. By exploring how boys are embedded in this community through occasions when they can dress up and act as men and play central roles in the drama of Saint Paulinus's life, we see how they become part of the community through embodied actions. They learn to tell stories about the feast and weave themselves in a long lineage of men who came before them. These narratives are pressed into their very skin as some get tattoos of the giglio. Their tattoos are inscriptions of their relationships with other men and the very medium through which they fashion their Catholic identity and their relationships with the saints. Masculine Catholic bodies are not born but made. Costumes, adornment, and tattoos demonstrate how men are embedded in this community and how devotion—a love of saints, tradition, parish, and other men—is written and worn on their bodies.

* * *

On the morning of Giglio Sunday, 2016, a huge crowd had gathered in front of a home on Skillman Avenue. Long sparkling streamers in red and gold draped down from the third story bay window of the house. Red and gold star-shaped balloons floated from the banisters of the stairway, and a long table piled with boxes of Italian cookies, trays of bagels, metal canteens of coffee, and vases full of roses flanked the house. The door was all set for a baroque exit, decorated lavishly and cloaked in cream brocade drapery.

In front of the house, a sea of people in red T-shirts waited, iPhones in hand, ready to take photos. Their T-shirts were printed with an image of a wooden boat with four sails on rough water. The sails read "Viva Nola, Viva Brooklyn." Across the top of the boat was printed "Joey Aragona," along the bottom "Turk."

Three little boys, the sailors, were assembled on the staircase, dressed in pleated pants of iridescent maroon taffeta, fitted up top and ballooned at the thigh. On their narrow shoulders they wore damask maroon and gold blazers, with ruched dip-dyed gold and red head wraps around their foreheads. They carried shiny, curved toy swords. The brass band assembled outside of the house began to beat a low drum to prepare the crowd. Trumpet blasts and confetti poppers erupted in unison as the curtains swung open. There was Joey pumping his arms in the air with intensity to the serpentine beat of the music. Joey too held a gold sword, and together he and the boys waved and pumped their swords in the air.

Joey's outfit was spectacular. On his slender frame he wore a red and gold tunic, down to his shins, with golden paisley shapes, embroidery, and white rhinestones. Even from my place at the side of the house I could see that his fingers and ears were bedecked in rhinestones. Thick rings hugged his fingers, and heavy circular earrings hung clipped from his lobes. Joey wore a thick groomed beard that highlighted his angular face and a tall cream ruby-studded turban with a train that draped down his shoulders. His gold earrings swung as he bared his teeth and waved his sword. At the bottom of the steps he triumphantly held his arms above his head, waving the sword back and forth; a priest blessed him

Figure 1.1. The 2016 Turk, Joey, lifted on his friends' shoulders. Photo by the author.

Figure 1.2. The 2016 boat, with inscription "In Loving Memory of Daddy / 20 Years in Heaven." Photo by the author.

with a few thick splashes of holy water and they embraced. As the crowd continued to whoop and cheer around him, Joey's gritted teeth melted into a smile and he looked so happy and humbled.

Joey was playing the Turk, transfigured into this character by his clothing and movements. Later he and the sailors climbed into a boat, high above the crowds of the feast during the Dance of the Giglio. Lifted on the shoulders of the men below, the boat traveled down North Eighth Street and around the corner to Havemeyer Street, with Joey standing triumphantly at the bow and the sailors inside throwing confetti and flowers onto the crowd and lifters below. Behind Joey stood a papier-mâché statue of San Paolino, a mast bearing the coat of arms of Nola, and a cursive inscription on the back of the boat that read, "In Loving Memory of Daddy / 20 Years in Heaven."

Down below, under the poles affixed to the boat, was Joe Speruta. Wearing dark sunglasses, Joe was one of the nearly hundred men assembled under the poles who worked to lift it through the streets until it met the giglio in a grand reenactment of the legend of San Paolino, when the Bishop of Nola sailed back to its shores on a sultan's ship, after being enslaved by invaders. For decades Joe had been on the crew lifting the boat and took pride in it. Always in dark sunglasses, in 2015, like the other hundreds of lifters, he wore a bright gold shirt and a red cap and bandana draped over his head. Joe squared his body under the pole, jutting his chest out, crossing his arms, and stiffening his back. His crossed arms were adorned with tattoos. One forearm sports a black-and-gray tattoo of Our Lady of Mount Carmel, seated on a cloud, with a halo of stars, offering the scapular. Spanning the length of his other forearm is a large tattoo of a giglio, with fine line details of crosses and saints. Lines of music wrap around the giglio and snake up and down his freckled arm. Joe's skin is always sticky with sweat, and between lifts in 2015 we laughed about how the confetti thrown from the boat littered his skin. Usually red under the hot sun, Joe always refuses my offer of sunscreen. His calves too bear tattoos that are visible below his khaki cargo shorts, the choice bottom for the lifters. Another giglio rises up the outside of his right calf, and on the inside is a portrait of Padre Pio. On the other calf is a bright yellow, red, and blue tattoo of the Knights of Columbus insignia, an eagle atop a globe.

Joey and Joe: Turk and lifter, sword and giglio, scapular and turban—although they occupy different roles and different levels of honor and prestige, through their bodily practice and adornment they replicate the imagery of the feast. Through material culture—dress, objects, tattoos, and other adornments—the men at the feast enact and construct history and memory, both personal and collective. Their bodies bear material inscriptions of the networks of allegiance and love that are forged through collective devotional practice.

Central to the feast and its male community is a hierarchy of roles that men can cycle through based on their work, commitment to planning the feast, and dedication to the parish. There are over three hundred lifters; with their strength they collaborate to make the giglio and the boat dance. Crews of forty lifters are directed by lieutenants, who achieve that role after over a decade of lifting and service to the parish. They command their crews, ensure they are moving in unison, and relay orders from the capos. The capos are the most honored men in the community, and it often takes them at least thirty years to ascend to that position. Capos control the giglio, command the brass band, and choose the type of lift and route of the giglio. While lifters are many, when a capo is in front of the giglio, he is the single point of authority and attention, and all those under him in the hierarchy are to obey his commands. The highest honor in the community is achieving the position of number one capo. While not all men ascend this hierarchy, what they do share is the know-how necessary to bear the weight of the giglio. No matter their role, men come to be a part of this community not necessarily or only through belief, but with their bodies.

By taking up the Turk's sword they enact the history of their patron saint but also write themselves into Brooklyn and even Nola's feast history, entering both a global and a local lineage. Tattoos of saints, the giglio, and Our Lady of Mount Carmel become media for shared stories of the feast—intertwined stories of friendship, mentorship, labor, and devotion. These inked inscriptions are evidence of love and dedication not only to the church but to other men. Young boys in the community have the opportunity to become sailors, playing mini-Turk, and they lift the children's giglio, a miniature lift that introduces them to the labor of the real lift. They can also play as children's capos, practicing the authority that the capos perform during

Figure 1.3. Joe lifting the boat, 2016. Photo by the author.

the Dance of the Giglio each year. They have everything in miniature: giglio, the swords, the lifters' T-shirts and bandanas, and temporary tattoos. These objects are central to creating and socializing a vital community of men of all ages who are dedicated to producing and sustaining this devotional tradition.

Tattoos

To understand why men get the giglio inscribed on their bodies, we must comprehend the Dance of the Giglio as a site of physical collective male action, a spectacle of strength and struggle in honor of San Paolino. During the Dance of the Giglio about a hundred twenty men converge under its aluminum poles for the lift. The men's bodies work in sync to bounce the structure, to move it down the street, and to spin it. As the sky fills with confetti, creating a magical atmosphere, the men arrange themselves into their lifting positions, their sweaty bodies and faces littered with tiny confetti flecks. One man can stand as synecdoche

Figure 1.4. Lifters gripping hands, 2016. Photo by the author.

for all the lifters. In sneakers, shorts, and their matching T-shirts, the men bend their knees together, their feet firmly planted on the ground, like interchangeable straining bodies. All of them moving in the same way, they raise their arms to grasp the poles. Once the band begins to play, they stiffen their upper bodies, straighten their legs, and begin to shuffle forward to move the giglio. The men at the corners, in a display of mutual support, with arms outstretched, pile their hands one on top of the other. Joe describes this physicality as helping them be in tune with one another: "It helps [you] feel the rhythm of the guys' bodies moving, to feel how their feet are moving. When you grip arms you become [more in tune], we try to move in unison and keep the corner steady. There are eight guys on the corner and when they lock up like that it's like having an extra corner on the pole. When we interlock it also forms a boundary, it forms a barrier from the crowd and the people around. It also helps with balance, you can feel a guy losing his strength and give him a boost, or moral support if you feel them losing."

The feast and the Dance of the Giglio have been a site of male unity throughout the twentieth century. Tucked into a bound booklet of all the feast meeting minutes from 1959 is a page written by a man named Lou Coppola titled "Re-united Again, But for a Day," a nostalgic publicity piece about how the feast is a place to see old buddies without the burdens of excuses or responsibilities.[1] "YOU CAN TAKE THE BOY OUT OF BROOKLYN, BUT YOU CAN'T TAKE BROOKLYN OUT OF THE BOY," he declares. He explains how on July 5, 1959, all of the old friends and Brooklyn boys, regardless of where they work or live, would gather to lift the giglio in honor of Saint Paulinus. The day had finally come for when they no longer had to lament

> gee, but I'd give the world to see that old gang of mine. . . . Not alone are you celebrating the meeting of your old buddies, but as a lifter of the Giglio or Boat, you're closer to your old buddies than you ever were. You're under the Giglio or Boat, shoulder to shoulder, your muscles tense and full of joy and excitement, hoping that you can lift the Giglio at the first command. It's here regardless of your place of business where old friends meet. . . . As for myself, God willing, I'll be there WILL YOU?

Today, just as it was for Lou Coppola over sixty years ago, the feast is a place of homosocial community, where men come together to participate in a public devotional spectacle, not only to strengthen their faith and bond to the saints and the church but also to strengthen their bonds to each other.

Lou Coppola chose print to express his love for the giglio, but some contemporary men choose the medium of skin and ink to express their ties to the ritual and the relationships they have forged there. At the feast tattoos have emerged as a particularly masculine mode of devotional material culture.[2] Rather than simply being expressions of belief, inner faith, and Catholic identity and of vertical bonds between men and the saints, tattoos are relational, by which I mean the saints are always inflected with loving connections to other people. A tattoo of a saint is not simply about an individual or personal devotion but is a devotion made and developed in relation to other men.[3] Love for specific saints is shared between fathers and sons, and mentors and friends.

According to German sociologist Georg Simmel, tattoos are the most permanent and visible expression of the individual self and personality. He categorizes them as adornment, akin to jewelry and clothing, objects and inscriptions that are "inexchangeable and personal" and thus work to "intensif[y] or enlarge the impression of the personality by operating as a sort of radiation emanating from it."[4] As adornments, tattoos are expressions of the self, public and visible projections of the individual. Scholars who have written on the intersections between religion and tattooing have largely been consistent with Simmel's analysis, understanding tattoos as individualized inscriptions that allow people to express their "true" and "inner" selves.

An increasing number of Americans are tattooed; the Pew Research Center found that 38 percent of millennials and 32 percent of Gen Xers have tattoos.[5] New York City was one of forty-seven cities that had "enacted ordinances prohibiting tattoos" by 1968, and tattooing remained illegal in the city until 1997 but has since become increasingly mainstream.[6] The mainstreaming of tattoos has moved the bodily practice outside the analytical realm of the subcultural and deviant and more into the realm of consumption and commodification. Tattoos have become media for "stories of the self"; the act of getting tattooed can be therapeutic, a means to commemorate triumph over difficulty, and narrate and perform a resilient self.[7] Getting tattooed is often a private spiritual experience.[8] For example, tattooed evangelical Christians, who favor images of crosses, praying hands, and scriptures on their "own private 'temple of the holy spirit'" understand the bricolage of religious images on skin as symbols of individual identity and "extreme expressions of extreme faith," inscriptions of their personal commitment to serve "the Lord forever."[9] But pain, catharsis, and discourses of spirituality do not much figure into the ways these men in Brooklyn talk about their tattoos.

The decidedly Catholic tattoos of men at the feast demonstrate the ways tattoos are much more than "exteriorizations of the self" and fleshly "affirmations of individual identity."[10] While tattoos serve as communicative devices that allow people to negotiate and narrate their personal lives and histories, the iconographically marked bodies of men at the feast challenge us to think beyond tattoos as individualist or mere symbols of belief or "insignia of faith."[11] The tattoo narratives of men in

Brooklyn reveal the ways their devotional lives are very much entangled with their relationships with other men.

Unlike the majority of tattooed Americans, who report that their tattoos are not visible, at the feast tattoos are writ upon the Catholic male body that is deliberately on display.[12] Italian and American flags, rosaries, saints, gigli, Madonnas, crosses are visible all over the bodies of lifters as they assemble under the giglio. These tattoos are much like the garlands and flags that hang from lampposts and the images of Our Lady of Mount Carmel that pervade the streets of the feast—they are central to the creation of the feast atmosphere and devotional, ethnic, communal, and celebratory time and space. Tattoos of the giglio do *social* work, and their meaning cannot be limited to single powerful moments of inscription (the act of getting tattooed) or to meaning making on an individual level. Rather, giglio tattoos are media for shared stories of the feast and function as repositories for feast histories. They are material, fleshy artifacts of commitment to a local Catholic masculinity that is contingent on shared obligations to the parish. Moreover, tattoos are efficacious. Much more than insignia, tattoos can also function as sacramentals. Like devotional objects, they are activated by communities of practice. Tattoos *do* stuff—they help men maintain devotional bonds to the saints and each other and offer protection and closeness.[13]

Every giglio is storied; each year the design elements change and the giglio is painted a new color or is completely remade to reflect the aesthetics and symbolic messages of that year's capo. Obscured in the spectacle of the giglio are the hours of labor, literal manpower, and personal meanings invested in its wood, aluminum, and papier-mâché form. The giglio seems to appear on the streets during early July, but there is an entire backstage process of labor, camaraderie, and meaning making behind it.

Neil's body is a patchwork of tattoos—among cartoon characters from the 1990s, voluptuous devil-girl pinups, and reapers and skulls, he has a giglio tattoo. Rising vertically on Neil's calf is a single-needle, all-black tattoo of the 2005 giglio. From far away it looks like any other giglio, but listening to Neil tell the story about why he got this one infuses this specific image with an emotional significance; it compresses and commemorates an extended temporal connection to the giglio. Among all of his years at the feast, 2005 was the most significant and the year he chose to commemorate on his body.

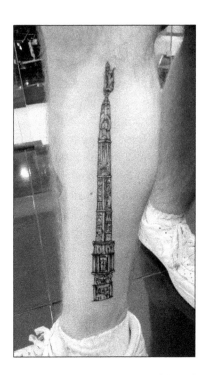

Figure 1.5. Neil's fine-line black tattoo of the 2005 giglio. Photo courtesy of Neil.

Neil, whom we met in the introduction, is now thirty years old and has been lifting since he was twelve. In addition to being a lifter and working on the giglio's construction in 2016, Neil was the chairman of the Children's Giglio Committee, meaning he built a miniature giglio that children would lift and coordinated with parents to sign up well over one hundred children to participate. As I sat with Neil and his then fiancée Amanda in an old neighborhood pizzeria, he reminisced about 2005, the year that a man named Joseph Dente was number one capo. Dente had recently lost a young son, and the giglio was a dedication to him, a reflection of the boy's place in heaven, and a remembrance of a little boy who loved the feast. The giglio was for "little Joey," and the men worked for months to craft a giglio that had the playfulness of a child's imagination. Both Neil and Joe Speruta have tattoos of the 2005 giglio, which had emotional resonance because it was a tribute but also because of the labor that they put into the facade. In Joe's words, "It meant a lot to me, especially with the amount of work we put in, sometimes ten to twelve hours a day on weekends, and after work we would go in and work three to four hours. It took us almost the whole year, we started after Labor Day and we were working until zero hour. . . . We had chicken wire moldings, I did a lot of the grunt work: papier-mâché, gluing, and we painted it blue, a turquoise blue. It was meant to represent heaven for Joey Jr." In Neil's words, "We broke our asses. At one point we were living in that basement with [our master artist], five nights a week, and on Saturday mornings. There is so much hidden meaning in the face."

Neil and Joe emphasize the work, in days, hours, and months, that they collectively put into the giglio. The giglio was not only an expression of love; making it required significant sacrifice in time and effort. Building and painting are devotional work for these men. Creating the giglio is a collaborative effort and a service to the feast and the church. The basement, according to Joe, is its own world and community. We sat in a bar one evening and Joe explained, pausing a long time between his words, that "the basement is like its own city. It's on the tip of my tongue, what is the word, it's on the tip of my tongue," he said turning his head from one side to another, wrinkling his brow thinking, "ecosystem! It's like its own ecosystem. It lives, it breathes, it grows." In this subterranean space of community and production, Neil and Joe labored on the face of the giglio, not only in honor of the capo but also in allegiance to the parish, and were devoting their time, year-round, to the production of the feast. This labor points to the importance of peripheral parish spaces, such as the workshop, as relational spaces of male bonding central to the meaning of their tattoos.

Joe often talks fondly of the 2005 giglio whenever we meet, bringing up pictures on his phone and explaining all the craft that went into it, elements only a member of the Giglio Committee would know. Its columns were made from corrugated cardboard, chicken wire, and papier-mâché and were painted to look like marble. An angel holding a banner that read "Ad Jesum Per Mariam" was made of an old mannequin, and in the center was a huge photograph of the church's statue of Our Lady of Mount Carmel, framed in gold and heavy glass. At the very bottom was a framed painting of a Tuscan landscape, in which the younger men all pasted pictures of themselves, to the chagrin of committee authorities. All these details are reflected in Neil's fine-line tattoo.

When they were building the 2005 giglio, the capo, Joe Dente, documented the whole process through photos. When it was complete he invited everyone who worked on it to a barbecue at his house—Neil explained that at the gathering "he had a big billboard [made], it was a huge collage of us working around his giglio. He gave all of us a framed copy. Mine on the back, because they used to make fun of me for wearing rubber gloves, said 'Most likely to be a surgeon.'" Neil brought this sentimental gift as a reference for his tattoo artist. Sticking out his leg he pointed out the details—the Tuscan landscape, complete with tiny trees, and the stars and rainbows for little Joey, the banner, and a smiling San Paolino. When he decided to get the tattoo, he explained, "I called Joe to ask his permission, I said to Joe, 'I'm thinking of getting a tattoo of a giglio, I want yours, I know what it means and where it came from,' and when I told him he teared up and said 'go for it.'" The tattoo not only was meaningful to Neil but also was integrated in a cycle of respect and admiration for an older man in the community. Tattoos not only spark narratives of labor but also are inscriptions that honor the male relationships that are forged through the love of the feast.

Joe Speruta has been a lifter for over twenty-five years and is a proud member of a lifting crew called the Cavemen. Joe is Lithuanian and Italian, and his parents met in Williamsburg. On his phone he keeps a picture of his mother as a little girl on the day of her First Communion and a picture of himself and his best friend on the day of their First Communion. Joe was a tall kid, with shiny red hair brushed to one side, and the only kid in a bright white suit. His best friend now lives in Chicago, but each year they reunite at the feast to party, drink, walk on processions, and lift. Joe's family has been involved with the feast for three generations. His father lifted in the sixties, and his grandfather threw famous block parties in the neighborhood. When he was a child, his parents moved away from Williamsburg to Maspeth, Queens, but sustained their ties to the feast. When he was a kid he used to hang out at a bakery on the street of the church to watch the giglio lifts, and one day he told me how he was scared of and in awe of the giglio: "I thought that it was alive and that it was coming for me."

Joe's skin is inscribed with two different images of the giglio that honor different male networks, his work in the basement, and his connection to his mentors in the feast. Each giglio signals different intimate relationships and temporal moments. One is the squared giglio design from the sixties when his father was a lifter. Like Neil, he used an object from the feast as a reference for the tattoo—a silky brown banner embroidered with an image of the giglio and Our Lady of Mount Carmel that used to be sold in the shrine and hung from parishioners' doors and windows. Joe understands his two tattoos as "two generations of giglios." On his forearm Joe has a tattoo of the 2005 giglio with lines of music from the feast song "O Giglio e Paradiso" wrapping around it. Music is central to the feast environment, and the giglio song that praises the "faithful and honest men" who "give the feast their hearts" is like a theme song for the Italian Americans of Williamsburg. Folklorist Joseph Sciorra has argued that the giglio is "an exclamation point proclaiming the community's continuing presence" in Williamsburg and the song "is its aural equivalent."[14] While Sciorra has argued that the song has become a symbol for the community, when inscribed on the body the music evokes not only a general, communal memory but an intimate, relational one as well. The song specifically honors men and their role as producers and laborers for the feast. Joe actually wrote out each music note for his tattoo artist in purple stenciling marker and was thus an active producer of his tattoo.

Telling the story of writing in the music himself prompted Joe to reminisce about his mentor in the community, a man named Sarge, and how their relationship revolved around music. Sarge invited Joe to play trumpet in the parish's folk band, took Joe under his wing, and got him involved in Mass and in parish life. Joe remembers as a young man, "I would sit on top of the steps [of the church] and that's how I got introduced to everyone. . . . The first year I lifted . . . I was lonely, I didn't know anyone, but once you hang out with these guys and have a beer, we were like family by the end. . . . What is so great about these people is that they embrace you as an equal." For years, all the guys at the feast would call him Little Anthony, referring to his father. One day, as we watched the giglio band play the song together, Joe got emotional. With downcast eyes he told me he wished Sarge were still here: "For such a small man he produced a big light. That is the only way I could put it. Even if you hated him he made you love him."

Joe remembers his time in the basement making the giglio: "For me it's one hundred percent dedication or zero. There was a group of eight to ten of us . . . all of us were the giglio junkies, anytime anywhere they needed us we would be there. Even in the wreck after [Hurricane] Sandy

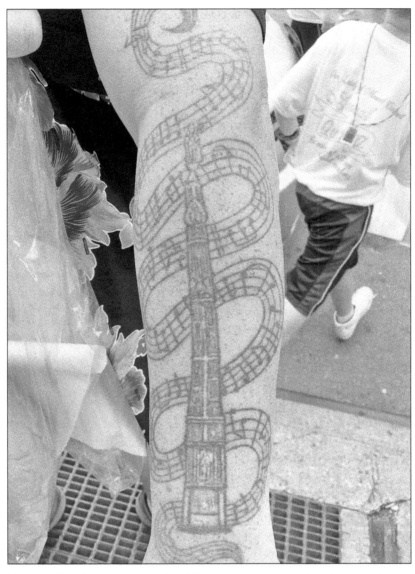

Figure 1.6. Joe's forearm tattoo of the giglio with lines of music. Photo by the author.

we were always there, always working. If they needed help on the procession they would call us to help, it is crazy but they could always count on us." Throughout our conversations Joe and Neil revisited the theme of male relationships. Joe described them as nurturing and as mentorships; they are intimate and important to his trajectory as a lifter. Through these stories, Joe reminded me, "I am going to lift forever."

Sal, an apprentice capo who is now in his fifties, grew up in Williamsburg and still lives in his childhood home. His involvement in the feast began when he was five and became a member of the rope gang, the troupe of children who would hold ropes to help with crowd control during the Dance of the Giglio. He started lifting in the early 1980s. He reminisced, "Wow, I remember getting pushed around a lot, all the old-timers were yelling at us all the time, my grandpa pushed me under. . . . I was nineteen or twenty when I lifted the big [giglio]. Whatever he instilled in me worked because I stayed, he just wanted that." Sal emphasizes the importance of instilling tradition the way the old-timers in the neighborhood did. As we sat in the Knights of Columbus council space across the street from the church, Sal pointed to his infant son sleeping next to us in his carriage. "That's what I'm trying to do with him," he said as he looked over lovingly in son's direction, "let him listen to the music." Sal told me about his life in the feast, his trajectory, his hopes for his son and for continuity. He wears a simple black image of the giglio on his bicep, but what it signals is the male relationships that he has forged throughout his life and the centrality of the feast to them. The giglio tattoo inscribes these memories and relationships on his skin.

These tattoos are not simply stories of the self but stories of the group; they are social in that they represent and honor relationships and create and inscribe solidarity. These men tattoo themselves into a narrative; they write themselves into feast history as makers of the giglio, as young lifters, as fathers raising subsequent generations of men dedicated to the feast. Other men too even get their children's names inscribed beside their giglio tattoos. The giglio is much more than an object or symbol of devotion to Saint Paulinus. For many in this community it is synonymous with family. These tattoos reveal these interpersonal connections and affections as central to the masculine involvement in the feast. Wearing a tattoo is a bodily practice that works to reaffirm a community identity, a connection with the parish and with tradition.

Tattoos are representations of the group, totemic decorations; in this case they are emblems of masculine solidarity created through the feast. What is most important about tattoos is their display, their contextualization within group life. Tattoos are intimate symbols of involvement, adornments that proclaim a group identity. They are actively worn and are an essential part of creating and entering the ritual environment of the feast. More than that, by materializing memories of labor and relationships they also extend the effervescent effects and feeling of groupness beyond feast time.[15]

Tattoos are concrete ways of connecting with the saints and the Virgin. Tattoos can become sacramentals, objects that "serve as a doorway between the secular and sacred world." Sacramentals are channels to the divine. Like rosaries or holy water, they are miniature sacraments that sanctify Catholics in their everyday contexts.[16] Joe has a tattoo of Our Lady of Mount Carmel on his forearm; it works as a devotional object for him.[17] Like other devotees of Our Lady, he always wears a scapular around his neck, for protection and to express his devotion to her. The scapular is a sacramental necklace, traditionally made of two small squares of wool and bearing an image of Our Lady of Mount Carmel; it hangs down the back and chest of devotees. The name scapular comes from the Latin word for shoulder blade, and was originally a long piece of cloth worn as part of a monastic habit as a sort of apron or as a badge of membership in a confraternity.[18] When Our Lady of Mount Carmel appeared to Saint Simon Stock in the thirteenth century atop Mount Carmel, she bestowed the scapular to the Carmelite order and instructed that they should wear the scapular and "that whoever dies wearing it will not suffer eternal fire, that is, wearing this, he will be saved."[19]

Joe, talking about his tattoo of Our Lady of Mount Carmel, likened it to the scapular and explained, "I work[ed] in a hospital and I wore my scapular every day, but because it is made of cloth they were worried about infection control. It gets gross in there. I didn't want to risk taking it off, I always have my scapular and I want her close to me, so I got the tattoo." Our Lady of Mount Carmel, in ink, replaces the worn scapular; her tattooed image is not merely decorative but is perceived to have the same power as a devotional object. The inked image is much more than an insignia or sign of devotion; it mediates sacred power through Joe's skin.

Saint tattoos are particularly generative for complicating devotion; through tattoo narratives we can see how these tattoos not only point to personal, individualized devotion to the saints but also are ways of representing intimate, earthly relationships. Saints become icons of love between people. Saint tattoos are storied with intimate relationships. Neil and Joe honor their relationships to their male kin, fathers and grandfathers, in material ways. Around his neck Neil wears a gold cross that used to belong to his father, and on his calf he has a tattoo of another cross that belonged to his father, with an inscription in Italian that reads "how do I live without the ones I love." As we stood outside the church one August morning, Neil told me, "The background is the sun breaking through the clouds, my father always said that that was when a soul is going to heaven." On the other calf, he has a tattoo of Saint Anthony, his father's patron saint. Every year Neil goes to Mass on Saint Anthony's feast day to get a scapular in honor of his father, often rushing out of the basement to get to Mass on time. A saint tattoo, much like the objects that once belonged to family members, functions as a powerful artifact of intimacy between humans and between humans and the divine, materializing those vertical and horizontal relationships.

Around his neck Neil wears a large gold crucifix, made from smooth gold cylinders, cut on a bias at the ends—on it hangs a thick Christ with long hair and a muscular body with abs carved into the gold. The detailing on Christ's toes, the cloth around his waist, the strands of his hair, the hint of a beard, and his despairing look are all carved lightly into the tiny gold body. Laying on Neil's chest with the crucifix is a giglio charm with small carved vines creating a swirling pattern across its tiny gold facade. The giglio charm was a confirmation gift that he received the year he began lifting, when he was twelve. Many lifters and men who hold positions within the feast have the giglio charm, cast in fourteen-karat gold or sterling silver. These giglio charms are specially made by Tivoli Jewelers, a local merchant. They wear this jewelry prominently during feast meetings and lifts. Their chains speak of their allegiance to the feast, to the lift, and to the saints and are often piled with other medals, crosses, and images of Our Lady of Mount Carmel.

Joe's stories of devotion to Our Lady of Mount Carmel and Neil's connections to Saint Anthony demonstrate the strong, embodied relationships Catholic men have with the saints, relationships that are strengthened through particular forms of material culture. These tattoos are also discursive, enabling the telling of stories about family bonds. In this way, tattoos constitute ongoing practice; they secure proximity to the saints and reinscribe their significance in men's lives. These narratives demonstrate how intimate relationships are mapped onto images of the saints. Devotional objects and images, whether three-dimensional or set in skin, inscribe love, sociality, loyalty, and community between friends, mentors, and loved ones at the feast. Through tattoos, we see how devotion is about both individual and communal approaches to the saints and how it is relational—how devotion is enacted with and in the relationships between men—simultaneously sustaining relationships and networks on earth and those between heaven and earth.

The Turk

Gold lamé, taffeta, gladiator sandals, brocade, and rhinestones are all part of a visual language and materiality that does not fit with the other masculine styling and aesthetics of the feast. The Turk is an example of aesthetic excess and play, play that is possible in embodying the position of a racial, ethnic, and religious other and in reenacting legendary hagiography. Lieutenants dress up in matching polos or baseball jerseys, emblazoned with their last names to differentiate themselves from the lifters in their matching cotton T-shirts printed with images of Our Lady of Mount Carmel and the giglio. Capos embody a more senior swagger in pressed polyester button-downs, loafers, and fedoras and hold canes, which they use when they command the giglio. The Turk's appearance sets him apart from the other ranks of men. He is a different kind of hero, chosen among men who are particularly visible in their service to the church, not just the feast. As one Turk put it when asked what makes someone worthy of being Turk, "The devotion to the parish, which is a big thing. A lot of people forget that. Being involved with the parish community, not just the feast. Coming to Masses, being involved, giving time to Our Lady. . . . What do you do to help the parish? . . . And secondly, it's how much time do you physically give to help make this feast happen? Do you work behind the scenes? Do you show up every night?" Men who become Turk are active behind the scenes and outside of the feast. They work in the rectory, coordinating dinners and parish fundraising, manage the shrine and the children's giglio, manage publicity, and sing on the giglio. They are men who are in the good graces of the executive board, the governing body of the feast, composed of past capos, the pastor, and the men in charge of feast finances who elect the Turk.

The Turk is the only figure during the Dance of the Giglio that is a theatrical representation from the life of Saint Paulinus (aka San Paolino). San Paolino appears only as a statue in cloth robes or papier-mâché representation at the very top of the giglio and at the back of the boat. In its most simplified form, a man named Danny, a self-proclaimed feast "die hard," explained the story of Saint Paulinus, "who was a bishop in the town of Nola. African marauders were taking children captive, and when Paulinus heard he went to go try to save the children, but he too was taken captive. A Turk[ish] sultan was moved by his sacrifice and went to Africa to save him and the children. When the people in Nola heard they erected a tower of lilies, lily is giglio in Italian, and they welcomed Paulinus as he sailed back." As the feast is a ritual that always receives publicity, the men are accustomed to telling this story in interviews (with journalists, filmmakers, and researchers), and it is the way feast promotional materials explain the roots of the event, but it is important to note that they know the historical inconsistencies in the narrative.

The feast of San Paolino, the fifth-century Bishop of Nola, was celebrated in June, around his feast day, June 22.[20] Paulinus was well known for his asceticism, caring for pilgrims and the poor, renouncing his patrician lifestyle, leaving his home behind, supporting the cult of Saint Felix, and serving the peasants of the Campania countryside. But the Dance of the Giglio commemorates the self-sacrificing Saint Paulinus, who defended the citizens of Nola from invaders and enslavement. Three years after he ascended to power in 590, Pope Gregory the Great wrote his *Dialogues*, about the lives of saints in Italy; in it he wrote about Saint Paulinus as the hero of Nola.[21] Gregory wrote that Paulinus was Bishop of Nola during the Vandal invasion of Campania. The Vandals, under the rule of Genseric, invaded Nola and enslaved Nolanis, taking them to the Vandal kingdom in North Africa.[22] Paulinus worked tirelessly to gather ransoms for the captives, but when a poor widow's son was taken prisoner and she beseeched him to gather a ransom to save her son, Paulinus could not gather the funds. Instead, Paulinus took his place and was taken to Africa and worked as a gardener for the son-in-law of the

Vandal king, never exposing his true identity as a bishop. Paulinus had the gift of prophecy and told the son-in-law that death would soon strike the king. The son-in-law had been having dreams about the king's death and was taken aback by Paulinus's prophecy. He urged Paulinus to tell him the truth about who he really was. When Paulinus revealed that he was a bishop, his master decided to allow him to return to Nola. Paulinus would not go back alone. According to Gregory he asked his master, "One thing there is wherein you may much pleasure me, and that is, to set at liberty all those that be of my city." On ships the slaves from Nola sailed back with Paulinus and Gregory declared that Paulinus "became himself for a time a servant alone, that afterward he might be made free with many."[23] Paulinus sailed back in ships full of wheat with the people from Campania. Scholars have discredited Gregory's story because the invasion of Nola occurred years after Paulinus's death (some scholars mark his death in 431, others in 441).[24]

Today on the feast website and in publicity materials, organizers circulate a story about Nola being overrun by North African pirates.[25] Instead of a Vandal prince, they state a Turkish sultan was inspired by Paolino's sacrifice and sailed back to Nola with Paolino and the other captives. The people of Nola, joyous about the return of their loved ones, met San Paolino on the shore carrying towers of lilies. This reception, according to feast literature, inspired the annual event in Nola, with various craftsmen and guilds constructing more spectacular displays each year; these displays evolved into the decorative wood and papier-mâché structure that immigrants continued to dance with when they moved to Brooklyn. Today in Nola, they lift eight monumental gigli.

The earliest known documentation of the giglio festivities dates to 1514, and the earliest known mention of the boat, or *barca*, is from 1744; another early mention is from 1853, in which the author wrote that there was a "boat upon which a young man dressed as a Turk [*un turco*] held a pomegranate blossom. Behind this boat followed a great war ship on waves supporting it." The author continued, "Sul bompresso stave un giovane, in vesti moreschi, l'aria divertita, fumando un sigaro."[26] A young man dressed in Moorish clothing stood on the bow, looking amused, smoking a cigar.[27] Prints from the mid- and late nineteenth century depict the boat in Nola as a large wooden ship, filled with turbaned men, carried on the shoulders of a mass of men. In the prints a

Turk dressed in a vest and cinched harem pants stands on the bow, holding a sword much like the one in Brooklyn.[28] It was not until 1958 that a boat and the Turk became part of the feast in Brooklyn, but the same imagery prevailed.

Through dressing up as the Turk, growing their beards, donning turbans, and wielding the sword, men enter a masculine lineage that stretches back to the 1950s, and more imaginatively stretches back to the time of Saint Paulinus. They use their performances as the Turk to commemorate and honor connections to male kin, to embody an "exotic," scandalous, and irreverent masculinity, and to solidify their place in history and enact their devotion to the saints.

In the figure of the Turk in the drama of the Dance of the Giglio, histories of encounter, Orientalist imaginings, and collective memory of southern Italy's enemies are compressed and overlaid. The figure of the Ottoman Turk was superimposed upon the figure of the Goth or Vandal invader, not just in Nola but throughout Italy. When Constantinople fell to the Ottomans in 1453, Renaissance writers likened the Ottoman threat to the invasion of the Goths and Vandals of the fifth century and refracted their fears through the lens of one of the "greatest tragedies of the ancient past."[29] To understand the threat of the Turk, writers likened them to "new barbarians," understanding them within the lens of distant history.[30] In the sixteenth and seventeenth centuries, the Kingdom of Naples, under the Spanish monarchy, was threatened by the raids of Barbary corsairs—Ottoman pirates. Saint Paulinus's hagiography, the story of a heroic bishop saving his people from invaders, was resonant with these threats to the coastal cities.[31]

In the Mediterranean imagination, Turks were not only violent invaders but exotic and "lustful."[32] In these Orientalist visions, the Turk and his harem loomed large. In the mid-1500s throughout Italy, right when the Dance of the Giglio was first documented, there was a fascination with the national costumes of the "other" like the Ottoman Turks. When the Holy League (which included the Kingdom of Naples, where Nola was located) defeated the Ottomans at the Battle of Lepanto in 1571, pageants, processions, and Masses were celebrated throughout the kingdoms of Italy. There was a dual fear and fascination with the image of the Turk in the Mediterranean, and European chroniclers often noted the ostentation and splendor of the Turkish armies and sultans, writing of their jeweled and adorned weapons, the plumes of their turbans, and the vibrant blue satin of their garments.[33]

The character of the Turk became unmoored from any geographic particularity and became a figure in drama, costume, art, and fashion. According to art historian Adam Jasienski, since the Middle Ages "the turban could be used to depict any non-Catholic individual."[34] It was immediate visual shorthand for difference. But Ottoman styles also became commodities coveted by clerics and royals alike. In Eastern Europe clergy wore brocade chasubles with Ottoman motifs that were imported from Italy. Noblemen wore long layered coats and vests with silhouettes that "muffled the body," emulating Ottoman fashions. In the fifteenth through seventeenth centuries in Florence and Rome it was a "fashionable fancy" to dress in turbans as the Turk became a figure in Renaissance and Baroque art.[35] If in the Mediterranean and broader European imagination the Turk was a figure that embodied enchantment and enemy, it still is charged in that way today, regarding not just race but also masculinity. There is a desire for dress-up and a bounded place and time where it is sanctioned. In Brooklyn today none of these historical resonances are necessarily overt or spoken about by the men. Other scholars have argued that because the dance focuses on the moment of "release-and-return" and reconciliation between the sultan and the people of Nola, "the resolution of ethnic antagonisms becomes the central message of the drama." Here I am interested in the Turk as devotion made into pageantry: devotion that allows men to transgress, to play with vibrant aesthetics.[36] In this hagiographical figure and racial other they get to transgress the sartorial standards of white heteronormativity; they can don jewels, rhinestones, and sequins *and* be celebrated for it. Being Turk is *fun* because of the freedom and opportunity to partake in dramatic display and play with traditionally masculine aesthetics.

One former Turk, Anthony, explained that the role is like no other in the feast; it is purely about having fun, not about responsibility, like the capos and lieutenants. Rather, when you are Turk "the honor is when you're at the house and hear the band coming [to pick you up]. You're up there, by yourself, you've got the sailors and it's your day, and you see everything from up there and its gorgeous. It's an experience. . . . It's a great honor that shows that you're respected. A helluva lot of fun and the easiest position because you're having fun up there."

Figure 1.7. Turk atop the boat, 2014. Photo by the author.

The most salient symbol for the Turk is a curved wooden sword, which has been passed from Turk to Turk for decades. Some years during the feast there is a celebration called Turk Night, which honors and reunites all the Turks, living and dead, stretching back to the second ever Turk, Sonny Mangone, who served from 1963 to 1966. Similar to Old Timer's Day, which typically takes place on the last day of the feast, where all the capos of years past return to command the giglio, Turk Night is a performance of a male lineage. In 2017 all the past Turks gathered at the top of the church steps; some had traveled back from outside of the city. From men in their eighties to the youngest Turk, Joey, who was twenty-one at the time, all the men gathered at the top of the steps in matching red polos that were embroidered with their names, the years they served as Turk, and an image of a wooden ship with three masts, the first one decorated with a seal of the papal keys.

In 2015 they did not yet have the matching polos but enacted succession in a different way. Turk Night coincided with the night lift of the giglio. As the sky darkened, the gold and maroon giglio moved through the streets, lit by bright white bulbs. All the Turks gathered on the steps and huddled together to take a group picture as their names were read from youngest to oldest. The men at the top of the steps took turns passing the wooden sword, and they each wielded it with their signature style. John, Turk in 2004, held the sword in both hands straight above his head and bent his torso from side to side. Phil, 2000–2001, gained momentum with his arm and thrust the sword in the air. Richie, 1982–83, acted like a swashbuckler, as if he was menacing someone in a sword fight, slithering his body backward, jutting his chin, and moving the sword in an S shape. Vinnie, 1978–79, posed with the sword coyly before moonwalking backward with it. Some of the men just waved the sword; others got more theatrical, like Joe Peluso, 1969–72, who stood triumphant with his arms up and sword drawn, as if waiting for applause. After performing with the sword, they walked down the stairs to the applause of the crowd that had gathered in front of the church. The band played a solemn song during the reading of a list of the deceased Turks. In 2017 the Turks climbed a ladder and piled into the boat, some donning their huge white and feathered turbans or their rhinestoned vests. They took turns at the bow of the boat, waving the sword as the lifters carried the boat down the street. In this ceremony the Turks expressed their belonging in a long line of men who worked for the church, were honored for their service, and were integral to the drama of the Dance of the Giglio through their embodied performance.

The Turk's sword is an exclusive object of pride; it is over fifty years old and made of heavy carved wood that is coated in new paint each year to match each Turk's color preferences. It is a precious object. Two past Turks, Phil and Anthony, explained the meaning of the sword to me: "It's an honor at the meeting [when the new Turk is announced] for the old Turk to give the sword to the new Turk. It's an honor that you're recognized for your hard work throughout the year," Anthony explained as Phil jokingly added, "The sword is passed down . . . we just like big swords." Each Turk customizes the sword. In 2014 Mark painted it a bright, shiny red, his favorite color and also a color that keeps *malocchia* (evil eye) away. In 2015 and 2016 Joey's sword was gold, with swirling cursive writing declaring across the sword, "Brooklyn is the Heart / Nola is the Soul" a saying that honored his recently deceased uncle and past capo Phillie Manna, who was one of the few people in Brooklyn with ties to the feast in Nola. Like the sword, Joey's boat with its inscription "In Loving Memory of Daddy, 20 Years in Heaven" broadcast his love for his male kin and located him in a lineage of feast leaders.

The Turks are responsible for the sword's safekeeping and understand it as a kind of sacred object that has to be protected and cared for. At one of my first feast meetings, Mark, Dan, and Phil—all former Turks—explained the sword's sacredness to me. One Turk had put star stickers all over the sword, and Mark took care to sand it down and repaint it. They told me that it is just a piece of wood with "seventeen layers of paint," but all expressed the anxiety they felt while keeping it in their homes leading up to the feast and how nervous they were when they finally waved the sword as the Turk on the boat. Mark was always anxious it would fly out of his hand and into the crowd. They assured each other that could never happen because that is why the sword is never held by the base. Leading up to the feast, Mark kept the sword on top of the dresser in his bedroom, high up so that he would not find his son waving and hacking around with it one day. Although he went out of his way to protect it, he admitted that if it was lost or broken he could probably make a new one and no one would notice "cover it in seventeen coats of paint and it would look the same," except to a former Turk who would be able to recognize its weight and the feeling of holding it. Turks thus have an exclusive embodied connection to tradition. They know how to hold the sword and exactly how heavy it is and have the privilege of temporarily owning an object that, through literal coats of paint but also through the aura of history, represents the feast.

Like the giglio, the sword is replicated in miniature and adorns the body of one past Turk, Dan. Dan is in his thirties, with milky fair skin, dark hair, and a thick black goatee; he served as Turk in 2007 and recently became an apprentice capo. Dan is a science teacher and has always been interested in going back to school for his doctorate. He is constantly calculating the years until he becomes number one capo, a role he has been preparing nearly his entire life for—his current estimate is 2037, when he is in his early sixties. He was "kid's capo" in 1994, the year his father died. He was head of the children's giglio for eleven years before becoming a lieutenant and even proposed to his wife in front of the children's giglio. One of the very first times I met him, down in the church's lower hall after a feast meeting, Dan pulled a thin sterling silver chain out of his shirt to reveal a charm in the shape of a curved sword. With pride he told me that it was custom made. In 2016 we walked as part of the Questua, a ritual in which crews of lifters and parishioners walk the neighborhood to pass out blessed bread and spread the news about the feast. Dan was clutching a handful of plastic bags with blessed bread as we shared our frustrations about explaining the feast and its rituals to people who had never heard of it. Dan fingered the thin silver chain around his neck and showed me the engraving on the back—7.8.07, marking the year he was Turk. His mother bought it for him and had a special cast made of the sword the year he became lieutenant in 2010.

While the Turks are central to the reenactment of San Paolino returning to Nola, the men seldom talk about how they imagine themselves reenacting hagiographical drama; rather the thing past Turks talk about most is their outfits as they try to one-up each other. Phil, who is now the deacon of the church, wore gold pleather pants, a sequined blue cape, a white tunic, and long strings of metallic Mardi Gras beads around his neck. In the pouring rain Phil walked through Williamsburg and under the overpass of the Brooklyn-Queens Expressway with an actual camel in tow, which he had dressed in a sheath of yellow fabric. Imagine the jarring sight of a camel walking through the streets of Brooklyn. John wore a blue and gold brocade coat lined with gold sequins and a tall matching turban and a troupe of belly dancers that carried a canopy over him as he walked and sensually fed him grapes—a performance the men joked was "very racial." Mark went back to school as an adult and has a degree in history and did research in order to pick what he thought was a more historically accurate outfit. He wore loose shorts, almost like culottes, a cream tunic with a cobalt sash that was heavily rhinestoned and beaded around the collar, a long cobalt vest with shiny beaded piping along the edges, and a headband rather than a turban. On his feet he wore tall brown gladiator sandals that grazed his knees and wrapped tightly around his calves. His sandals were a sacrifice; after wearing them the whole day he had absolutely bloody feet, joking that he looked like he had stigmata. Mark explained that it annoyed him that the Turk's costumes were never historically correct. "There were no Muslims back then, North Africa was under Roman control—so why would they wear turbans? And anyway, the sultans that wore turbans they were huge turbans." Mark continued that for the sake of being historically correct he refused to dress "as an Arab."

One past Turk told me that post-9/11, when there used to be cops stationed in the subways with assault rifles, he once got stopped and had his bag searched. As he waited for the search to be over, he told me he touched his face and remembered his beard: "Oh I get it. . . . Sunglasses, full beard, tan, backpack. . . . I get it, I look like a terrorist." When Joey was Turk, people watching the lifts in the crowd noted that he looked "Arabic." Their donning of the turban prepares them to be heralded rather than being profiled and is not a point of "fixation" or "anxiety"; the exaggerated costume turban and full beard, in the context of the feast ritual, accrues positive meaning rather than real state surveillance.[37]

The Turk is an Orientalist foil to the capos and lieutenants—setting up a binary between authority/power/discipline and play/sensuality/excess.[38] The Turk's costume is an exoticized, Orientalist, Disneyfied imagining. As scholar Sam Baltimore has written about musical adaptations of Aladdin, in order to create mainstream Orientalist entertainment there must still be a "face of respectable, heterosexual, white maleness that so often serves as a gossamer-thin veil over campy Orientalist fantasy."[39]

Figure 1.8. Neil, Turk in 2018, making his debut. Photo by the author.

That same veil is essential to the serious business of Catholic ritual. Between the exotic animals, the sexualized dancers, and the seemingly transformative qualities of dress and beard, the Turk is the exception, an aesthetically excessive foil, in a community that otherwise privileges white, male, seemingly heterosexual bodies dressed in cargo shorts and T-shirts. This performance enables them to embody a masculinity that is flamboyant and in direct contrast to the uniformity of the lifters and the senior authority and formality of the capos. If the lifters are penitential and disciplined, the Turk is their visual opposite.

Neil was in the running but did not become Turk in 2017, but leading up to the vote and announcement he imagined what his boat would look like. As we stood outside the church before the meeting when the new Turk would be announced, he dragged a cigarette and told me, "I'm nervous. I already know how I would paint the boat . . . simple, just red and white. And I already know exactly what I would put on my sail. It would be my father's cross in the middle." He gestured down to his leg, where his father's cross is tattooed. "With angel wings behind it. . . . On the right there would be an angel in blue for my grandfather. The red and white is actually because when I was a kid," he turned his head to the side and smiled so wide I could see his pointy incisors, and his eyes wrinkled at the sides, "my dad had a 1990 red Cadillac Seville, it was a cherry red with a white vinyl top. It was beautiful. And you could see him from a mile away, you always knew it was him and he always said I have to get rid of this car, I don't need people knowing where the fuck I am." Through this imagined boat he would honor his male kin. In his imaginings we see how it is an aspirational role, and its meanings rely explicitly on its materiality and its connections to male networks of affection. Neil finally became Turk in 2018.

From Brooklyn to Nola

Nola and Williamsburg, Brooklyn, are 4,394 miles apart. The year I visited along with a group of men from Brooklyn, travel between the two places required a car ride to the airport, a direct flight from JFK to Naples offered through Meridiana Airlines, an affordable, convenient option that no longer exists, and a train ride or taxi between Naples and Nola. One is an ultra-gentrified neighborhood founded in the nineteenth century, once an Italian enclave, consistently mourned, claimed, loved, and protected by Italian American Catholics. The other is an ancient town in the shadow of Vesuvius. What binds them are networks of real and imagined ancestry: ties of blood, but more interestingly ties of devotion and ritual. Even those who are largely not fluent in Italian and not bound to the town by family history or remaining connections still navigate its Catholic ritual landscape with know-how. Nola as the origin place of the giglio is imagined as a natal landscape of sorts: an affective landscape of wonder, sentimentality, and nostalgia. Nola feels like home—not just emotionally, but in the body and through the body.

Nola and its gigli are enchanted. I use that concept within David Morgan's framework: images and objects "operate as the tokens of enchantment by deftly integrating the individual into larger communities or networks"; they are "instruments or technologies that connect bodies to places and to one another; productively integrating humans into their physical and social ecologies."[40] To visit Nola today is to connect with centuries of artisans, lifters, devotees, and San Paolino himself and to locate oneself within a broader, and more global, Catholic history. To travel to Nola is to link Brooklyn to southern Italy and North Africa. Men make those links through travel, but also through costuming, ritual, and hagiographic play. Even before they get to Nola they have had a lifetime of building bodily competency and adorning themselves to serve and honor its patron saint.

When he was a little boy of only four, Joey left the country for the first time and traveled with his family to Nola. He was born in Brooklyn, but on this very first trip to Italy he met all his Italian uncles and met the devotional object that would become the center of his Catholic practice and identity for years to come. As he fell asleep one night, in his family's house nestled on a narrow cobblestoned street, Joey saw two wooden towers outside his window. Even as he recounted this story as a man, he conveyed the aura of childhood enchantment. The next morning he saw another set of towers floating down the street through his window. They passed just as the sun was rising. These towers, tapering wooden and papier-mâché obelisks, were four of the eight gigli.[41] This first vision of the gigli, monumental and animated, remained with Joey all these years.

At twenty-five years old, Joey told me that that almost magical night was a turning point for him. "The first time I saw the geels [short for giglios] that's what made me always love the geels in America, that first experience." When Joey made his confirmation, he chose the patron of Nola as his saint. Describing his devotion, he told me, "I pray to San Paolin, actually my confirmation name is Paolino. So I do have a big devotion to San Paolin"; in the characteristic New York Italian American style, he dropped the vowel at the end of Paolino: San Paolin. When Joey was nine, he put on shiny gold harem pants that ballooned out at his ankles, a matching gold vest, and a thick fake mustache. He wielded a plastic sword and played the role of a sailor on the ship that carried San Paolino back to his people. Instead of sailing on the Mediterranean, Joey rode on a ship hoisted high above the streets of Williamsburg, sailing through the crowds, and past his parish, on the shoulders of lifters. Joey threw confetti, waved his sword, danced to the music of the brass band, and came to know San Paolino through playing a scene from his saintly life. Joey loved the giglio so much that when he was thirteen his friends jokingly gave him the nickname Joey Giglio and it stuck. In 2018 Joey was the very first American Turk in Nola; Nolani feast authorities were impressed with his outfit, what he called a Muslim wedding suit, when he played Turk in Brooklyn in 2015–16. People in Nola saw pictures of Joey's lavish getup on Facebook and requested his presence at the 2018 feast. To Joey, being a good Turk on either side of the Atlantic requires "being joyful, wanting to dance with the geel in rhythm with the boat. Dancing to the music, being respectful." In summer 2018, a year before being named Turk in 2019, Joe Mascia was able to visit Nola for the very first time. Reflecting on his time in Nola, Joe said, "Just walking through the streets in Nola, it felt like I was home, there's no words to describe that. . . . Like it was a place I'd never been to before, but I felt like I was there."

These men shared the ineffability of their first experience seeing the gigli in Nola. Like Joey, who was too young to have words to describe the gigli passing by his window, Joe Mascia, now thirty-two, stood on Joey's balcony and watched as the gigli went by: "One of them actually passed by Joey's balcony and it was just like the most awesome experience, I can't. I—words can't even describe, videos can't describe the giglio being like two feet [away] that you can reach out and touch it, not just the bottom, like you're in the middle of the tower cuz you're up higher." Neil traveled to Nola by train and saw a giglio as soon as he disembarked. He said he was "speechless": "We got off the train and there were no words to describe the feeling of getting off and having it right there." There is no better way to describe the gigli than as enchanted. That day, awestruck and running around Nola to find all eight of the gigli, Neil, by way of Facebook and YouTube, already knew so much about their histories, crews, and past designs. He low-fived his wife, and said if I get to lift, "I'm gonna cry." "I'm gonna cry" was Neil's refrain throughout the day, as we wandered around searching for the statue of San Paolino in the center of the city and found a column embedded in an older building and learned from another Brooklyn man that it was a column from Paolino's time. Time and space collapsed in the travel from Brooklyn to Nola.

Affordable air travel, Facebook pages celebrating all things giglio, a network of friends and kin involved in the feast, and YouTube videos that allow New York men to virtually visit Nola, learn its traditions, and know its ritual environments are all part of the formation of the global body of the feast. "Brooklyn is the heart, Nola is the soul" is a slogan that has become increasingly popular in Brooklyn. In this translocal body, if Brooklyn is the heart, the men formed in its traditions, seeking a return to a small town that is either a real or imagined site of heritage and ancestry, are its limbs and sinews, shoulders, fingers, and, most of all, blood. To understand the body of the feast is to understand how men share embodied ways of knowing and feeling. That bodily knowledge helps them navigate a ritual landscape that is at once completely unknown and completely familiar.

Men from Brooklyn might not speak Italian, relying on technologies like Google Translate to mediate conversations, but they do speak the same body language as lifters from Nola. Regardless of language or ancestry, men from Nola and from Brooklyn share techniques of the body. Those techniques are the very movements of devotion, as much about bodily fluency as about belief. When Brooklyn men lift in Nola, they quickly learn how to rock their bodies back and forth to turn, to take baby steps through precariously narrow and bumpy cobblestone streets. They hone these techniques through listening to the music, through learning exactly what note of a song to lock their knees and square their shoulders to collectively lift the giglio off the ground. In the natal home of the giglio, I have seen men, emerging from a successful lift, cry through dark glasses, hug each other, jump, dance, and celebrate together, giddy with joy, intermingling their sweat below the unbearable Campania sun. Whether in Brooklyn or in Nola, these men share a devotion they know with their bones, feet, shoulders, and costumed bodies—a devotion they enact together.[42] These men cross the Atlantic with their friends, with fellow parishioners, and with hopes of accessing some origin experience. They fly to Italy for their love of the feast and for their devotion, a love and devotion they have been cultivating their whole lives. But they often do not have words for their devotion.

Among the men in Brooklyn I learned that direct questioning was not the way to access their devotional lives. I learned to watch, to hear, and sometimes to feel and learn with them, to see how they inculcate bodily expertise, acquire deep knowledge of how to construct a giglio, carry a saint, and handle blessed objects. This is not to characterize men as stoic or restrained interlocutors, but to account for the ways kinesthetics and bodily competencies were privileged over discursive accounts of devotion. When I asked Joe Mascia, after years of knowing him and seeing his devotion, whether lifting is part of his devotional practice, he simply said, "Absolutely, absolutely." When I asked him why, he honestly didn't know what to say—quite the talkative guy, he was stumped for a second: "It just you know, you just, I'm trying to think of the right words. It's just your devotion for the saints and you feel like you're doing your penance. You know, like, the more pain, the more penance, you know what I'm saying." This was a recycled answer, the answer maybe he thought I wanted to hear, the answer I expected, or the answer he heard others give to journalists and reporters. Joe's devotional practice and commitment to the parish were not enacted during Mass—which he often attended virtually by live streaming it. Rather he enacts devotion by managing social media for the church (@OLMCFEAST), ensuring thousands show up to the feast, setting up the technology to enable live streaming, and uploading homilies to Facebook. Joe enacts his devotion by using his unique skills to serve the parish and the saints. Throughout our interview, Joe told me at least seven times that he could not put into words his experience in Nola. He privileged body over meaning. What he did do was mime how he moved his body under the poles. He could talk at length about the contrast between the steel poles in Brooklyn and the more authentic wooden poles in Nola. In Brooklyn, "it's just the unforgiving steel pushing down on you. . . . The metal and the weight is just pushing down on your back and on your legs." But in Nola the wood has "so much more flex to it . . . it's just so evenly distributed because it just flexes. . . . Everyone's actually carrying their own weight, there's no fake lifters there. And just the flex, it was just unbelievable."

As we sat in the rectory of the parish, between bites of a huge tinfoil-wrapped sausage and pepper sandwich, Joe used his body to describe his experience in Nola: "The second lift I ever took, we turned, we did a 360, and when I talk about baby steps as we were turning, they were half a baby step and you're just slowly—and as you're going your shoulder is moving." He began swaying his shoulders up and down in a wave, or like the pirate boat ride at Coney Island, swift back and forth, one shoulder up, then the other up, acting out the motion of the steps and the shoulder sync, and continued, "The giglio is bouncing as you're turning and it's just unbelievable." What was striking for him was the corporate and corporeal movement. The memory was held not just through photos or stories but through embodied imprints and in situ pedagogy through which he exported his bodily knowledge about lifting to another context. If Nola felt like home in an uncanny way, it was not only its landscape but the familiarity he felt in his body.

Devotional memory is "archived in the body."[43] The sense memory of lifting, of bearing weight on one's shoulders, pivoting, working in sync, is a particularly gendered, devotional memory, one central to the masculine body of the feast. Anthropologists of Catholicism have been working on discerning and theorizing the Catholic sensorium—the body logics, "gestural and experiential repertoire[s]" that "under[pin] Catholic understandings of the world."[44] Religious studies scholar Matthew Cressler, in his work on Black Catholic converts, also found "the ways Catholics moved their bodies in the world" to be central, perhaps more so than assent to beliefs. Catholic identity and devotion to the saints are products of a pedagogical process of "repetition and habituation."[45] While lifting the giglio is not a pan-Catholic technique of the body, not ordinary like kneeling or extraordinary like experiencing a vision or locution, it is the embodied practice that unites Catholic men from Brooklyn to Nola in shared bodily devotion to San Paolino.

The kinesthetics of this devotion are especially salient in the absence of shared language. When one of the local leaders pointed to the boat and said "under," Joe said the one word in Italian he was sure of, "si," and let himself be grabbed by the arm and put under the boat. As an American, he was honored. He lifted for three hours, from three thirty to six thirty in the morning. Like Joey, his first experience with the Nolani machines was by sunrise: "You're lifting and the sun is coming up there is no experience that could ever change that. It's just a once in a lifetime—well obviously not a once in a lifetime—but for the first time, it was just the best experience of my life to be lifting . . . the boat as the sun is coming up, and you're pulling into the piazza." While they skipped Mass in Nola, missing the liturgy that is supposed to unite Catholics across the globe, the men were linked through the shared bodily techniques of processing and lifting and the collective experience. In Joe's words, "All the giglios are surrounding you, and the crowds! and the music! . . . then! San Paolin [*sic*] comes out of the church! and they are playing the San Paolino hymn and [he] goes to every giglio and blesses it and it was just unbelievable." In 2019, when Joe was named Turk in Brooklyn, it was the capstone to the devotional commitments that he expressed in his Brooklyn parish, but also in his travel to Nola.

Joe had always dreamed of being Turk, ever since he was a kid. When he was younger he often worried about the future of the feast: "From the time I was a kid I always worried, is this feast going to be around when I get older? Is this feast going to be around for me to be Turk? Is this feast going to be around for me to be a lieutenant? Because as a kid you want those things." Joe, like so many others, often talked about how the feast is "deeply rooted into our blood." The discourse of blood implies that love for the feast is inherent rather than cultivated. Children learn to love the feast, as Joe said, from the time they are in a carriage. They are brought on processions; they learn to admire and emulate lifters; they listen to the music. But most importantly, especially for boys, they experience the rituals and materiality of the feast in miniature. Through material and performative processes young boys are made into generations of men committed to the feast.

Everything in Miniature

On July 10, 2014, a crowd of children gathered in front of the church for the children's giglio lift. Temporary tattoos, the kind that peel and flake and wrinkle with the movement of the skin, adorned the biceps and forearms of a few little boys, and around their wrists they wore green, white, and red rubber wristbands that read "Giglio." The temporary tattoos of the giglio in the ubiquitous shape of the tower in the green, white, and red of the Italian flag are sold around the corner from the church. The kids looked like lifters in miniature in their matching white shirts printed with a purple line drawing of the giglio floating among puffy clouds. Along with the T-shirts the children wore white golf hats and bandanas tied neatly around their necks. Some wore silver and gold chains with small crucifixes, and others had red and white carnations tucked into the brims of their hats. One of the boys, a husky kid of about ten, stood much taller than the others; the sleeves of his tee were frayed from scissor work, and the large (temporary) giglio tattoo rose the length of his exposed, fleshy bicep. Rather than in a neat bow around his neck, his bandana was tied around his forehead, giving him a more rugged look. Like many of the other children, his cheeks were rosy from standing in the sun.

The crowd of kids gathered with their parents for the tradition of the children's lift. In 2014 the children's giglio was about twenty feet tall and made in the same architectural style as that year's giglio, with gray marbleized painting, windows, cornices, and gilded *putti* adornments. Like its larger counterpart, the children's giglio was dressed in white streamers, draped with the American and Italian flags, and topped with a statue of San Paolino. Although the children's giglio is a lift in miniature, complete with little capos dressed in slacks, button-downs, and fedoras, who meekly shout the commands to the little lifters, one detail sets it apart—girls. Little girls lift the children's giglio. They too wear the lifter T-shirts and white hats and gather under the wooden poles of the giglio. Long ponytails and braids drape over their shoulders. Some wear pink and purple sneakers, hoop earrings, ribbons in their hair, and T-shirts customized with hand-cut fringe; one little girl even wore red lipstick for the occasion.

During the lift some of the children were resilient, but others com-plained their arms were sore. They rolled their eyes and fidgeted as they wondered when they would finally be able to take off their hats. Their whines and complaints were assuaged by their parents, who took videos with iPhones in hand and passed them water bottles. The kids' capo raised his cane, waving it in the air to commence the lift, and was in-structed by men in the crowd to get his cane up high and wave it, like the capos do. He walked backward, gesturing with his hands that the kids should move forward. It is a big moment for children when they get to play capo. In 2015 one little capo was nervous before the lift and brought two dollars to the Our Lady of Mount Carmel statue, telling a shrine worker he wanted to give her the dollars "so she can pray for me that I won't mess up."

The older boys stood under the poles of the giglio gritting their teeth, grimacing, and puffing out their chests, emulating the adult lifters. They emphasized the difficulty of the lift. One boy, who was about eight years old and the son of an apprentice capo, gave a particularly impressive performance. As he walked he took small, calculated steps, the same as the lifters on the giglio. He had his bandana tied around his head and pumped his fist and stamped his foot along to the music as the giglio bounced. As the giglio turned he marched sideways, scrunching his face with strain and rolling his tongue over his bottom lip. When the chil-dren moved forward he balanced the pole on his shoulder and pumped both his fists along with the music, and his brow furrowed. When they dropped the giglio, he rose in relief from the weight. He looked like a mini lifter, with the same gestures and the same real and performed strain. As the giglio music came on, he pointed up to the large giglio on the corner, as if in dedication, bent his knees, jutted out his chin, and lifted his weight up.

As parents watch their children, proud and impressed to see them dance the giglio, and watch their little shoulders bearing the weight of the mini tower, many in the crowd express the innateness of lifting. "The second they lift, it's like they've been doing it forever," "It's in their blood," and "It's in their DNA" are sentiments parents often express at the feast. They are always eager to support their children, to encourage them to continue, even when they get too hot, too sweaty, or too tired.

John was proud to see his nephew as a little capo; the young boy of about nine wore a straw fedora, a neatly pressed robin-egg-blue button-down shirt, nicely creased khakis, and a brand-new pair of navy leather boat shoes. His small wooden cane was decorated in curly blue ribbons to match his outfit. John proudly hugged him and later expressed, "[It's a] positive sign that young kids are obsessed with taking the torch. They are fascinated by it. It's in their blood."

Before the children began the lift in 2014, the pastor of the church blessed them and told them, "You're getting a blessing because what you do for us is give us a promise that this feast has a nice long future, because you could be doing this for another fifty or sixty years, so it is wonderful [that] you are promising us that what we do is important, and that you want to keep it up." Taking on a role at the feast as a child is ideally the start of a lifelong dedication to the tradition. As we have seen, many men have narratives about starting out in the feast as soda boys, running errands and helping out where they could, or serving as part of the rope gang. Some men, like Richie, got the opportunity to be a sailor on the Turk's boat, a high honor for little boys. Reflecting on being a sailor at age seven, when his uncle was Turk in 1982, Richie told me, "When you grow up around this, it is in your blood, really."

Inculcating a love of the feast and knowledge of and dedication to its rituals is not just a matter of blood and nature. Rather, it is a process that is performative, embodied, and material. Children, particularly young boys, learn the embodied repertoires of the feast. They learn to carry the cane and wield the authority of the capos. They learn to wave swords when they play sailors on the boat; they pretend to be lifters, knowing full well that one day they will actually get to lift the giglio. All the roles available to men of the feast, the ones that bestow them with glory and honor, are available in miniature to little boys. "Taking the torch" is not just about being born into a certain family but is a pedagogical process that involves repetitive and cyclical performance, embodied training, and the material things that allow little boys and young men to imagine themselves as lifters, lieutenants, Turks, and capos and practice these roles. When little boys dance along to the giglio music, walk on processions, and watch the lift, their parents and onlookers say things like "this guy's gonna run the feast!" Their relatives call out to them to lift their swords higher, to wave their canes, and to speak up as they say the commands into the mic of the miniature giglio.

Since the 1990s little girls have been allowed to be children's lifters, and they can also become capos for the kids' giglio, but they do not get to wholly share in the material culture and pedagogy that makes *men* at the feast.[46] Girls have typically not gotten to share the objects and performances that train little boys how to play the Turk, how to dress as a capo, or how to imagine themselves as one day "running the feast." The first year the boat was danced at the feast, girls and young women rode with the Turk. In 1959 the Boat Committee proposed putting boys on the boat instead because the girls were "unmanageable."[47]

It is important to note that in 1994 the Vatican's Congregation for Divine Worship and the Sacraments issued a letter clarifying a 1983 change in canon law on lay liturgical servers, communicating that both men and women, boys and girls, could serve at the altar. Girls began lifting the children's giglio, perforating the all-male ritual at the very time that girls were also newly seen at the altar.[48] The Vatican was quick to assert that having female altar servers in no way opened the possibility of women's ordination. But the presence of altar girls was not without controversy. Still a decade later some US priests and cardinals in Rome critiqued the presence of girls and women at the altar, arguing that they feminize the Church and hurt priestly vocations. As the conservative cardinal Raymond Burke put it, "Young boys don't want to do things with girls. It's just natural."[49] Priests who have decided not to allow girls to be altar servers have insisted that "being male and female is a charism given by God that enables a person to do certain things and not other things," marking the altar as a distinctly male space with roles suitable only for boys and men.[50] While girls have very much been part of the children's giglio lifts, they evolve into teenagers and women who have no official roles at the feast, except as spectators, volunteers, supporters, and romantic partners. From a young age girls understand that their roles later on will be different from their fathers' and brothers'.

Women have an intense love of the feast; they know its history and relish its rituals, and their love for the feast is also relational. In 1995 Marie Langone, the sister of Gerard Langone (2017's number one capo), penned a letter that appeared in the parish bulletin about her love for the feast.[51] Each year she awaited the feast, and as soon as it came she changed the answering machine so it would play "O' Giglio e Paradiso." She went out to buy new clothes for Giglio Sunday and would "cook up a storm." Marie wrote that for many years her friends had "listened patiently to what used to be my most fervent desire—being the 'prima capa'—the first female to command the Giglio." She continued, "Tradition dictates that the commanding and dancing of the Giglio be done by men. This is as it should be. With this in mind, I have finally put my dream of being 'prima capa' to rest, preferring to savor the different joys and emotions I experience on this day." She reminisced about walking on candlelit processions for Our Lady of Mount Carmel, singing hymns with her grandmother, mother, and aunts, and the hours they spent cooking together and sharing food with relatives in the yard of their home. "On Giglio Sunday, the vision of my father and uncles lifting that magnificent structure remains in my heart." She recounted all of her male relatives who honor the memories of their loved ones by partaking in the feast traditions. Her brothers were lieutenants and lifters, and her young godsons and cousins were lifting under the children's giglio. She ended the letter with, "We are bound by tradition to play a role and doing it to the best of our ability is what keeps our tradition alive." Although Marie passed in 1999, Gerard dedicates every single lift he commands to "his sister, Marie, in heaven." In her words and reflections on tradition and male and female roles, there are obvious resonances between the giglio tradition and the priesthood and male hierarchy, and the way women have had to settle for only supporting roles in both.

My first year of fieldwork, I met Priscilla (pseudonym), the preteen daughter of an apprentice capo. We both watched as the men put the face on the giglio, hoisting the ten-foot-tall pieces up on a pulley system and securing it to its aluminum framework. As we watched, she explained all the rituals of the feast to me and quizzed me on its history, pointing to capos and making sure I knew their names. She proudly explained how her dad is now an apprentice capo and during the Line of the March everyone arrives at their house to pick him up and they exit the house wearing matching outfits as a family in honor of her dad. She helped him pick an outfit and flipped through pictures on her iPhone of her dad in the fitting room in different combos of summery button-down shirts and white slacks and the white overalls she wore to match him that she assured me were very "in." She and her sisters made signs honoring their father to hang outside the house. As we watched the young men climb the beams of the giglio, she pointed out her older sisters' boyfriends, a lifter and a lieutenant, and she bragged about lifting the kids' giglio and the one year she was capo. During the Questua ritual of giving out blessed bread, we walked with the all-male Greenpoint crew because her father was one of the leaders. While all the guys drank scotch out of red cups, we tagged along as the only two girls on the procession, and she was bold about entering businesses to sell bread. While she was the only girl with the all-male crew, when I asked about her older sisters, she explained that when they were young they too used to help with the Questua, but now that they are older they stay home and help their mom prepare the breakfast for the Line of the March, the procession where capos are picked up from homes in the neighborhood. She understood and fully articulated knowing that as she got older she would no longer participate in the same kinds of activities as boys and men and would follow in the steps of her mother and sisters who worked to support their father during the feast.

Marie Langone, like Priscilla, articulates a love for the feast that is relational, an expression of love between kin, a devotion that sustains both horizontal and vertical ties. While women love the feast, from a young age they understand that they "phase out" of its public rituals and transition to other roles in its gendered division of labor. While little girls tag along with their dads and learn feast history, those who continue to be involved are more likely to become shrine workers, the girlfriends of lifters, spectators cheering on their partners, and sisters or wives of capos who work on decorating the homes for processions and coordinating breakfasts and catering. Unlike boys, girls have not had full access to the developmental materiality that leads them through different roles and levels of authority at the feast. In 2018 and 2019 two girls played sailors on the boat, and many made up the lifters of the children's giglio. In 2019 a teenage girl, related to a feast organizer, stood in the crowd watching the children's lift. She turned to her friend who was asking about whether she ever lifted the little giglio and said, "I was not involved and girls aren't allowed to do the big giglio, so there is really no point."

By looking at feast materiality—the body of the feast and its adornment, inking, and training—we see how gender is made and performed through material media, how it is constructed, imitated, and embodied through costumes, objects, and ink. Dedication to the feast, to tradition, and to a homosocial community is cultivated through bodies of men, as they grow their beards, wave their swords, wear tattoos, paint the giglio, and lift together.

2

Manual Labor and the Artistry of Devotion in the Basement

One spring I was at an antique store in Indianapolis. It was a huge warehouse of room upon room, a veritable Crystal Palace of stuff. In a corner of one of the rooms—a city of clutter—among ceramic pigs and aging souvenirs was a stunning, albeit homey, image of a female saint painted on what looked like tin. She knelt in front of an altar where there sat wilting roses and a lonely rosary. She wore a voluminous black habit, her face and neck framed by a white cowl. She was pretty. Although she was lost in meditation, she was not alone. Cherubs holding flower crowns danced above her and played in heavenly light. Behind her was an angel crowning her with a crown of thorns. Her gaze was one of intense love with a hint of anguish. She looked down at a crucifix she held in her hands, and her fingers delicately touched the edges of the corpus. In her forehead was a thorn that had lodged itself in her skin. I knew immediately that it was Saint Rita, the nun from Cascia, Italy, who so desired to intimately share in Christ's suffering that she was pierced by a thorn, leaving a wound that remained open until her death. I did not know this because of any robust Catholic education or any of my own family's devotion to the saints. I'm not Italian American, and the only saint who figured prominently in my memory as a childhood was San Lázaro, with his wounds and crutches, the much more Puerto Rican choice of my grandmother. Growing up I had done my sacraments, but the last time I had gone to Mass outside of research was probably the day I wore a purple dress for my confirmation when I was in eighth grade. Actions like making the sign of the cross and praying the Our Father and Hail Mary were engrained in me, but I did not have a catalogic knowledge about the saints and their attributes until I began spending lots of time at Brooklyn's Our Lady of Mount Carmel (OLMC). I can recognize this image as Saint Rita (nun in a black habit plus crucifix plus thorn plus roses) because I had worked in the basement of OLMC alongside men who build and paint the giglio and make the saints that stud its face. By painting Saint Rita, I had to come to know her.

Much like an antique store, the basement is ordered disorder. Catalogued chaos. The same way that Rita was hidden in the store, she too stands in the corner of the basement of the church. In the basement religious objects are not given any reverential positions. Saint statues are wrapped in plastic, like corpses on crime shows. The faces of papier-mâché saints are often devoid of color, actually whitewashed: primed and ready for paint colors. The work that occurs on them is much like autopsies, amputations, and operations: their hands replaced, their necks reformed, and decayed and broken pieces removed so that they may be made whole again. Sometimes their heads have to be made anew or transplanted and their necks severed. Skinny baby cherubs formed of paper and glue snooze on beds of wire and planks of wood. Tangles of cords, dusty drills, and milk crates full of spray foam and tools abound.

By exploring the subterranean space of the basement, we will see that it is a vital site where men learn to embody values and skills, like craft, creativity, and dedication—skills that are masculinized and cultivated in all-male spaces. In the basement they learn and demonstrate fluency in Catholic iconography and negotiate questions of sacred presence. In short, to explore the peripheral and literally underground space of the basement is to understand Catholic pedagogy and the particular gendered processes through which young men become embedded in the community through competence in the artistry of devotion. The basement offers a site to understand how men transmit religious and embodied knowledge and how shared devotional labor structures male relationships. Woodwork, painting, and building are manual labor and devotional labor—they are the very means through which men enact their commitment to the parish and the saints. In this space commitment is about getting your hands dirty, about long hours of work and weekends sacrificed, about runs to Home Depot and handling the broken bodies of saints.

The drama of any devotional celebration, ceremony, or sacred object is made possible by a whole apparatus of things, people, and processes usually and deliberately kept unseen. Looking at the basement as a backstage space gives us a glimpse at sacred and ritual objects under construction, and provides a viewfinder to the labor essential to creating a "devotionally evocative spectacle."[1] The focus here is on production *as* a religious act rather than the use of already-complete objects *in* religious acts. The basement offers a view of the often messy processes through which ordinary materials become something *more* than ordinary.[2] As network theorist Bruno Latour put it, "What we fabricate goes beyond us."[3] The saints on the giglio decay, break, sink into disrepair.[4] In the basement we see how men negotiate tactile, even intimate interactions with saintly bodies, many of which they have constructed with their own hands. In the basement wood, paint, and papier-mâché are mediums and materials, but also *more.*

I spent far more time in the church basement than anywhere else, and I want to both take seriously the work that goes on there and also table the "seriousness" that scholars of religion are always asking for. The basement is subterranean because the values and rules that govern interactions in the basement are different from those "upstairs." It does not necessitate a cohesive display of piety or a spectacular performance of religious identity. The basement is also a place that is fun, that is about friends who gather to make something, to teach and learn from one another; doing this collective labor is also about integration in a masculine culture of camaraderie and joking. To accomplish all of this is also to place myself in the basement. For years I was part of the Giglio Committee, and I spent many Saturdays down in the basement. This chapter then also describes the embodied process of ethnography and how I gained an education in the culture, skills, and know-how of the basement.

When ethnographers enter a community, we entangle ourselves with people and their lives, and then we are supposed to leave. We amass hundreds of pages of field notes and thousands of photos to tell a story of a place in time. Ethnographers attend to how our intersectional identities set us apart from our interlocutors and acknowledge how our entanglement in webs of power and social and cultural capital differentiate us from those we study. But as ethnographers, we also have our bodies, our ways of knowing, our gender performances, and our styles. That physicality matters to our vantage point, the spaces we occupy, and the sensory way we navigate the field. So as I explore masculinity, materiality, and embodiment, I too want to account for how I moved through space and the embodied knowledge I now share with my interlocutors. There are times when I felt seamless, like an insider, and times where I felt weird and strange, like an outsider, and that affect matters to this eth-

nographic research.[5] Feeling difference matters to ethnography. Sometimes ethnography is about achieving seamlessness, but other times it's
viscerally awkward, and unpacking those moments, and my interlocutors' reactions, is central to understanding my ethnographic method.

Ethnographic subjects, our euphemized interlocutors, whom we
hang out with and talk to, question and investigate us as much as we
investigate them. They are conscious of being under our gaze. The men
in Brooklyn joked with me about that gaze often. They all knew I was
studying religion but liked to joke that at the end of the project I would
unveil it as a psychology experiment. As we worked in the basement,
Mark, one of the men I was closest to, often with a large paintbrush in
hand, would joke with us, "I'm telling you, she is really doing a psychology experiment on us. And you're gonna fail, no one is going to believe
you, that we are this crazy. She's doing psychology. I keep telling her she
is going to fail." One day he joked, "They're gonna have to come see for
themselves. You could do show and tell." They imagined me toting them
to Princeton to be observed by a slew of professors with clipboards.
Hunched behind a giglio piece, another man added, "Freud would walk
out on us. Freud would have a field day with us, we lift a giant phallus!"
Mark agreed, "We are her thesis." I laughed too and assured them, "You
are my thesis, just not my *psychology* thesis."

Ethnographic authority is not a given; it is performed and constructed. As an ethnographer, I wanted to be the one doing the observing
and gathering the data, but when that was turned on me, I felt strange. In
2017 a documentary filmmaker whose father grew up in Williamsburg
began to attend feast meetings with a team who wielded cameras and tall
microphone booms. As I sat in a feast meeting taking notes in a note-
book and on my phone, I felt the gaze of the camera. I found one of the
filmmakers twisting her wrist to zoom her lens, focusing on me. They
had never asked me who I was, so what did they think of this woman in
this meeting? I thought, "Me? I am just a researcher, certainly I am no
subject for a film." I shifted in my seat uncomfortably, conscious they
had probably caught all the moments when I looked "on," persistently
taking notes, and all the moments when I looked "off," laughing, joking
around, whispering side comments to those who sat at my table. Weeks
later the filmmakers were in the church basement, where I worked in my
Vans and dingy jeans with holes at the thighs, splattered and smeared

with paint. I was not a picture of professionalism. I tried to look diligent as I worked to apply gold paint to molded filigrees.

This was a moment when I felt both insiderness and outsiderness palpably, viscerally. With that gaze I became hyperconscious of my performance as an ethnographer and tried to make it overt and marked for the camera, rather than for the everyday rhythms of relationality with those I worked with. Later when the cameras were gone, Mark and I discussed why I felt weird about being in the documentary, and I explained, "I'm a researcher, I'm down here painting with you guys but I'm from Princeton, I don't know I just felt weird about it." Mark laughed, "You don't want your psychology project filmed?" Mark gave me a neatly packaged defense for my labor in the basement. He told me I should tell my colleagues, "You had to get your hands dirty and be in it and help out. You say, 'Well they don't accept outsiders so I had to get in and do it.' You're like Jane Goodall among the apes. She had to get in with the chimps, she had to be a gorilla." "She had to assimilate!" Neil called out from behind a pillar. This joke persisted. I was Jane, and they imagined each other as apes: "the gray one," "the big one," and "the small one: the dwarf" who is in charge.

In our conversations, many scholars have remarked, with their analytical hat on, that the giglio is a phallus. The men in the basement know that and joke about it. They too know what the work of ethnography is; they think critically about what it means to be ethnographic subjects and joke about that too. The basement was this kind of dialogic space that is key to understanding the work of ethnography. Ethnography is a craft that I learned, embodied, and worked out situationally as our relationships developed and as I learned their craft of making the giglio. The ethnographer's craft happens in these moments when ethnographic authority short-circuits, when it is questioned, joked about, and challenged. This is the kind of methodological story I tell in the following pages: in the basement they challenged me, they taught me things, and they laughed at me and with me. That is all part and parcel of how they interact with each other and how they socialize and are socialized into this Catholic community.

Devotional Labor

Elaine Peña's theory of devotional labor is instructive in considering the constellation of practices that go into producing the feast. In *Performing Piety*, Peña's ethnography of Guadalupan devotees, she focuses on an all-female pilgrimage to Guadalupe's apparition site at Tepeyac, a sidewalk shrine erected in a Chicago neighborhood, and a gymnasium that functions as a sanctuary for Masses and feast day celebrations.[6] Devotional labor encompasses all the things devotees do as they engage with Guadalupe and each other to create and maintain sacred space. Sweeping a shrine, washing rose petals, lighting candles, genuflecting, walking on pilgrimage, and even singing are all bodily outputs. Describing these actions as devotional labor helps us consider not only the way those actions put people in relationship with the divine but also how those actions embed them in broader social networks of support and trust. Devotional labor thus has regenerative effects, social and even economic benefits, what Peña calls devotional capital. This is not to put forth a functional definition of religion or to say people do religious acts just for the benefits they get from them. Rather, it is to see how to sweep a shrine, make food for a festival, or go on pilgrimage does the work of making a space sacred. All of these acts also have broader effects. Undocumented migrants who spend time at a Guadalupan shrine and work to keep it clean and beautiful not only demonstrate their love for the Virgin but through their very presence and dedication make connections with others who offer jobs, child care, and advice on navigating political processes and the health care system. To "be in good standing with Guadalupe," to maintain sacred spaces in her honor, meant you were in "good standing with your fellow devotees."[7]

While the men in Brooklyn do not live in precarity as those in Peña's study, devotional labor is a useful concept for thinking about the many ways they contribute to their community and the relationships and recognition they gain from that work. As one man put it, "I work for seven months in the church basement volunteering for the church." He understands that work as a sacrifice, as a good that he is doing for the parish. All those acts of manual labor are much more for the men of OLMC—they are acts of devotion. One morning I painted alongside a man who has been involved with the feast for nearly forty years; he told me, "I try to explain to people, this is a calling. This is like a calling you get from God. Some people never heard of the giglio, or don't know what it is, they have no idea of the construction." Work in the basement is consequential. One Saturday as we worked long hours another man said with a laugh, "After working down here if I go to hell something is wrong. . . . This has to count for something in the afterlife." Constructing, painting, and refurbishing the giglio are part and parcel of Catholic practice for these men. In a community governed by a hierarchy of roles that men can ascend, the basement offers an arena to demonstrate that one is committed and worthy of moving up the ranks. Those who work in the basement also prove they are upstanding men in the community. They are publicly honored in Masses, win awards, and are given other positions of authority in the planning and organization of the feast.

Back Stages

Performances, like celebrations of a feast day, rituals, and processions, occur before a set of observers, whether human or sacred. For example, on July 16 a procession for Our Lady of Mount Carmel is the central event of the feast. After a morning Mass, her devotees wait patiently outside of the church while her statue is carried out and placed upon a flower-bedecked metal float. All around her are bright yellow floral arrangements donated by parish families and bouquets tenderly placed at her feet by visiting devotees. A priest blesses the crowd with holy water. The bishop and other priests often join along, all in their vestments, heightening the solemnity and official status of the occasion. All of this announces to the public and passersby that there is a religious event happening. In sociologist Erving Goffman's classic theory of performance and regions, this is the "front region." A performance is framed by a setting, what Goffman refers to as "expressive equipment," which includes clothing, decor, bodily postures, and scenery.[8] During the procession for Our Lady of Mount Carmel, for example, the setting includes devotees dressed in tan and brown (her colors) and wearing brown scapulars over their chests and back, outward signs of their devotion. It also includes the statue as the focal point of the ritual. That focal point is established through decorations and/or devotional gestures like singing with hands and arms raised in praise or walking while gathered around the float. Individuals during a performance work to "embody certain standards." They are to act as devotees.[9]

Goffman argues that during a procession or any other performance there is usually "only one focus of visual attention," like the sight of devotees collectively walking or the movement of the float. An observer inside the crowd will see the other processors. An observer outside of the performance might see the float in passing and have a more panoramic view of the collective. Similarly, during the Dance of the Giglio observers will see lifters in matching T-shirts straining under the poles. They will see capos marching to the music while wielding their canes and using them as props as they tell the lifters to straighten their legs, lift higher, or bounce the giglio. They will see the giglio as a complete and seamless object, a towering display of artistry and the dance as a polished performance.

On the other hand, a back region or backstage is the place where "ceremonial equipment" is "hidden so that the audience will not see the treatment accorded to them." The backstage is where "the capacity of a performance to express something beyond itself may be painstakingly fabricated."[10] The backstage is where the statue is refurbished and cared for, where the flowers are arranged, the float decorated, and where the devotees and clergy get ready for the day. Labor, fabrication, preparation, and training are backstage activities. All of these activities prepare for the feast day and give the statue or the giglio an air of sacrality and importance. Back stages are sites of religious transmission, where people gain proficiency by learning the techniques, norms, and values of their traditions, and negotiate and construct the sacrality of religious objects.[11] Belonging in any religious community is achieved through a process of gaining skills and knowledge, of learning ways of moving, speaking, and acting as member, a process of "gradual habituation."[12] The basement is a place where members of the feast community are as much under construction and preparation as the giglio itself.

Creativity and Dedication

As I explore in the next chapter, discursively and financially the feast is the backbone of the parish. Its revenue allows the church to keep its doors open, maintain its budget, and fund projects and repairs. In addition to recounting changes to the urban landscape, at the end of feast meetings the pastor often prayed for the men's "work, creativity and talent" and reminded them how important their labor is to "the health of the parish and to keep[ing] it alive above all else." In March 2016 he delivered messages about the necessity and gravity of their work, telling them, "I can only rely on the love of the parish [that] I hear spoken of so much transformed into creative energy." He reminded them how their allegiance to their parish not only is an emotional tie but should be expressed through output and labor. Even as they work on seemingly mundane things, like choosing T-shirt colors, selling raffles, and constructing a new bandstand, feast organizers are consistently reminded that their sweat and countless hours of work matter. They come to understand all of their efforts under the rubric of working for the church. That work is also important for gaining respect in the community.

As the Dance of the Giglio is governed by a hierarchy, through years of commitment to the parish and the feast, select men ascend to the pinnacle of achievement: number one capo. A literal lifetime of dedication is behind every man who holds this position. By the time he gets there he has most likely served on multiple planning committees and spent up to five decades committed to the feast. The number one chooses the colors of the giglio and is honored on processions through the neighborhood. People don T-shirts with his name. Most of all he decides and commands the giglio lifts. The roles of lifter, capo, and lieutenant have most often commanded scholarly and media attention as they are the most spectacular on the public stage. But I am interested in the many other positions men can hold—like member of the Giglio Committee, in charge of painting and construction, and head of the Children's Giglio Committee, in charge of recruiting children and building the mini giglio kids will lift in emulation of the dance. This committee work is how men come to be worthy of those positions in the eyes of others.

Each year during Giglio Sunday Mass, before an overflowing church, the monsignor awards one feast organizer the pastor's award. He describes the men who deserve the award as those who "worked very hard to make this feast what it is, giving not only all of their talents but more time than we could ever imagine." Honorees are praised for their "endless commitment" and stand out as the men who are "the most selfless and the most dedicated" to the parish and feast. In 2016 the pastor explained that the "feast doesn't just happen" but takes weeks and months to complete and is about "blood, sweat, tears, laughter and joy." Mark, one of the newest lieutenants and the man who had led the giglio painting for the previous two years, won the award. Mark has a sharp humor, delivered with a devious smile under his signature goatee. Those he knows often became the butt of cutting jokes and endearment, but he seems reserved and quiet among those he doesn't know. Having worked in the basement with Mark and being sensitive myself, I teared up as I sat in the pews watching his family cheer for him when he went up to receive the award. Later that night as he reflected on the award, he smiled and hung his head down, looking humbled, unable to articulate how he felt when his name was called. Then he laughed, "There is nowhere for me to go from here . . . but there is a light at the end of the tunnel . . . NASA is still working on the calculations," with their top mathematicians crunching the numbers to figure out just how many years he would have to wait until he became number one. Neil calculated that it would take thirty-four more years. Thinking about that time span, Mark said his son would be "old enough to be married and under the poles by then," glimpsing into his future.

While most men involved in the feast became part of the community through their fathers and grandfathers, Mark forged his own ties: "I never would have imagined this. Not being from the neighborhood and most of these guys they have a father, a grandfather that did this, but I had no one, I had to do this myself. But my mother and my father hated it. My grandmother lived on Bedford [Avenue] and every summer I would stay with her and she would take me to the feast to play games." He remembers watching women process with Our Lady of Mount Carmel and that as a child he thought "the giglio was huge." As a kid he even built little giglios himself. Mark is now in his forties but became a lifter when he was seventeen, later met and married a girl from the neighborhood, and after more than twenty years of lifting became a lieutenant in 2015. His work in the basement is central to his reputation as an upstanding man in the parish and his path to one day becoming a capo, the pinnacle of manhood in the community.

Neil started working in the basement when he was fifteen and nearly a decade later, in 2017, he was given even more responsibility and tasked with building the children's giglio. He hand carved flat Styrofoam sheets to mimic stones and brick, molded little saints, even used pool noodles to make columns. Although he once lifted the children's giglio when he was a kid, as a member of the Giglio Committee he learned to display mastery and a pride and proficiency in iconography and craft that he accumulated over his years of involvement. I learned about his creativity when he asked me to paint the saints on the children's giglio. I got to see up close the care he took in carving and the ways he learned new skills in the basement. I witnessed the very first time he used the table saw. He was cautious and somewhat terrified and told me, "The day I don't have to use it is a happy day. I like all my ten!" As it whirred away slicing the wood, Neil was relieved to still have all his fingers. Neil built an entirely new wooden skeleton for the children's giglio, although he had never worked with wood on that scale before. The previous summer a former capo brought him a model giglio kit from his trip to Nola. Neil worked to build the model in his house with a hot glue gun and instructions entirely in Italian. It was in practicing with this miniature gift that he was able to figure out how to make the wooden skeleton of a giglio and can now construct an architecturally sound tower. Neil was so proud when his first children's giglio was displayed in front of the church. In 2019 he was named one of the newest lieutenants, demonstrating not only the importance of all those years he has been involved but also the consequential nature of the work he has done in the basement.

Men like Mark and Neil are active in the parish and on their way to becoming capos one day, but they understand that they have decades of labor before them. In the basement we see how men are integral to the maintenance of Catholic objects and how they materially forge relationships to the saints and the parish. While construction may seem like "grunt work," this space alerts us to the varied embodied engagements of Catholic men and the gendered routes through which they approach devotional labor.

In March 2015 the feast planning season got off to a rocky start. Many worried that the feast was in jeopardy because of infighting and that younger generations were not as dedicated to its survival. Some of the older men decried that the "kids" (men in their twenties) were not respectful of their authority. Fewer young men had volunteered to help with the giglio, so it sat in the basement largely unfinished. It was in this tense environment and this vacuum of volunteers that some of the men recruited me to help work on the giglio. As past capos and feast leaders thanked me for my work, they simultaneously lamented that the basement was once full of kids and young men. For four consecutive feasts I was part of the basement crew and was dubbed "the artist" by many of the men.

After having spent a year attending feast meetings and events, I expressed interest in visiting the basement to watch them work. Before I visited for the first time, Neil texted me to ask, "Do you have any artistic talent?" I replied, "I have painted before & took some art classes, drawing I am not good at, but I am pretty precise :)." The next Saturday when I got to the basement, Neil wore latex gloves and was working with a tub of glue and strips of brown paper to apply a new layer of papier-mâché to the giglio pieces to prepare them for a new coat of paint. The giglio's face was made up of six pieces, or facades, secured to a crisscrossing metal structure and can be replaced and remade. Under the last year's peeling paper, I noticed that the pieces were made of Styrofoam upon wood frames, getting a glimpse at the usually hidden anatomy. Neil asked if I would help out and laughed that the gloves would be too big on me. I put on the blue plastic gloves, and of course my hands were swimming in them as I struggled to grab a piece of paper with my plastic-wrapped fingers. He picked one up and quickly coated each side in the thick glue before placing it on the giglio piece. I had put down only one strip when Pat, a former capo and longtime feast leader, walked in. We greeted each other with a handshake and cheek kiss, a customary greeting—it was the first time that I was meeting him personally, although I always saw him sitting with the executive board during feast meetings. That year Pat was the head of the Giglio Committee, doing more overseeing than actual construction. He looked around and surveyed the work as I glued up another piece of paper and stuck it on.

"Well, can she paint?" Pat asked Neil. "Yea, that's why I brought her!" "Well, what's she doing doing papier-mâché??" Pat asked, widening his eyes as I stood there with the glue brush in my gloved hands. I took them off and walked over with him to the piece of the giglio with a Sacred Heart of Jesus at the center. The robes were messily painted in splotches of red and brown. He looked at the Sacred Heart and was displeased. "Jesus looks like an Indian!" he exclaimed, pointing to the painted skin tone, an eerie peach red, like a cartoon sunburn, which looked like the result of a brush covered in red paint and not washed off properly. This passing comment reflected how Christian figures are racialized as white and how the politics of "proper" representation and race are always at work in the making of devotional objects. To be legible as Jesus meant the Sacred Heart had to have the right skin tone. Unhappy with the shoddy paint job, he pulled out a small piece of shiny paper with an image of the Sacred Heart of Jesus on it for reference. Neil brought reference images of Saint Anthony printed on computer paper. They walked me through the attributes and colors for each saint. Pat found me a triangular piece of wood to serve as my palette, which I would use for years to come, and I began sifting through a metal container of small acrylic paint squirt bottles.

I busied myself mixing up a peach skin tone, a mix of sand, coral, and light brown paints, to match the reference images of a clearly white Christ. Pat took a look at my work. "She's an artist!" he declared. There was a floating set of stairs in the basement and I climbed on top, almost skimming the concrete rafters of the ceiling, to reach the giglio piece. I began painting over the face, restoring Jesus to a more iconographically appropriate skin color. Pat was impressed, and I continued on painting, making the inner robes bright white and the outer robes a vibrant red. To match the picture I added in light gold striations radiating out of the flaming heart in the center of Christ's body and used gold highlights to emphasize the thorns around it. Satisfied with my skills, he told Neil, "She can come whenever she can. . . . She's a painter. . . . You see, a woman comes in and she's more talented than us. We don't know what we're doing." Pat thanked me for my willingness to help and also couched it in broader concerns about a dearth of volunteers: "We used to have many, now it's the precious few."

I worked for weeks alongside seven or eight men, but I told no one else of my work on the giglio. I feared that others would be angry that I was messing with tradition. So I was surprised when former capos visited the basement and excitedly surveyed my work and told me the saints looked beautiful. That year's capo embraced me and said, "It looks beautiful, thank you for your work. You are building my geel, you don't know how valuable that is." I became a laborer for the feast, the only woman in the homosocial spaces of the parish. As I spent more time

Figure 2.1. The Sacred Heart of Jesus, made of papier-mâché and spray foam, and the "artist's" palette. Photo by the author.

working on the feast, I was able to complain alongside other men about the giglio gobbling up my weekends. When it finally went into the street I was able to stand back with them and look at our handiwork. When someone remarked that it was the "most beautiful geel" in years or that they hated the color scheme, I shared in the pride and dismay.

Mark arrived in the early morning every weekend to paint, repair the giglio, and manage the small team of us in the basement. When we started work in 2016, the basement was crowded with the dismembered giglio in an odd combination of whitewashing and hints of 2015's beige, maroon, and gold scheme. Bo, that year's number one, chose a stone blue for the giglio. In the basement we learned to respect the capo's wishes, to work not only to make an aesthetically pleasing giglio but also within the confines of the capo's authority. All the lifters would wear blue T-shirts silkscreened with images of the giglio and San Paolino. Mark darted back and forth from Home Depot to the church getting swatches and samples to perfectly match the blue the capo had chosen for his T-shirts, even having Home Depot scan the shirt and mix paint to match. Mark chose chrome silver as a coordinating paint color and combined his own authority and design sensibilities with the necessary deference to the capo.

In the basement we learned tiers of deference and respect. We worked below Mark, taking his orders and instruction, and he worked to please the capos and the men above him in the hierarchy. Though not yet officially chairman of the committee, Mark was our teacher. His humor always masked his humility. Through crude joking Mark made sure the other men worked hard and instilled a culture of accountability with quips like, "While I was down here doing eighty-five percent of the work, you were beating your meat" when he saw others slacking. When others made suggestions he did not like, he would shoot back, "What did I tell you about thinking?," jokingly letting them know they were down there to follow orders. I too became included through being the butt of jokes, especially about my ability to paint eyes. One of the men told me, "This is a tough crowd get used to it," and with time I did, shrugging off insults, retorting with my own quips, and eventually getting better at painting eyes.

I learned how young men are trained and disciplined in the values of giglio artistry. With its complex architectural design complete with cornices, blind arcades, niches, and columns, the giglio is designed to be viewed from the ground and from a distance. It thus requires a different kind of artistry that values not precision or detail work but a special attention to contrasting paint colors for the effect of architectural texture. The giglio is like a color puzzle, and it was only when I worked with Mark to test color schemes that I learned the importance of thinking in what he calls "giglio dimensions" and came to understand how slight contrasts in colors help the forms of the giglio stand out when it is on the street and getting hit by the bright sun. When we made bad color suggestions or became too detail-oriented, Mark chided us that we needed to think in three dimensions: "You are not thinking in giglio dimensions, in sixty feet off the ground," he scolded, explaining that it would be a waste of time to paint details that will "disappear . . . once it goes in the air."

The Giglio Committee works with limited resources, so the men have to be proficient in improvising to create saint iconography. They use ninety-year-old cement molds that look like rock forms to create the saints for the face of the giglio. In the final product each saint is equipped with its own iconographic elements. Saint Anthony has robes, lilies, and a ring of hair. Saint Joseph is bearded and holds a Christ Child. Saint Rita has a long habit and holds a cross and flowers. Mount Carmel has a crown and a Christ Child and holds scapulars, and San Paolino has a bishop's crozier and a book, reflecting Paulinus's prolific writing and rhetorical prowess.[13] Despite this varied cast of saints, actually only a few molds exist, and the men do the work of creating hybrid saints. Their handiwork and ingenuity are readable on the bodies of the saints—products of circumstance and artistry. There is no Mount Carmel mold, only a mold of Saint Rita, so they add a crown, replace the roses that adorn her body with a Christ Child, and add a strip of hair and flowing robes to turn a mold of a nun into a figure legible as the Virgin Mary. Neil explained that they have molds of Jesus and Saint Anthony. To make a saint discernible as Joseph, Neil said "[he] got the baby, cut off the lilies, add the beard," and from those elements they created an identifiable Saint Joseph out of the existing molds. Neil followed the same model on the children's giglio. He transformed a small mold of the Sacred Heart of Jesus into Saint Paulinus by crafting a bishop's miter, creating a cupped hand to hold a bishop's staff and a book, and papering over the Sacred Heart.

Figure 2.2. Concrete mold for Saint Rita with nun's habit, cross, and flowers visible in the layers of concrete. Photo by the author.

In 2018 the committee made a new San Paolino from the concrete mold. They carefully placed wet strips of papier-mâché into the crevices of the mold to ensure each feature would be in relief. His nose was molded carefully so that his thin lips, cheekbones, and full beard were modulated in the final product. He had a miter and surprisingly detailed garments. On his chest was a pectoral cross, with cords wrapped around his waist. What this mold of San Paolino did not have was a right hand. He was a bishop, but sans an extremity he could not offer a benediction. This is where the creativity and literal bricolage that are so important to the work in basement came in. They bought a mannequin hand, the kind that would be used to display costume jewelry like rings and bracelets. The long delicate fingers were slightly bent, which in a store might have made them look feminine, but the way the pinky and ring finger were lowered and the index and middle fingers slightly erect made it look like the nonchalant hand was offering a benediction. They used spray foam to attach the hand, fashioning a sling of painter's tape so that the transplant would stay on. From a distance no one could tell that this emotive hand did not belong to Paolino's body. For the crozier they used a broom stick. Neil tried to bend a metal rod into the scroll that usually tops a crozier, but when that failed he capped the stick with a golden cross.

They pieced together an accessorized body identifiable as Saint Paulinus, and it was my job to paint him. They brought out a painting of San Paolino on a canvas that had been stored in the basement. He was wearing golden yellow robes, his beard filled with waves of gray and white, his garments and miter woven with gold filigree, his gaze solemn. This painting was to be my source, and to paint San Paolino I had to spend a lot of time looking at his image, to try to emulate his gaze, the weight of his garments, and the way his gold vestments caught the light, hinting at shoulders and limbs hidden beneath the robes. When I finished he was completely legible to any insider as San Paolino and stood as tall as me.

As a painter I was immersed in the informal pedagogy of the basement. I learned just how important and contentious the shade of red paint used for the Sacred Heart of Jesus' robes and flaming heart was. I learned that a golden mustard yellow and brown were the colors to paint Mount Carmel and that any image of a Madonna and Christ Child painted those colors would be legible as Mount Carmel. They coached me on color choices and bickered over how young or old saints should look or what color their hair should be based on their hagiographies. This included "proper" racial representation. Saints and angels were to be white: peachy skin tone, which I mixed out of pink, peach "fleshtone," and tan paints. And if the color veered too tan, they told me to bring the color down a notch or lighten it up a bit. In the basement men circulate stories about the saints, how San Paolino should have blonde hair and blue eyes because of his French heritage and how Rita should look pretty with painted rosy cheeks and lips.

In the basement men lightheartedly joked about presence and the vital nature of Catholic objects. There was simultaneously an attitude of reverence and irreverence. The Giglio Committee joked about creepy saints, deformed angels, and statues watching them, but simultaneously understood the sacrality of these objects made with their own hands that were blessed by the priest and used in devotional performances. When the angels suffered broken wrists, they carefully mended them with masking tape, saying things like "bandage him up and say a prayer," while jokingly making the sign of the cross. It is important to note that they used personified, affectionate language to talk about objects at all scales, from life-sized papier-mâché figures of San Paolino to the small angels mounted on the giglio. Sometimes as Neil toted a papier-mâché San Paolino through the basement and interacted with the saint's body in a tactile way, he said things like "Excuse my right hand, Paulie."

Bodies and Squeamishness

Men participate in the cycle of creation, damage, and repair. As they dance the giglio, the saints often break, and men are the ones who have to do the work of mending their broken necks and backs. Squeamishness and humor accompany these inappropriate but necessary reparative actions.

In 2014, during especially rigorous bouncing, Mount Carmel's head nearly fell off. That year people were especially worried about the fate of the feast. In the shrine workers often lamented the dearth of people attending novenas and Masses. One shrine worker, who had worked there every year for thirty-one years, shook her head at the emptiness and said, "There are only ten people in church, there used to be at least two hundred. . . . I feel like we don't have a parish anymore, I feel like we have a church": a building without community. That year it rained torrentially during the feast, which many people interpreted to mean Our Lady of Mount Carmel was "teaching us a lesson." During the night lift the papier-mâché head of Our Lady of Mount Carmel on the giglio broke. Her head hung low, severed, bobbing but never quite falling off. With each bounce of the giglio it was thrown up and down, an eerie sight in the darkness. Some people said it was because they no longer prioritized devotion to the Blessed Mother.[14] Some constructed a narrative about Our Lady's disappointment. Whereas rain could simply be a feature of unpredictable summer weather and the broken neck the result of wear and tear, the odd dangling head on the giglio seemed to indicate something more.

The basement was the place to repair Our Lady of Mount Carmel's broken neck. Mark used a table saw to remove her head, and as he mimed the action for us he told us how uncomfortable he felt doing it. "It just didn't look right" to cut the head off a saint, he exclaimed, shaking his head. The severed head sat around the basement. Next to it was the severed head of the Christ Child that had been in her arms. When some of the guys complained that it was weird, perhaps watching them and creeping them out, and asked if they could put a sheet over it or get rid of it, Mark affirmed that they couldn't, explaining, "They're blessed, we can't." The papier-mâché head sat on a shelf in the basement, painted in a stone gray and wearing a golden crown. New heads were added to the decapitated bodies of OLMC and the Christ Child, but the set oddly did not quite match the bodies. It resulted in the Christ Child having an elongated almost serpentine neck, even longer than those in Mannerist paintings. When I told Mark about my interest in ideas about presence the next year, he pointed over to the plaster image of OLMC and the heads and said, "Well you can say it is a pile of junk and paper and plastic, or its Mount Carmel up there. You can say the same thing about the one in the church—is it just paint and plaster, or is it Mount Carmel?"

The statue of San Paolino that stands atop the giglio was also damaged. He stood for months at the back of the basement with a broken back and his benediction fingers pointing up to the ceiling. To repair San Paolino, Neil, Mark, and Sal ripped off the thick canvas garments that were securely stapled to his body. The fabric was stubborn with the staples stuck deep within the torso, and Neil had to push against his body to yank away the heavy robes while Sal steadied the statue. As they forcefully disrobed him and revealed a rusted, naked torso, they shook

Figure 2.3. Heads sitting on a shelf in the basement. From left to right: Our Lady of Mount Carmel, the Christ Child, and two angel heads: one made of a mannequin, the other made of papier-mâché. Photo by the author.

their heads and said, "This feels so wrong," obviously disturbed. Because San Paolino stands at the top of the giglio and weathers rain throughout the feast, he was moldy, and as the men tore the fabric from his body the thick staples left little holes surrounded by rust stains on his torso. San Paolino stood naked, a torso made of metal and asbestos and metal legs that ended in thick boot-like feet. They hung him by the neck from a pipe with a piece of twine so that they could use fiberglass to repair his back. Neil, steadying the statue as it hung, laughed and shuddered, "I feel like I'm giving him a prostate exam!" As we all laughed, they told me not to think they are bad people for hanging San Paolino. I joked with them that between hanging, dismembering, and beheading saints, they had some really weird stuff going on down there.

Figure 2.4. Broken and disrobed statue of San Paolino. Photo by the author.

The basement offers an interesting case for how statues and objects under construction are treated (or not) as objects of presence. In other contexts, people relate intimately to religious statues and images. They caress them, speak to them, and care for them; they change their garments, pile them with money and jewelry, place offerings at their feet, and negotiate with them, making promises and offering votives in gratitude.[15] All of these pious acts are most often bestowed upon already-complete statues and objects, but they are not the kinds of practices that take place in the basement. Scholar of material religion Amy Whitehead argues that religious statuaries are not "merely wooden artifacts or religious art—they are 'statue persons.'"[16] In acts of devotion, maintenance, care, gift giving, and offering, people enter into relational engagements with statues and "objects" of devotion become "subjects" of devotion, brought into "co-relational being" in "moments of active relating."[17] The papier-mâché saints on the giglio might never be fit for placement in a chapel—they are functional objects, not to be set in a church niche or before rows of candles. People most likely would not kneel before these papier-mâché saints, and yet Paolino's asbestos anatomy is likened to that of a man. Rita, even though she was molded with their hands, is still "she." Even a store-bought angel is "he." "It"—the depersonalized way to mark nonhuman objects—is seldom heard in the basement. As Whitehead notes, statues are "spoken to and about in ways which are similar to how humans speak to or about each other" and "gendered reference is an indication of personhood."[18]

This is what I meant about objects and saints in the basement becoming more than ordinary, even if they are molded from mundane hardware store materials. "What is the genesis of this surplus?" is how anthropologist of material religion Birgit Meyer posed the question. How might attention to religious fabrication help us understand how objects become *more*?[19] In the basement the entire process endows these objects with some sort of specialness. The use of heirloom molds; the deep knowledge of iconography; the paint that renders those molds legible as the saints; the familiarity with the bodily forms of the saints and their hands, necks, and torsos; and the knowledge that damaged objects have been blessed or that new objects are destined to be blessed and are to be the focal point of an important ritual. They are different from the saints in the chapel upstairs, as they were not made in factories or by professionally trained artisans.[20] They are not destined to stand above kneelers or on altars. They might not be worthy for the sanctuary, but they are worthy for the giglio and are a point of pride for those who work in the basement. The networks and sediments of memory, ritual use, craft, and artistry are important to understand how papier-mâché saints and angels become more, even if in jest. To make saints and angels for the giglio is to create convincing images of them, intelligible bodily and iconographic forms with the materials at hand. That intelligibility might underlie the uncanniness of those objects. They are paper and paint and glue, but in the dark they seem "creepy," and in the intimate backstage acts of repair, handling their bodies feels awkward because they are *more*.

Homosociality, Ethnography, and Joking

Joe captured the importance of camaraderie and labor as he reminisced about his tireless work in the basement: "In the basement all the guys would be having fun, building all day, making fun of each other and in the midst of it we build the giglio." Homosocial spaces have been traditionally defined as sites where people gather and seek enjoyment with company of the same sex in ways that are not necessarily erotic or romantic, sites where men "cultivate a sense of camaraderie and closeness."[21] The Catholic parish is a ripe site of homosociality, not only in the context of the all-male clergy, but in the gathering spaces of laymen, those spaces hidden or not central to official liturgies and rituals. In the basement, through labor and craft, that camaraderie is made and achieved.

While handmade objects and craft are usually coded feminine, the stuff of domestic devotions, men achieve belonging and competence in a masculine community through those very kinds of practices. In her groundbreaking study of Christian material culture, Colleen McDannell argued that the "material dimension of American Christianity has been ignored," in part, because "longstanding theological and intellectual interpretations of art, objects, and places have associated material expressions of religion with certain types of people," namely "women, children, and other illiterates."[22] The basement defies a logic that places institutional authority and administration in the hands of men and objects and relationships in the hands of women.[23] In the case of the feast, men do both. In the context of the feast, the framework of homosociality allows us to see how masculinity is made and expressed through material religious practices. The basement's spatial context and homosociality does the work of masculinizing those practices.

While the basement is a place where men practice craft and creativity, it is also a place where the banter, competition, and humor more traditionally associated with homosocial spaces are prevalent. In the basement, along with discussions of iconography and memories of feasts past, the men banter with each other. They make jokes about masturbation and compare their weights and taunt each other about their appearance. As they paint and build they call each other fat and short and stupid and incompetent. Sociologist of group culture Gary Alan Fine has argued that "sets of humorous references" in social interaction mark affiliation, designate insiders and outsiders, and are mechanisms of social control.[24] Joking is one way in which "unofficial, unstated, but crucial values are expressed."[25] In his study of restaurant kitchens Fine examined the ways teasing and "coarse joking" are parts of the informal norms that structure male-dominated work spaces and argues that women in these kinds of spaces need to adapt to and become adept themselves in masculine "humor performances" in order to fit in.[26]

The basement is a place where men engage in manual labor and creative and artistic work, but it also exhibits some of the features of other male-dominated spaces: like competition, one-upmanship, and joking. In the basement banter centered on issues of skill and artistic ability, competency with tools, and occupation. Neil worked in IT and often was made fun of for being a nerd and a tech guy who "sits on his ass." Mark was a delivery driver, and Tony (name modified) was a union mechanic who worked on motorcycles as well. Tony was tall with gray hair. Three thick silver hoops adorned his ears, two in one ear and a single in the other. He always wore yellow-tinted glasses and black long-sleeved shirts. He rode a motorcycle and often talked about his "bike." Tony had expertise and tricks the other men did not. When Neil was having trouble cutting foam in the shape of stones with wire, Tony knew that they needed a hot knife. In the absence of the official tool, he heated a knife on the stove, as if they were in "medieval times." It took me a while to get to know Tony. At first I thought he was mean, as he seldom returned my greetings and smiles, but the more I got to know him, the more I figured him out. He would talk about me in the third person, and when I talked about how many years I had been researching the feast, he would make comments like, "This is why kids take so long and don't get jobs." He would watch my work quietly with arms crossed. When I was in earshot he would mumble "eyeballs," knowing I would hear his critiques of my skills. Whenever I would reveal the smallest bit of offense or show any indication that his comments were hurting my feelings, he would say things like "this is a tough crowd, get used to it." It was when I challenged Tony that I finally got in on the joke, proved to him I could "withstand ridicule," a central feature of masculine belonging in the community; after that we began to talk, work together, and get to know each other.[27]

One day in the basement we were trying to figure out what to order for lunch; I leaned up against the cabinets that held the tools and the paint, looking at the menu on my phone. Talking about me in the third person, Tony inspected one of the angels on a giglio piece. The angel had peachy skin and blank eyes—its eye sockets empty and painted in the same color as the rest of its body. Tony said, "Alyssa can come in and paint the eyes white with a pupil," pointing out the elementary way he thought I represented eyes with a half-moon of white paint and a dark center. Feeling kind of annoyed about this constant jab, I told him, "I painted over all of them, you wanna give it a shot and show me how it's done?" He looked at me and in a measured, warning voice, drawing out his words, said, "Alyssa . . . don't challenge me." I challenged, "You can relieve me of that job, it's my burden." Mark laughed, "It's her burden!" giddy that I challenged Tony. After that we became friends and he and I worked well together; we shared opinions on which wood stain to use on the doors of the giglio and how to get the best brick effect on the foam stones. He valued my opinions, telling others he thought that I had a good eye, and I valued his input. Tony, recalling Mark's Jane Goodall joke about how I was a researcher becoming one with the apes, joked that he would be the "gray one" or the "arrogant one." Next time he made fun of me and Mark came to my defense, he clarified, "If I don't pick on her, how will she know I like her? Because if I don't like someone I just won't talk to them." He even said, "You might be the first girl lieutenant" and added, "that's something they would never do here, have a girl."

One conversation in particular stands out: one day over lunch Mark and Tony compared occupational injuries. There was talk of blood, stitches, and bones visible under cut flesh. More than just an example of competitiveness, this conversation was an explicit instance where the men talked about and valorized their experiences as blue-collar workers and emphasized their embodied manual labor.

After Tony and I had established our rapport, one day we all sat in the lower hall at a long table eating—they had steak sandwiches and I had an avocado salad, a choice I predictably took flack for. Tony began to tell us about a friend of his who was drilling a steel cable one day when the drill went right into his hand and he just backed the drill out, put a rag on it, and continued working. Tony had his own injury story: one day he cut his finger open with a razor blade. It opened all the way down to the knuckle, and the skin on his thumb was basically a flap covering the bone underneath. He calmly rode his bike home from work, "real calm," and told his wife to bring a rag outside before they went to the hospital. Mark too had a bloody story to share. He chimed in that he once cut his head open on a piece of razor wire while he was on the job and needed eighteen stitches, two on the artery inside and sixteen on the outside. I inadvertently made a cutting joke, the kind the men leveled against each other about the relative ease and comfort of others' jobs. I said, "Wait, why are you doing dangerous stuff at work, isn't it just boxes?" When I said that, Neil busted out laughing, throwing his head back, his mouth wide open, releasing a loud cackling laugh that went on and on. When he finally took a breath, he got out, "She said it's just moving boxes" through bursts of laughter that shook his body. He and Tony pretended to pick up boxes, holding their elbows at right angles and moving their outstretched palms like robots. Even as Mark clarified he had been working in air conditioning repair and was not a delivery driver at the time, Neil mimed Mark's incompetence picking up a box and hitting himself in the face with it, throwing his head back dramatically as if a box hit him right in the nose. "Alyssa wins today" they said. It was a day when my initiation into their joking culture and masculine banter was most explicit and salient. Earlier that day we had been talking about *The Walking Dead*, Mark's favorite TV show; I expressed that I was no longer watching the new season. "What too violent for you?" he asked. When I responded "I don't mind the violence," Mark said aloud to the room, quoting me, "'I don't mind the violence,' That's why we like her." It was a perfect preamble to our talk of blood-spattered ER tables, open wounds, and long needles of anesthetic inserted into skulls, as they competed with their gory stories of staying calm and getting through pain.

While some have productively probed the barriers to access for female ethnographers and ultimately concluded that women researchers' "access to backstage regions and masculine discourse will almost certainly be limited," in my fieldwork at the feast I found gendered boundaries to be strikingly more flexible than I had imagined.[28] My forays into the peripheral and homosocial spaces of the feast, like the basement, are indicative of the situational and performative character of gender in fieldwork and, for me, the possibility of crossing gendered boundaries through embodied ethnographic practices. Because I too underwent the enskillment central to the basement, I could belong in that space.[29] As I painted, as the men brought me prayer cards and printouts of saint images for me to use as artistic reference, as I loyally represented saint iconography and demonstrated competence in giglio artistry, I was learning to become a proficient member of the Giglio Committee and a practitioner of this local masculine Catholic craft.[30] Being part of the basement crew meant I was also included in other spaces and celebrations typically devoid of women.

One night at the feast my husband and I joined the lieutenants and some members of the Giglio Committee at a local bar to celebrate a successful night of lifting. It was the first time in the three years I had known them that I brought my partner to the feast. As a woman researcher I deliberately never brought my then fiancé to the church or the feast; I often told anyone who inquired why I had not yet brought him that I consider this work and I wanted to keep that separate. When they brought it up, asking me if my fiancé (whom they often called "the boyfriend") cared that I spent my Saturdays in the basement or that I stayed at the feast until the late hours of the night, I would shoot back "I do what I want." I often heard some of the men talking about how their wives complained that they spent so much time working on the giglio or preparing for the feast, and they would reason that they should deal with it because it was just twelve days out of the year or that they should know what to expect already. Sometimes they would say that wives are "feast widows." In the words of one man, "You're a widower for two weeks. I knew what I was getting into, my wife knows." In my responses I had the same irreverent tone, the same response about him already knowing that this was what I did with my time. This was not just a case of adopting their language and public attitude toward their relationships. My strategic refusal to bring my now husband to the feast was also to prevent the men associating me with a partner waiting for my return. I wanted them to understand that I was an ethnographer first and that the feast was my priority too. Some even told me my husband was now one of these "feast widows." That night I learned the benefit of bringing my partner along; for the first time I got invited to the bar for the after-lift ritual.

As Mark welcomed us into the basement of the Whiskey Brooklyn, a dimly lit bar, he lifted up his arms, "This is all part of the fiasco, you never saw it before, but now you have. This is all part of the fiasco that is the feast." We sat at the bar taking Fireball shots, listening to stories about union work and boiler explosions, and sharing in the elation over the success of the lifts. Neil told my husband as we stood outside for their smoke break, "We finally got to the point where we can be ourselves around her without being like . . . oh shit." "But we take good care of her," Mark said as he put his arm around me. Mark and Neil are longtime friends and work together in the basement on the giglio. Mark, because he is older and occupies a higher position in the feast hierarchy, always pokes fun at Neil by ordering him around and cautioning him not to think too hard. That night Mark explained, "She is in now. She's one of us. You know how I knew? Because she zinged Neil. One day I told Neil he was right, and he said 'what?' because he couldn't hear me. And she was just there, painting." He put his head down and mimed holding a brush in his hands and painting nonchalantly. He continued, "She says 'he's not used to hearing he's right.' She didn't even look up." Mark told this story multiple times to different people, warning them, "Just a heads-up, she's sharp, she has some zingers. She zinged Neil, I almost peed myself!"

This exchange is just one that shows the doubleness of gender within my fieldwork. On one hand I would shrug off any concern about leaving home to work for the feast, subverting gendered expectations and boundaries in the community. I would swiftly deliver and take jokes and insults and operate within the norms of behavior in the basement, but I also acknowledge that there was likely some self-censorship when I was around. In the basement I made very real friendships that exceed the language of methodology. But more technically I had negotiated a liminal position in the field; through socialization and practiced skill I became a woman researcher who belonged in the masculine spaces of the feast, but situationally and relationally I also easily occupied the position of wife, girl, and woman they should watch out and care for.

3

Making Money, Keeping the Parish Alive

John moved through the feast in tattered cargo shorts, his pockets heavy, the fabric around them spliced, as if slit with a small knife, revealing the white lining. This had been his uniform for the first week of the 2017 feast: a T-shirt and the same pair of oversized cargos. He is the only person I have ever seen put so many pockets to use. The pockets were filled with money. Folded stacks of bills and rolls of neatly packed quarters weighed his shorts down. By the end of the second week of the feast his shorts were completely torn and he had to wear an old size-36 pair from when he was heavier. They ballooned around his legs but got the job done, serving their functional purpose as he darted around the arteries of the feast. From the rectory he usually went to the ticket booths on Havemeyer and Meeker streets where women volunteers sat in metal booths selling ride tickets individually and by the sheet. Then he stopped off at the "Nevada" stand on Havemeyer situated at the foot of the church steps, where his mother worked during the feast. It was a small stand that sold peel-away gambling tickets, called Nevadas. People stood in front, peeling off the strips of paper board to see if they had matched three fruits. The losers littered the ground in piles like paperboard snow. From Nevada he went into the lower hall of the church to the café where you could get anything from cappuccinos and sangria to cannoli and *sfogliatelle*, the classic breakfast pastry from Naples. Then he went to the flea market where older women poked through porcelain tea sets and figurines. Lastly, John stopped at the "beer trap" on North Ninth, a tented space where volunteers slung cold Brooklyn Brewery IPAs to restock beer and pick up their cash, soggy with condensation. On his rounds John looked busy as hell. His phone vibrated with requests. It buzzed with volunteers requesting singles and quarters or relief from their posts, with texts from his mother, and with complaints about unsanctioned booths. As he rushed he rattled off numbers so he could remember which money belonged to which booth and kept moving through the crowded streets of feast. I know his frantic path because for three consecutive feasts I often was right behind him, shadowing, helping, memorizing the totals of each pickup, and counting money at the night's end.

John's path and his heavy pockets demonstrate the importance of two things: labor of the financial and logistical sort, and money—its circulation, accumulation, accounting, and central role in the feast. While the feast is an occasion for devotion, it is also an occasion to make money. Those two aims are not separate but part and parcel of one another. To be devoted to the saints, the feast, tradition, and the church is to help make money to sustain the parish. This chapter is about money and finances, how it is collected, earmarked, and accounted for, and the labor John and other parishioners do backstage to keep the feast running and profitable. It considers the history of feast planning and the central role money and discourses of work, effort, and success have played in masculinizing and valorizing men's work at the feast. A focus on money, its circulation, and its symbolic import to the community is to understand the symbiotic link between the feast and the parish, and more broadly the link between devotional activities and the realities of sustaining an institution. Like the basement, the "money room" in the rectory is a site of backstage practice and embodied and discursive training. Fundraising is a devotional practice. Dollars and cents are not secondary to Catholic devotion. They are intertwined with intergenerational bonds between men, loyalties to the church, and ideas about survival and community longevity. Counting, collecting, and soliciting money is religious work.

The money room is a place where parishioners and feast organizers express their dedication to the church in ways that are not immediately visible on the streets during processions and giglio lifts. The money room is the hub where every dollar collected during a day's work goes, from offerings to ride ticket sales. Every dollar tenderly folded and dropped in the offering basket and every dollar spent on candles or given to Our Lady of Mount Carmel with love and devotion ends up in the money room. Just as a child watching the giglio in awe does not know the process by which it became a seamless devotional object, devotees and visitors do not follow the paths of their dollars as they are totaled. These dollars become figures that point to the feast's success and the church's survival or contribute to fears of its demise. More bodies on processions and more visitors to the shrine have both religious and financial import. Here, devotion translates to dollars.

Keeping the Parish Alive: Money and the Catholic Ethic

Scholars who have studied giving and tithing in American Christian churches have discovered that discourses and practices around giving and money vary with denomination. Cultures around finances and giving money in a church are one way in which congregations and congregants "work out what is sacred to them."[1] In churches, "mundane money becomes sacralized giving" through different discourses, practices, and logics that undergird why congregants give money and how religious leaders frame giving. In a comparative ethnographic study, sociologists found that in an evangelical church congregants understand giving through the lens of individual spiritual health, whereas in a mainline Protestant church giving is a sign of the "community's spiritual and fiscal health."[2] In their book *Passing the Plate*, Christian Smith, Michel Emerson, and Patricia Snell argued that among Catholic churches, a "Pay-the-Bills" church culture dominates discussions of money from the pulpit and parishioners' understandings of why they give. Within a Pay-the-Bills congregational culture, clergy take a practical approach to discussions of money. They explain to parishioners that the church needs them and that giving is a necessity to maintain a church. They often discuss things like repairs, maintenance, bills, building work, and financial need. Within such a culture, money is about the present needs of the church, and leaders and congregants frame it through the lens of obligation.[3] What sets the Shrine Church of Our Lady of Mount Carmel (OLMC) apart from the parishes in these studies is that the financial health of the parish centers in a large part around the feast. The feast is about not just promoting giving but encouraging people to *work* to make money. In this Catholic community money talk is not simply about bills and repairs; rather it is located in broader, more consequential discourses about the life and death of the parish.

At the feast money is bound up in networks of social relations and communal discourses that imbue it with social and religious significance. Sociologist Viviana Zelizer has argued that money has social and subjective meaning in addition to its market or use value—the meaning of money is qualitatively different across contexts and spaces. Although modern currency seems physically homogenous and stable in its value, it is used by different social actors in qualitatively unique ways.[4] Using, saving, collecting, and storing money are governed by sets of values, norms, and "networks of social relations."[5] The meaning of money is "socially constructed and context specific," rather than stable based on economic value.[6] At the feast money has both symbolic and practice-oriented dimensions. In the months leading up to the feast, talk of money is one of the most salient aspects of feast planning meetings. At each meeting organizers account for and report donation totals and the number of raffle ticket books sold by lifters. These amounts are signs of readiness for the feast and are, more importantly, symbolic measures of the overall health and fate of the parish. At the feast organizers understand money through a frame of survival. A profitable feast ensures the parish will remain "alive."

At the first feast meeting in March 2017, OLMC's newest pastor walked into the meeting right before it was set to begin. Men were milling around the lower hall and settled at tables with their friends, family members, or affinity groups. Many still had their coats on and sat hunched over the tables. It was the day the new pastor of the church would make his first appearance as moderator of the feast, so everything he said mattered and set the tone for the coming months. Monsignor Jamie walked into the room wearing black slacks and his collar. His clothes looked pressed and crisp black. He was wearing a slate gray blazer that I could tell was tailored. It was not boxy around the shoulders but fitted and draped nicely. His hair was dark black, high, and combed back in a natural and wispy pompadour. His skin was tan, and his Brooklyn accent was thick. He opened with a prayer. With closed eyes he dedicated all efforts to God, saying, "Everything we do for the feast and parish is for Your glory and Your honor." He prayed that the feast "continue to inspire new generations in the Catholic faith" that the feast had instilled in all of those gathered on that day. His prayer looked both forward and backward. He prayed that everyone work together and hard to keep the feast going, and dedicated their work and efforts to the glory of God. At the close of the prayer we all crossed ourselves and repeated, "Our Lady of Mount Carmel, Pray for Us," "San Paolino, Pray for Us"—these kinds of "brief exclamatory prayers" are more formally termed pious ejaculations.[7]

Because it was the very first meeting, there was a lot to get through. Two women from the Smithsonian were there, hoping to work with the feast on a contribution for the annual Folk Life Festival, the 2017 theme focused on youth, migration, community culture, and heritage. They were interested in the feast as a demonstration of the enduring spirit of community across generations, especially in a gentrifying neighborhood. There were more new faces as well, people who carried cameras and sound equipment. Two documentary filmmakers were there, and the lead filmmaker introduced himself as someone whose father grew up in the neighborhood. He explained that he wants to make a "film that is a portrait of this neighborhood and tradition over generations."

At the end of the meeting Monsignor Jamie stood to talk. He did not remain standing or seated behind the table but walked in front of the table, confident and swaggering with his hands tucked in his front pockets and his blazer tucked behind them. He took one hand out of his pocket as he began talking, and I noticed a thick gold ring on his pinky with a dark almost black signet stone in the center. Monsignor Jamie was stationed at OLMC when he was a seminarian, and when he was here he worked every single day of the feast. He requested placement at the parish twice before but never got it. This is the story he told about how, although new, he had been around the feast for a very long time. He explained to the men how his career in the Development office of the Diocese of Brooklyn had prepared him to become pastor at this "crucial time" in the parish's history, with the neighborhood changing and old-timers moving and passing on.

> It's so important for us to keep this feast alive and make it the center of this parish as it has been for many years. . . . More so than before, this feast has kept the parish alive. . . . When they . . . built this church, they never thought it would survive and that's why it doesn't look like a church. It looks like they felt they could always use it as a community center or a hall in case the parish closed. . . . But the parish survived and people fought to keep it alive. Many of your parents and grandparents did that. . . . One of the things that kept it alive was this feast. [It is] so important for us to keep this feast alive for the sake of the parish, but also

for the hard work that our parents and grandparents put into this parish and it's very important that we do that in their honor as well. You know a lot of times everything comes down to money. It's not all about money. Yes, the money keeps the feast going, the money we raise keeps the parish going . . . the money that we raise will help keep this parish the center of this neighborhood, but it's all about the spirit and the faith that comes out of it. . . . We have to work together. . . . A house divided will fall, and we have to work together . . . and make decisions that are going to benefit the whole parish [and] the whole feast.

This meeting was particularly salient because it was the new pastor's first formal introduction, but it was largely like many of the other meetings, where each year it seemed there were new filmmakers. It was full of mundane updates, bickering and occasional spats, and the pastor and chairman calling people to order and reminding them of the importance of unity. There were lamentations over the changing neighborhood and discussions of strategies to get more people to attend the feast. Each year, as meetings progress and the feast nears, one of the main goals is to have lieutenants deliver reports on the number of lifters in their crew, the number of raffle books they have distributed, and the number of books returned. Each lifter has to sell five books of raffle tickets, each worth twenty dollars. A central purpose of subsequent meetings is hearing the lieutenants' reports, which typically sound like this: "thirty-seven men [lifters] twenty-five [books] out, ten in." At the meetings many routine topics seem to boil down to questions of money and fundraising. While documentary filmmakers and Smithsonian representatives came hoping to capture a community's vitality, perhaps with romantic ideas of perseverance in the face of gentrification, and enduring tradition over generations, the feast is not just a question of tradition. For the pastor and the organizers, the stakes are much higher. Survival is at stake. All of these more sentimental registers are soaked in talk of the bottom line.

Pastors and feast organizers anthropomorphize the parish. Money correlates to parish health. Without high net profits, hard work, and dedicated fundraising, the parish could perish. Condominiums, bike paths, garages, and new residents are all worrisome symbols of change and threats to the parish. The previous pastor consistently reminded feast organizers that, especially in a gentrified neighborhood, "we have to keep the feast the profit that it is for the parish." Without the money from the feast, the parish could suffer and die, but through hard work, aggressive fundraising, cooperation, and devotion to Our Lady of Mount Carmel, the men keep the parish alive. These discourses of life and death make feast organizing high stakes and are prevalent in homosocial gatherings and spaces like the meetings. These discourses valorize men's labor as productive, vital, and all-important. Keeping the parish alive then becomes a masculine duty, the responsibility of male feast organizers who get out there to solicit, sell raffle books, and recruit lifters and children for the children's giglio.

When pastors refer to the feast as the lifeblood of the parish, it is a metaphor that not only speaks to vitality, life, and survival but also evokes families, lineage, bonds, and bloodlines. Obligation to the feast and the parish extends beyond the contemporary moment. Money is wrapped up in discourses of life and death and intergenerational bonds, burdens, and responsibilities. Continued labor for the feast not only benefits the church but honors the legacy of friends and family who came before. In previous chapters I have argued that participation in the feast and its devotions is a means of honoring and sustaining bonds between men, be they kin, friends, or mentors. So when pastors deliver speeches about the feast and working hard to honor the contributions and efforts of parishioners past, they are evoking those blood ties, and linking obligations today to the sacrifices, work, and memory of those in the past.

The language of helping the church *live* is prevalent not only among male organizers and clerical leaders but also among women volunteers. Debbie has been volunteering for the feast for years. Although she is a resident of Astoria, Queens, she commutes to OLMC every day during the feast to work in one of the ride booths. Often for six hours at a time, Debbie sits with another volunteer in a booth on North Eighth Street, selling sheets of tickets to families. I first started talking to her in 2016. One day I was sitting in the money room in the rectory and she came in to report to John to begin her shift in the ticket booth. Pointing her chin to me, she said to John, "While she's here we should put her to work." John told her, "Trust me I keep her very busy. And I'll let you know, Alyssa painted most of the geel." "No! really?" she said, her mouth agape. I could not tell whether she was shocked, pleasantly surprised, or scandalized, so I tried to temper the amount of responsibility John attributed to me. "Well Mark painted most of it, I just worked on some of the saints." "Absolutely beautiful, absolutely beautiful," she responded with widened eyes, which eased my anxiety. After that, Debbie and I became friends. As a high school teacher with a wealth of knowledge about Italian American culture and foodways, she often shared book recommendations with me and dubbed me an honorary Italian. She has black hair that is often pulled in a bun and often wears denim shorts, with a big T-shirt tied at her hips and flip-flops for her shifts in the booth. Debbie is Calabrian and Sicilian and grew up in Howard Beach.

That year at the end of the feast, I rode the Ferris wheel with Debbie, and we made this a tradition. We climbed in the little swaying metal car and rode to the top of the wheel. As we looked over the flower garlands that marked the boundary of the feast and the roofs of the church and old buildings in the neighborhood, she sat across from me in big black sunglasses, and we both took panoramic photos of the feast from above. In that Ferris wheel gondola she explained how she got involved in working for the feast. She told me her father started a feast in Howard Beach and it failed horribly, but one day she was at Mass at OLMC and a local leader, Richie Cats, stood up and said, "The feast is how our church lives in a changing neighborhood so please if you could donate any of your time, even just a few hours, we have applications, that would help." She continued, "I didn't think of it, I left church, went to my car and I heard my father's voice 'Debbie, it's for the church,' and I turned back around and went in the rectory and [a rectory worker] was there. He handed me an application like he knew what I was there for. I heard my father's voice." She explained that when she filled out the application, "I circled 'flea market' because I'm terrible with money and there you just stand, take a dollar and don't make change but then John calls me three days later—I had forgotten—and he says would you be open to doing something else? And that's how I started. I heard my father's voice, 'Debbie, it's for the church.'"

Sociologists argue that money can be "sacralized" and transformed from mundane into sacred money when "dollars and cents shed their instrumental-use value and take on substantively-rational, 'non-economic' significance."[8] At the feast, money has moral meaning. Money binds feast organizers to the parish and implicates them in the labor of sustaining the church. Raising money and working with money locate them in intergenerational networks of parishioners and kin bonded to the parish through sentiment, neighborhood, and familial networks. Debbie frames this story of how she began volunteering through two lenses: a connection to her father and the idea that the feast is how the church "lives" in a changing neighborhood. Although she paints herself as "terrible with money," she wound up in a role where her primary task is handling money. Working with money, as a volunteer, is important because it is for the church. It keeps it alive and honors her father.

While some are passionate about volunteering for the church, many note that the work of the volunteers goes unappreciated and unnoticed. Workers often critiqued pastors for not acknowledging the labor of the women workers, for not providing food or water to those women who had been out in the heat all day working the booths and the shrine. One volunteer suggested, "I think someone needs to talk to [the pastor] about some things that are important like thanking the workers. You think that you could walk around and say hello and say thank you . . . these people are donating their time taking off from work and getting babysitters," importantly noting the differential costs of their labor. Some wanted more acknowledgment of the years and hours they have committed, a recognition that they work all day with no relief. They suggested things that leadership could do to acknowledge the sacrifices of the volunteers: "You think we can get some Poland Spring?" or "You can buy cookies. [You] think you can walk around and offer some cookies?" One told me, "I'm happy if the church is prospering," but said, "the workers, we work hard. He doesn't see it that way."

It is important to note this frustration. While there are formal mechanisms of recognition in place for men who dedicate time and labor to the feast all year, like the pastor's award and promotions, there is no similar formal means through which women workers gain praise for their dedication and labor during the weeks of the feast. By focusing on "men's work," I highlight the construction of laymen's authority within religious institutions. To discuss the poles of women's work and official hierarchies of male leadership leaves us without analytical tools to understand how laymen occupy more informal positions of power within churches, how they imbue their work with religious meaning, and how they form intergenerational bonds of love, duty, and responsibility. My aim is to interrogate and understand how laymen valorize their labor within religious institutions. My focus on men's labor at OLMC does not take male power and authority as a given but works to unpack men's organizational labor and constructions of "productivity" and "dedication." Men construct and embody masculinities through their church work and sustain networks of male authority and a gendered division of labor.

Masculinity and Church Work

The focus on money, success, and ideas of their work as productive and integral to the parish's survival also masculinizes feast planning work. Feast meetings are the place where lay and clerical leaders instruct the men to come together to cooperate and unify. When they gossip and feud, leaders chide them to stop being "petty" and to "be men," build up revenue, and bring in the "bucks" by taking on responsibilities and working for the good of their church. Feast meetings are the place where men hear disciplining messages like this one from Monsignor Jamie: "There shouldn't be a reason you can't sell a raffle book of a hundred dollars. Kids at school sell a hundred dollars' worth of chocolate, you can sell a hundred dollars' worth of raffles." Feast meetings are also the place where men compete over who works the hardest, is the most dedicated, and is the most productive for the church and feast. When things get heated and arguments break out, they competitively affirm their hard work, as one man did by saying, "I bust my ass here all the time. If everyone did what I did we would [make] half a million, and we would have no problem."

Men use ideas about productive and organized work to draw distinctions between men's and women's work for the feast. For example, men actively feminize work for the flea market. The flea market is often bustling and staffed by older women. In 2014 tables in the lower hall were abundant with saint figurines and boxes of prayer cards. Parishioners donated everything from antique brass jewelry and novelty salt and pepper shakers to crystal picture frames and piles of scrap fabric that crowded the tables. The flea market accepts donations in the months prior to the feast and then sells the donated items in the church's gym or lower hall during the feast.

In 2015 the sister who coordinated the flea market was no longer running it. At the first meeting that year the general chairman announced that they needed a volunteer to help with the flea market: "Last year it brought in thirteen thousand dollars. Our total from the feast was two hundred sixty thousand, so thirteen is a lot. Most of it comes through donations, and we are already getting donations." The men at the meeting snickered, and the chairman looked at the group with his eyebrows raised and chin pointed down. One man, a past capo who was always outspoken and irreverent in the meetings, said, "Don't we have women to do that?" He seemed to wonder what this group of men had to do with the flea market. "We do, but we need help sorting all of the donations that are coming in," the chairman responded. A few weeks later at another meeting, he announced again that the flea market needed some help. So far they had gotten many donations that had not been sorted yet, and he had been telling people to hold off on further donations until they could get some more help. "The flea market last year made about thirteen thousand, and that's with no money put in. We have the ladies who run it, but as I mentioned last time we needed someone to oversee and help out." It is notable that he used words like "oversee" and "take charge" to paint this as important executive work. Some called it the "junk freak market," and although the flea market makes money, men characterized it as women's work. To them it is not organized but full of junk and is staffed and frequented by women, and all in all the labor of collecting donations and selling them seems to take no significant effort. For them, it is inconsequential and thus feminized.

The men of the feast have official channels of recognition for their work in the form of promotions and the pastor's award. In the previous chapter I looked to the basement as a site of devotional labor, where through work with paint, papier-mâché, and wood, the male members of the Giglio Committee demonstrate their skill, knowledge, and dedication to feast tradition. Labor in the basement is one very physical way men are initiated into lifelong labor for the feast and learn to embody ideals of masculinity that value creativity and productivity. Mark won recognition for his time and labor in the basement as the recipient of the pastor's award in 2016. In 2015 John won the pastor's award for a very different kind of labor. While Mark could measure his labor through the successful completion of the giglio and beautiful paint job, John's labor was measured not only in time (hours spent) but in permits and dollars.

Mark's work was physical and visible, whereas John's was largely logistical and invisible.

On July 12, 2015, the church filled with people in gold and maroon T-shirts: lifters and friends and family of that year's number one capo, Bo, crowded the pews. John zipped around the church working as an usher, seating people in designated pews for this packed Mass, which was in such high demand that people often had to get tickets to be seated. His family sat in the third row, and he zoomed by, scolding them for sitting in the wrong pew. He had no idea that they were seated up front because he was receiving an award. I sat with his mother—a thin, tan woman with a perfectly highlighted blonde bob, a school principal and a grandmother of eight. She gushed that he has always been like this: always busy and always achieving. As we waited for Mass to begin she told me how he received a full ride to Regis High School, a private Catholic school, a full ride to Fordham, a job at IBM, and a fully funded MBA. She described her son as someone who likes to be in control and aware of everything, so his family sitting in the wrong pew really agitated him. Monsignor Calise explained as he stood before a crowded Giglio Sunday Mass,

> Every once in a while you meet people who want to do something good for the feast, but they really do want to keep it as quiet as possible, and attract as little attention to themselves as possible. Now the odd thing about that is that when you find someone that is so service-directed and want to keep it on the low key, it makes you want to say thank you all the more loudly. It's been my privilege over these last seven years to present the pastor's award to a lot of people who've worked very hard to make this feast what it is, giving not only all of their talents but more time than we could ever imagine and certainly this year's honoree stands out as one of the most selfless, and the most dedicated. So in recognition of your endless commitment and dedication to the parish and Feast of Our Lady of Mount Carmel, on July 12, 2015 . . . please join me in presenting this year's pastors award to John.

In a gray T-shirt and cargo shorts, John approached and kissed the monsignor on the cheek before quickly posing for two photos.

John and Mark represent two different kinds of feast men—one who dedicates his time and service in the form of physical labor and one who dedicates his time and service in the form of "professional" labor. Mark lifts, is a lieutenant, paints, and creates. While he does backstage labor, the products of his labor, like successful lifts and a good-looking giglio, are highly visible in the front stage. John files permits, does paperwork, interfaces with municipal agencies, writes solicitation letters, and does the accounting. He is often hidden away in the rectory during the feast, not lifting but delegating and managing. These are two different kinds of labor that have been built into the structure of feast planning and production since the 1950s and are representative of different masculinities at the feast.

While the giglio is the structure that epitomizes the Giglio Committee's (and Mark's) manual and creative labor, a very different kind of structure captures the "business" side of the feast and labor of a more financial and executive sort: the Century Board. Made of wood and metal, the Century Board holds shiny brown plaques printed with yellow letters, the colors of Mount Carmel. Each plaque is printed with the names of businesses, families, and individuals who donate money to the feast and church. The bigger the donation, the bigger the plaque. The names of donors stay up all year round and include business like Cross Country Savings Bank as well as Italian classics such as Bamonte's restaurant, Grimaldi's pizza, and contractors, realtors, plumbers, funeral homes, and construction/building material companies. Plaques also hold family names and commemorate loved ones who have passed. Donors become part of the Century Club and receive a T-shirt, and their plaque is displayed throughout the year. The smallest plaques are for donors of one thousand dollars, and various tiers of "Special" large plaques at the top of the board range from fifteen hundred to five thousand dollars.

Each year solicitation letters ask donors to contribute to the church. In 2015 the letter that went out to potential Century Club members noted that it was a significant year for the Catholic Church in the United States because Pope Francis would be visiting in the fall. "Before the Pope's arrival, there will be another significant moment for the Catholic Church, right here in Brooklyn—the 128th Annual Feast of Our Lady of Mount Carmel and San Paolino of Nola!" The letter continued, "Each time you offer your prayers at Novena, attend Mass, process through the streets and participate in the dancing of the giglio, you are showing the face of Christ to our neighbors and loved ones." It ended encouraging donors to join their "extended parish family to celebrate our faith, to live the Gospel, and to enjoy another Feast" and asked, "As always, please keep the spiritual and temporal success of the Feast in your prayers."

The Century Board is so important because its sponsorship model is a high-margin and low-cost way to raise revenue for the church. In the back of the basement I discovered the small workshop where each Century Board plaque is produced. The small dark room contained a few desks, a sign reading OLMC Print Shop Est. 1999, rolls of yellow plastic used for the font, and a printing machine. Small black-and-white portraits of past pastors and San Paolino were taped to the walls. Framed photos of men on the annual Usher's Retreat lined the walls and tables. The photos showed men barbecuing and having fun in what looked like a cabin in the woods.

During feast meetings one of the central topics of discussion is the progress of the Century Board. In 2016 members of the executive board asked the men gathered for the meeting if each of them could take solicitation letters and try to bring in one or two donors. As the executive board explained in 2016, "The Century Board is the best bang for our buck, it costs $1.25 or $2.50 to make those signs. We have a machine back here and we make it ourselves. That's almost one hundred percent profit. . . . This is where we lack effort, and last year we paid the price. It was one of the worst netting feasts, the least money the feast made in ten years." Because they produce the signs themselves, the Century Board is inexpensive. The general chairman explained that overall fundraising was down and expenses were up and that everyone needed to put in extra effort, bring in one extra donor, or sell one extra raffle book because it was really tough last year. In the 1990s the Century Board often made $175,000, but by 2015 it did not break $100,000. The chairman concluded, "We like to have fun on the streets and down here, but we have to work."

Scholars like Gail Bederman and Beth Wenger, focusing in on the first half of the twentieth century, found that men often mix the discourses and practices of work, business, and religion as a means of masculinizing church work and charity. The 1911–12 Men and Religion Forward Movement (M&RFM), a nationwide interdenominational Protestant religious revival, proclaimed that men needed to "vitalize" churches by repopulating them and providing virile church work as opposed to futile

and feminized committee work.⁹ The M&RFM, founded by Fred Smith
of the YMCA's religious work department, swept the nation, holding
conferences and meetings in seventy-six cities and over one thousand
towns. The goal of the movement was to create a "truly masculinized
religion" by putting religion "in congruence with the world of twentieth
century business and politics."¹⁰ The M&RFM, with its slogan "More
Men for Religion, More Religion for Men," sought to find the three million men it claimed were missing from church pews, decrying a Protestant church whose attendees were two-thirds women.¹¹ As a counter to
domestic, maternal faith, the movement held outdoor Christian Con-
gresses in places like New York City's Union Square. It bought billboards
over Times Square and Broadway that lit up at night, declaring, "The
Church Wants Men in Her Work for Man." The movement advertised
men and boys conventions where "experts" on men's religion would be
speaking. These advertisements often appeared in sports sections, next
to columns on football and baseball and ads for burlesque houses and
automobiles, declaring that sports is not enough for a well-rounded
man—he needs both pleasure and spirit.¹² They called on men to speak
to their clergymen and to meld sport, business, and religion in their
lives. Although at these institutes men pledged their lives to Christ, the
movement was not "old-fashioned" evangelism but a new corporate
campaign of evangelism through advertising.

The M&RFM discursively created a crisis of feminization and worked
to masculinize faith and "recodify religion as manly" so that men could
move in the spheres of both church and business. Movement activists
argued that men needed "manly outlets in church work itself." Blend-
ing the world of modern corporate business and religion through advertising campaigns was not enough. Rather, church work needed to
change in order for men to think it was important and meaningful—
more "important" than the work women did for their churches. Leader
Fred Smith believed that men needed a "man's job to do in church work."
He complained, "I found one church committee of twenty-three men—
men capable of organizing a bank or running a railroad—engaged in the
work of buying a rug for the vestry floor."¹³ Men needed action-oriented
work, according to the movement. Interestingly, the movement also
used the language of survival and death to describe churches without
men. According to one campaign in Providence, "Unless men and boys

were attracted to church by some definite program of work for them to do, the church will die."[14]

Beth Wenger's study of the Federation for the Support of Jewish Philanthropic Societies of New York City from 1880 to 1945 argues that in these years Jewish philanthropy became gendered and masculinized. At the turn of the twentieth century male Jewish leaders called for the consolidation of charitable organizations into philanthropic federations. These federations acted as umbrella structures that would fundraise through annual campaigns and disburse money to "constituent" organizations.[15] As charity and philanthropy became consolidated, men increasingly identified their philanthropic efforts as organized, efficient, scientific, and systematic, as opposed to the more "benevolent" activities of women, driven more by kindness than efficient organization.[16] Both the federation and the M&RFM reflected the rise of corporate culture. The federation, like the M&RFM, represented its work with masculine rhetoric and defined its efforts as strategic, relying on skill, success, preparation and precision, and business acumen.[17] While women's charity was "sweet," based in events like bazaars, philanthropic work was done out of a sense of duty and responsibility.[18]

What is interesting about the planning and committee work of the feast is that it is much like the work that federation men and M&RFM activists critiqued: selling raffle tickets, choosing T-shirt colors, and planning processions. How then is feast planning considered men's work? While many scholars have written about the feast, focusing in on the Dance of the Giglio, the authority of the capos, and the physicality of the lifters, taking a broad temporal look at the feast reveals men doing other kinds of work.

The meeting minutes from the 1950s and 1960s reveal the spectrum of roles men took on and the day-to-day decisions they made about the feast. They discussed the merits of crew-neck over V-neck T-shirts and took requisite votes. They decided color combinations for their hats and neckerchiefs.[19] Polka dot or plaid hats for those giving out blessed bread on the Questua? Blue slacks or khaki? Red scarves and purple hats or just all brown for the lift? The minutes from 1957 to 1961 reveal that men chose "chicken dinners" for *pranza* (lunch) on the day of the lift.[20] They reviewed fabric swatches and visited bakeries. They decided on souvenirs and tokens like medals, prayer cards, and letter openers for donors. Sometimes the minutes very sternly read "First Order of Business; SLACKS."[21] In 1961 a Slacks Committee formed to review colors and prices for the matching slacks all the lifters would wear. Blue, brown, and gold were the colors on the table, and three men were in charge of the pants situation.

The minutes for May 5, 1961, read, "The all important decision on the PANTS was discussed next." It is interesting to note that in the hundreds of pages of notes, the secretary of the meetings is seldom mentioned. One secretary, Marion Ambrosino, was mentioned once because she was absent one day and a man had to fill in to take minutes, but the note of her absence suggests that while these meetings were largely homosocial, there was often a woman present. While it is impossible to know, perhaps it is her sarcastic tone when the minutes mention the "all-important" pants decision. The chairman of the Slacks Committee presented the room with two swatches, one "light gold," the other a "dull brown." The men ultimately decided on a "deep gold." Conflict ensued when some men were angry that they had to pay an extra twenty-five cents to order pants over a size 40, and they voted on that as well.[22] This was the minutia of meetings. No matter if they were bickering about kerchiefs or discussing the price of confetti and lumber, all of their time was framed around the idea of work and productivity in service of the feast's success.

Discourses of work and effort valorized men's labor and imbued it with broader meaning for the parish. In May 1959, Father Frank Varriale ended the meeting by telling the men, "Each man is to feel he is an adequate part of the feast, every individual is important no matter how big or small his job may be. . . . Everyone's help is needed to make this another successful year. Above all . . . keep in mind always that everything we do, we do for God."[23] A 1959 letter by Lou Coppola, a lieutenant and member of the Publicity Committee, suggesting that deceased members of the committee or *paranza* (lifters) be honored with a bronze plaque, captured those ideas: "Year after year we go on planning and preparing for the day to celebrate our wonderful feast. We search our minds in every direction for ideas to make the feast a success." The plaque would ensure that they "not be forgotten for their faith, loyalty, and effort for a successful feast."[24] The language of success and work presented the efforts of all committee men as executive labor. They made decisions, called shots, and contributed to the church; their jobs mattered. The resilience of these discourses helps us understand how the labor of women volunteers and workers seems ancillary. Selling ride tickets and flea market wares is the administrative counterpart to the valorized "decision-making work" men do.

Success meant money, even in the 1950s and early 1960s. In 1957 and in 2017 alike, the men were told by their priests and lay feast leaders that they had to work hard, "hustle," and "bring in the money."[25] While it may seem that there is a heightened focus on money because the parish is embattled because of gentrification, money has been a central concern of feast organizers since the 1950s. In 1954 the Society of San Paolino and the parish formed the Cooperative Feast. Whereas a mutual aid society formed by Nolani immigrants, the Societá M.S. (Mutuo Soccorso) San Paolino, founded the Dance of the Giglio, the Cooperative Feast brought the giglio and devotion to San Paolino under the authority of the parish and created a joint feast that celebrated both San Paolino and Our Lady of Mount Carmel.[26] This happened at a time when across America there was a heightened focus on parish finances. Scholars trace this midcentury concern to suburbanization and the construction of new parishes and schools in the places Catholics were moving as they left cities. New buildings meant parishes had debt and had to raise money to fund the construction of schools, convents, rectories, and churches.[27] According to historian Jay Dolan, "Bingo signs became commonplace, and fundraising events defined the church year much in the same way as Easter or Christmas. . . . An endless round of fundraising events took place: card parties, dinners, raffles, picnics, entertainments, and fashion shows. They culminated in the largest event of all, the parish festival, or bazaar."[28] The feast was all of these things, plus an ethnic devotional tradition rolled into one. Although OLMC is not a suburban parish, after its church building was torn down to make way for the Brooklyn-Queens Expressway, its new building was completed in 1950 and its school opened in 1953. So like suburban parishes, it too experienced new construction midcentury. At this time money seemed to be the primary concern of clerical leaders. According to historian Robert Orsi, young clergy "knew that what mattered to their superiors was not how well they cured souls but how carefully they shepherded the bottom line. . . . Many serious pastoral duties, such as visiting the sick, were assigned to men who had proven inept at raising funds and buildings, the 'real work' of the clergy." As Orsi writes, "Smart priests knew: saints were a good investment."[29] Devotions and bazaars proved to be reliable sources of revenue, and the feast had both. Meeting minutes from the late 1950s and early 1960s show that solicitation and fundraising were at the center of the feast-planning process.

The meeting on the night of April 29, 1958, provides just one example of a meeting where money was the central concern. On that night the men of the Cooperative Feast Committee gathered in the church's lower hall from nine thirty to eleven fifty, opening their meeting with a prayer. Perhaps the meetings were so late to accommodate everyone's work schedules; perhaps they were all tired from a long day. This day was different because lifters were invited to the meeting. While the meetings were largely composed of men who made up committees like the Entertainment, Publicity, and Solicitations Committees, they were extending an invitation to lifters. Lifters largely did not participate in bimonthly meetings; rather they collected their hats and shirts before the feast, gave money to order matching pants, and showed up for dress rehearsals. But in 1958 Father Ricigliano welcomed the lifters present to become a part of the Solicitations Committee. He made it very clear that they would not be "compelled to solicit," but bringing them into the meeting was a way of welcoming them to take an interest "in what takes place planning months in advance."[30]

After talking about lifts and logistics, the conversation turned to entertainment and publicity. The chairman of the Giglio Committee reported that repairing the giglio and buying new lumber and labor would cost $2,100. That year, 1958, was the first time they incorporated the boat into the Dance of the Giglio. Mr. Mirando, chairman of the Fact Finding Committee regarding the boat, reported that it would cost $1,558, including each enumerated cost, for decor, lighting, construction, confetti, and food for one hundred lifters. At that meeting the men voted to approve the boat. Father Frank Varriale set the year's fundraising goal at $10,000, which would cover basic expenses, and reminded the men "to keep in mind the fact that solicitations is the foundation of the feast, without it we would have nothing."[31]

Throughout the years for which there are minutes and archival records, reports about money and solicitations were one of the main features of the feast meetings. Usually the priest—the feast moderator—would deliver a message about how the men had to set aside personal animosity, refrain from gossiping and complaining outside of the meetings, and "above all always cooperate with one another." On April 23, 1957, Father Frank told the men, "Our present income is very low and is definitely not encouraging," now that Easter was over it was time to "show a very marked improvement." He admonished them for "a poor showing!" in how many raffle books they had sold thus far. When they were not being scolded for poor efforts in fundraising, the men were figuring out how to make the process more effective. They talked about organizing groups and teams and pairing "weak men" and "shy men" with "strong men" to go house to house canvassing in Williamsburg and in Nassau and Suffolk counties.[32] Each meeting was punctuated with a report on how much money was received at the meeting and raised so far. At the end of the 1957 feast it had grossed over $60,000; after expenses $35,000 were disbursed to the church—nearly $9,000 from solicitations.

The division of labor at the feast was not simply about loyalty and shared work but about the skills of each man. Men who worked as carpenters and home decorators took charge of building the giglio, assembling pulley rigs to hoist up the pieces, and painting the papier-mâché angels.[33] The Publicity Committee specifically sought men who could type in order to write press releases. In 1958, the year following its inauguration, the body of the meeting "agreed that a business man head the Century Club committee to contact other business men who seem to be prospects for this club."[34] The Century Board did not yet exist, instead club members had their names put on panels on the giglio. At the next meeting the Century Club and Solicitations Committee merged, "with a business man as chairman." This man, Mario Bosone, had his own travel agency and managed pool halls.[35] According to the minutes, "business men" and "professional men" were to particularly take charge of bringing in large donations for the Century Club.

The feast is a devotional spectacle that relies on physical strength, authority, and craftsmanship, but this early emphasis on "business and professional men" resonates with today's division of labor at the feast. It particularly illuminates John's role as the behind-the-scenes money manager, especially as a man with an MBA who not only is knowledgeable about finances but also fundraises for a living. John's role at the feast depends on his professional skill, education, management abilities, precision, reliability, and trustworthiness. While feast publicity documents from the 1950s present the Dance of the Giglio as a "devoted tribute to the church," we see in this review of early planning meetings that devotion and money have always gone hand in hand at the feast.

The Money Room

In 2014 John sat in a room in the rectory at the head of a long wooden table, surrounded by old metal boxes. The boxes were covered in chipping paint and old curling duct tape in the place of labels. They showed their age and functioned as an old-fashioned system for managing funds at the feast. John organized money based on where it came from: the shrine, the rides, the flea market, and so forth. John's wife sat at the table as well; she was pregnant at the time and wore denim shorts. She ate a plate of pasta salad and ripped raffle tickets. As this was my first time in the money room I did not yet understand his system of organization and accounting. John sat counting bills, large stacks of twenties and hundreds. He organized the bills into piles that he then placed at the lip of the money counting machine. The machine was old, thick, and yellowing. Its plug extended across the room. He ran the bills through the machine, holding the thick stack at just the right angle to feed them through, and with a quick whirring sound it ate and spit out the bills and displayed the number in red analog letters. He turned to me impatiently: "So what do you want to know?" It was characteristic John: blunt and abrasive yet warm all at the same time. I asked him to explain what he does, and that was the beginning of my time in the money room. The very next year, 2015, he recruited me to the money crew.

That day John explained to me that on a nightly basis he managed the group of volunteers who help out because of their devotion to the parish. He explained that these people help the feast succeed. According to John, despite the changing number of parishioners and neighborhood change "it is still the same concept: to maximize money raised during the feast." He ran through the different roles volunteers have—working in the shrine, the café, or the beer garden—and that all the proceeds raised from these spots and the rents collected from the stands outside help the church.

John continued, "I have tiers of responsibility that I love. Volunteers take care of themselves, especially in the shrine and café. My phone is constantly ringing, so that's a pain in the ass. But everyone tries to squeeze in time to work." John's participation in the feast began when he was a child, and his continued involvement and progression in roles is a story of male mentorship. He explained, "First I volunteered as a soda boy. . . . Water was later, it was only soda then," he said with a laugh. "Coke, root beer, I would give cans and make the rounds and fill up. . . . I became an altar boy when I was six or seven, a few years after, in my own progression, I worked as a sacristan on Sundays, opening the church and stuff. Monsignor Cassato . . . asked if I wanted to go in the money room, I was elated at the time because it was the whole center of everything that happened. It [all] ended there." He continued, "So that's how I progressed to where I am [and doing] the money every night. I am responsible for all the proceeds and closing out. The boxes go out when we open for the night, and they come in and we count them. I manage the feast books and coordinate the rectory staff. They record and I reconcile." He explained the importance of all of this work and fundraising: "The feast and the parish are interdependent, you have to understand how important the feast is to keep this community active, and keep the place going. That is where my passion is."

On Giglio Sunday in 2017, we were in the rectory having a late night; not only did we have to count all the money from the day, we also had to "prove out the rides" (which meant to reconcile the amount of tickets sold with the actual cash that came in). John just finished totaling up for the day—$24,845—and as he tallied up the beer money and compared it to the previous year, he said, "Holy shit, holy shit, this year we made $8,158 on beer, and last year only did five grand, holy shit." He was elated that they were breaking records. After that, we went outside, and as we walked down the steps of the shrine, he told me how sometimes he thinks he got his MBA just so he could run all of this. Later he told me, "My thing is really a calling. I know I have a regular job and I make a good salary, but I do what I do for the church." What makes John particularly drawn to and qualified for this role at the feast? His MBA is important, as is his professional experience. John sees his work for the church not simply as an extension of his expertise in finance and fundraising but as a calling and a mission, one that is particularly tied to bonds of love and mentorship he forged at the feast and in the parish.

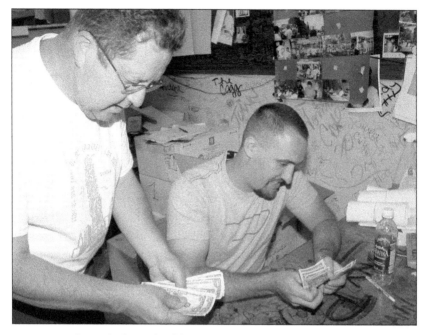

Figure 3.1. Richie and John in the old money room, 2004. Photo courtesy of OLMCFEAST.

The more I got to know John the more I heard about the money room of the past. It was a hidden room upstairs behind the church basketball court, making it even more of a literal and metaphorical backstage. John and his best friend Phil would often reminisce about their nights in the money room when they were younger. They would rattle off all the names that were scrawled over the walls and the inside jokes they had there. It seemed to be the stuff of legend; every inch of the walls were signed with the names of people who visited—it seemed like the ultimate place at the feast that mixed labor, business, and fun. One slow day in 2014 John and Phil took me to the old money room. I was so excited to see this hub, this mine of feast memories that I had heard them talk about with such fondness and excitement. They still sounded like little boys who felt lucky to see the men's secret hangout, and it seemed not to have lost that magic that it had for them as they were growing up. As we walked through the halls, some people warned us that the money room may have already been painted over. Phil and John were visibly shaken, surprised that it possibly could be gone, especially before the legendary space was documented with photographs. We walked into the gym and into the darkness behind the stage where there was a small room. It was almost hidden, heightening the magic of the reveal. But when John opened the door, all we saw was four white walls and a sad window with bars over it. The light was not working, so we stood in the center of the room; it was still light outside, right before dusk. John and Phil looked around, bewildered, their mouths open, as if trying to piece together everything that was here before, trying to stitch together memories and mental pictures and superimpose them onto the blank walls. The sun set and the room darkened. In the darkness they lamented the white walls. They scanned the room as if looking for their names on the wall. Quickly John began to walk around the room, gesturing to physically represent the images he seemed to be collecting in his mind for me. He walked throughout the space pointing to corners of the room with both his arms, as if placing furniture. He was amped up by the loss of the space.

> Here there used to be a table; here was the coin machine—we had a slot machine in here even though they were illegal. . . . Every inch of the walls were covered with names. It doesn't matter who you were, you came in here you were given a marker and you scan for an empty space, the names went back to the eighties. There were shelves with money boxes. We wrote the totals on [black] boards on the walls. There was always a minimum of four men counting the money. I remember the nights, [monsignor] fell asleep counting money in a chair in the corner. This was the center of the feast.

As John walked around the small room, re-creating it with his memories for me, lightning flashed outside, which Phil and John interpreted as a "sign." John continued saying that every night there was a police escort stationed outside the door as they counted the money and they used to walk "right out on the street" with all the cash as they brought it to the rectory. As John told this flurry of stories, more thunder and lightning struck. "I guess this really is the end of an era," they said. As we left the room and shut the door behind us, I felt a sense of sorrow for the room I never saw or experienced. I understood the way Phil and John miss the space that looms so large in their memories as men and as boys.

Money Work

The police who are assigned to work the feast have a small break room downstairs right outside the lower hall, and John has a good rapport with all of them. One day I stood with John as he spoke to two police officers. John shook their hands and asked them if they needed anything. One of them was obviously new to his feast assignment, and his partner told him about John: "If you need anything, he's the man. He is the man, behind the man, behind the scenes that makes the feast run." When they left I laughed and nudged John, telling him that I loved that description. That police officer was right. The day at the feast begins and ends with John: the rides open, beer gets stocked, and the café, flea market, and shrine all open for business when John doles out the money boxes. I learned about the networks and paths all the money takes to get to the centralized money room in the rectory when John recruited me for his counting team.

John is obsessed with counting his steps and his miles. He is the kind of person who wakes up at four o'clock every morning, eats the same breakfast of shredded wheat with blueberries, and is go-go-go at the feast until midnight or one o'clock. During the feast we often spend hours every day together. I help him make money drop-offs and pick-ups and help him count. We take trips to the café for cappuccinos at the end of the night and check up on all of the volunteers. He has a frantic agitated energy that is always a source of laughter for me as I trail him at the feast. John is simultaneously always overwhelmed and in control. He often looks down at his phone to check his step count and missed calls. In 2017 on Giglio Sunday, John's phone buzzed all day. He told me he got fifty-four phone calls just that day, when usually he gets none because he is antisocial. One day he was so proud in an exasperated kind of way, telling me that on opening day of the feast "I left the house at nine o'clock, and I did 8.7 miles and forty-five flights just on this property!"

John is tall, with increasingly graying short buzzed hair and a light beard. He has a big smile that looks exactly like his mother's—toothy and wide, revealing all of his gums and the dark recesses of his cheeks. John likes to work out but hates nature. He prefers running around Juniper Park, a city park in Middle Village, Queens, to a hike. He sets goals and likes to stick to them. Often after a long day of working at the feast he heads to the park to get his final miles in for the day, even if it is midnight. John works hard and works all the time, and his roles at the feast and his job often blend together because he is the head of the diocese's Catholic Foundation and fundraises for a living. John was Turk for a year in 2004, and on Turk Night, when he has to gather with all the other Turks to be honored, he often cringes: "You know I don't like to be out in public." John really does prefer his behind-the-scenes work to more public-facing roles like those of the capos, lieutenants, and lifters. He told me as the feast was ending in 2017, "[This year] I killed myself. I'm ready for it to be over. Twelve days it comes and goes and it's a lot of aggravation but if I didn't have it I don't know what my life would be like." That same day, when he was frustrated talking about all of his work, he said, "For God's sake, I don't think it will get me into heaven but maybe it will shave some time off purgatory."

One of the very first days I spent time with John in 2014, we went out to a bar with Phil and one of John's coworkers at the diocese. John had been complaining that for so many people at the feast "everything is about lifting the cane"—meaning that the giglio lift, the hierarchy, and path to becoming capo often overshadow the needs of the parish, which in his opinion should always be the priority. That day as we sat around a wooden booth in the basement of the Whiskey Brooklyn, John drank a vodka and tonic. I asked him if he understands his work recruiting volunteers, doing finances, and securing permits as "religious work." He was resolute and said "absolutely," and told me about the many hours he spends working on the feast, and how it is central to his identity and role as a parishioner and a Catholic.

My first day working in the money room I had to learn about organization and earmarking—the way the money is sorted and handled differently based on its source. That first day I learned the rules of working in the money room. Number one: always lie. And number two: always look/act busy. As I walked around with John making money pickups, he told me, "You have to always act like you are so busy, and if someone complains you tell them you will come back then don't." Looking busy involves rushing around, not stopping or lingering with anyone too much, looking like you are doing business, and then going right back into the rectory. The "always lie" rule comes from the tradition in the 1990s and 2000s in the old money room. Back then everyone would compete to see which location made the most money. They would line up to get their boxes counted and see their totals written on the walls, but John told me that the key was to "never let them know what's up. That is the rule, always lie." He jokingly warned me, "If you're honest, you gotta go." I learned that what John meant was that what happens in the money room stays there—it is private, and to work there, around so much cash, you have to be trustworthy and be willing to keep talk of totals to yourself. It is similar to working in the basement on the giglio, where, although committee members knew the details of its design and colors, when talking to others they were purposefully vague.

The other money room worker is a parishioner in his mid-twenties named Sabier, who lives on the Southside of Williamsburg. Unlike all of the other men who give their time to the feast, Sabier is Mexican and not Italian. He worked in the rectory on weekends, taking phone calls and letting visitors in, and did all sorts of other work around the parish, like helping in the sacristy and filling bowls with unconsecrated hosts to prepare for Mass. Sabier loves zeppoles, and there is always a greasy bag of them on the table. Like John, Sabier is professionally trained for this work. He works as an accountant and knows about finance, and John always says that Sabier could take over for him. They often sit talking about spreadsheets, Excel, and QuickBooks. Sabier loves alternative music like the Red Hot Chili Peppers and Fall Out Boy, and we often bonded over Game of Thrones. In 2017 Denise, Sabier's sister, also began helping out. Denise is short, with thick wavy hair and long eyelashes; she looks like a mini version of her brother. They played in a kickball league in the neighborhood and often came to the feast tired from double-header games. Denise worked in the rectory, as did Sabier, and I have seen her make phone calls to priests to arrange for them to do Spanish Mass, set up taxis, do computer work, and hang out with other rectory workers in the Nevada booth. Denise loves chocolate ices and zeppoles and is outspoken, candid, and knowledgeable about feast finances. She is critical of the culture of insular dating at the feast (lieutenants and others who hold ranks often date "neighborhood girls" and those who come from feast families) and rolls her eyes whenever she talks about it. She knows how to prepare deposit slips, and at night we gather and rubber-band piles of money, stuffing thousands of dollars into plastic deposit bags. She taught me how to separate the collection, novena, and raffle money from the other cash collected at the feast. Their work in the money room is an extension of their roles as rectory workers and dedicated parishioners.

Each day's business began and ended in the money room. Each night, somewhere between ten and eleven thirty, based on when the police shut down the rides, people from the café, shrine, and flea market filed in with their money boxes, often with police escorts. Some had boxes full of messy stacks of money, but the flea market box was always full of neatly packed, paper clipped, and tied stacks of money. When Concetta, a woman who worked in the flea market, came in, John always said hello to her in a loving singsongy voice as she handed over her red peeling metal box and said, "I give you my treasure." The flea market workers counted their bills and tied them up with a long blue notepad paper with the total making it much easier to work through that box. The women who worked in the ride booths left their tall metal boxes filled with messy bills, loose quarters, and reams of ride tickets. The two men who worked the beer trap from 2014 to 2016 would come in later than the rest without a money box, unloading their pockets onto the table, and we would sort through their soggy stacks of bills. The shrine workers brought in their yellow plastic boxes where they collect candle money and "ribbon money."

The statue of OLMC that stands in the shrine is draped daily with a yellow ribbon. A shrine worker usually sits right next to the statue, not only guarding it and giving out scapulars, but also collecting offerings from devotees. They pin the dollars that devotees offer to the ribbon, and OLMC wears this long sash of bills. Periodically throughout the day Anthony or Nicky, two shrine workers, will bring the ribbon money into the rectory. While no longer attached to the ribbon, the bills are usually still pierced with sharp metal pins and run in a long vertical line, making shrine money and its accounting materially different from the other locations. Sometimes John gets on Anthony's case about how much stock he orders for the shrine and how over budget he goes. One day John told him, "I wanted to hang you because you spent twenty-two hundred bucks on scapulars." Anthony assured him, "We could make that back in one day. The ribbon is pure profit and the candles are going like hot cakes." The ribbon is not the only garment of bills the statue wears. On the processions the statue is outfitted with a cape of bills; at the center there is usually a check. This thousand-dollar donation comes each year from a man who insists OLMC wear the money like a blanket. The ribbon is interesting because people offer bills to OLMC out of love, devotion, and obligation. These bills have multiple meanings. They are perhaps votive, or hopeful offerings, gifts to OLMC or the church. These bills are emotionally and religiously charged but are simultaneously "pure profit" for the feast. One day Nicky was frantic when he came in the rectory to drop off the ribbon money. He was wearing a red polo, dark sunglasses, and his scapular. He explained how he told Anthony that he could not take the ribbon money down as people were looking, "because they think things! . . . I give them a scapular and a card and they're waiting, I asked 'Do you need more scapulars?' . . . [They say] 'I want to see you pin the money.' They make me feel like I'm robbing!"

"De-pinning" is a job in and of itself in the rectory, and doing it quickly and doing it well is a laudable skill. The shrine workers painstakingly put the pins through the bills, sometimes forcing one pin through three bills. In the money room you have to learn how to de-pin. My first feast working in the money room Anthony came in with a box full of fives, tens, and ones strung together with pins. He asked me if I knew how to remove pins, and I tried my best to quickly remove those that punctured the dollars, piling them on the side. Their tiny metal tips dug into my fingertips as I pulled them out and stacked the bills in front of me. Later, Richie Cats came in and asked if I knew how to pin money. He asked to look at my hands, and when I flashed him my fingers, with their gold rings and aqua nails, he said, "No, this won't do, they are too fragile." Anthony and Richie told me how they were both kicked off of ribbon duty and that they could not be pinners because they were no good at it. They had to hide their faces in shame, Richie said, covering his face and cowering. There is a method: you have to get the pin through multiple bills and twist and stick it. De-pinning is the process of extracting the tiny, sharp pins that pierce through multiple bills of money, feeling their sharp metal heads under the skin of your nails as you latch and pull them out. While it seems mundane, this task, like all the others in the money room, matters. People consider pinning and de-pinning a learned skill, a point of pride.

That first day they trained me how to do all the counting and record keeping. There is a fleet of money boxes. There are deep gray metal boxes that go to the ride booths filled with fives, tens, twenties, and rolls of quarters as well as books and rolls of ride tickets. Each box has to be prepared with precisely the right amount of change. All tickets, whether in rolls of single tickets or sheets of twenty and forty, have sequential starting numbers that need to be recorded on a sheet. At night we note down the last ticket number and subtracted to find out how many tickets had been sold. It is important to get this right because the church shares profits with the coordinator of the rides, and his share needs to be set aside. Each box needs to be counted, and every denomination of bill needs to be noted, reported to John, and written down on the account-ability sheet for that location. Everything has to be counted by hand and checked by the money counter. I learned John likes the money all facing the same way and how they throw all the coins in a big box and rubber-band and pack bills in hundred-dollar denominations and put everything else in the wooden "bank" in the front of the table. Work-ing on the money requires training and embodied knowledge: learning just the right way to gently tip dollars into the counting machine so that they do not jam or go sputtering all over the table, to rip raffles right on the perforation, and to rapidly and meticulously count stacks of money.

The money room has its own discourse. All the work with the ride tickets and figuring out the shares and the profits from each location is called "proving." When each box has been counted, the denominations of the bills noted and recorded, and when all of that has been reported to John, then it is okay to "kill" the money. For example, if I am counting the money from the café, I note how many tens, twenties, singles, and so on are in the box and calculate the total. John checks my work, then I remake the box with the starting change. Only after I have recorded all the totals can I kill the money. To kill it means to put it in the general bank by denomination. I could hand someone a huge stack of money and say "kill it," and they will know I mean to put it in the wooden bank at the front of the table. In order for cash to become generalized money, part of the pot of money that is the "bank," it needs to go through that accounting process. Learning the right lingo is important. In 2017 the money room got a new worker, Joe Mascia. In addition to lifting and managing all the social media for the feast, Joe filled in for me while I was doing research in Italy, and John was not shy about disciplining him. As he counted money, Joe would pass along stacks of bills and ask us,

"Can you dead this?" and John would scold, "Dead is not a verb!" making sure Joe knew "kill it" was the right way to say it.

John is a disciplinarian and is sarcastic and stern in a funny way. When people are late, when they do things wrong, when they take days off from the feast, John holds them accountable. When one day I took charge of running the bills through the machine, everyone passed me their stacks and I helped them confirm whether their counts were accurate. It was a rowdy day in the money room, as we had been eating ices, shooting rubber band guns, and generally being irreverent, to John's dismay. As I was running the stacks, John noticed Joe's counts were off; Joe defended himself by complaining that one money counter is not enough, that we needed one on the other side of the table. It was the Wednesday after Giglio Sunday and Joe had not come to help out in two days. John shot back, "We used to do this for years with no money counter. You haven't been here! You can't come back after two and a half days and request things. You text me on Giglio Sunday and say I'm going to go home and take a break and you come back today. I don't know what union you belong to that you're on break for two and a half days!" John has a tic: when he is stressed or overwhelmed he tightens his jaw, and gnashes his lower teeth, as if readjusting his mouth machinery, and on days like that one, when there was too much to count, John really worked his jaw.

There is a right way and wrong way to do things in the money room and to work there you have to learn how to be on time, to be accurate, how to talk the right way, and earmark and organize the money properly. For John, all of this is how he enacts his love for his parish, and he learned all of these accountability systems and practices from his mentor. Counting money is not simply mundane for John but is imbued with love and sentiment and it helps him stay connected to his church and his mentors from the past. One of those mentors is Richie Cats, a former Turk and capo, whom John credits with teaching him everything he knows:

> I credit everything I know about running the feast to Richie Cats—he is my mentor. [He] has really has been like my second dad when I am at my second home of Our Lady of Mount Carmel. From the time I was a soda boy, I was always fascinated by how he kept everything in order and

was constantly entertained by his never ending jokes and storytelling. I couldn't wait to get to the feast to hear what he would say or see what he would do. He ran that feast night after night, caught up with countless old friends, drank plenty of beers, and found a way to make everyone laugh. I would leave some nights wondering how we made it through the night and proved out on our counting. It was a whirlwind. Richie was always the go-to person and I was the sidekick, ready and willing to do anything he asked. . . . Every committee, every person with a position, every pastor, ultimately came to Richie for advice, to figure out how to get something done. He is what made the feast tick. And I absorbed every moment of it. I would meet Richie early every night to get things going, would drive home with him at night and would call him first thing in the morning to get ready for the next day. One of my greatest honors was at a general board meeting when . . . Richie stood up and named me as his replacement as Bazaar chairman. As much as I have learned, as much as I have "taken over," I don't feel I could ever run the feast the way he did—natural, hard-working and funny as hell.[36]

On the final day of the 2017 feast, I asked John again, like I did in 2014, to tell me how he got involved in doing work for the feast. He whined about how busy he was and that he needed to finish counting and get to work and complained that he could not talk and concentrate on counting. I persisted, and when I told him "this is my work," he conceded and began his story again. This time around his story was laced with more accounts of his affection for Monsignor Cassato, the pastor from 1985 to 2001, and the great influence the priest had on his life. Earlier that day I met Monsignor Cassato, who is like a living legend. He is the man, John said, who "revived a dying parish" when he became pastor in the 1980s. I was in the rectory with John getting ready to drop off ride tickets. I had a thick pack of yellow tickets in my arms, and John balanced three metal money boxes, and as we were ready to leave we saw Monsignor Cassato sitting on a chair in the main wing of the rectory, through a sliver of open door. Monsignor Cassato is tall, with thick cheeks, a shadow of dark mustache on his upper lip, salt-and-pepper slicked-back hair, and deep lines of forehead and smile wrinkles that hint to his expressiveness. Monsignor Cassato was on John's mind as he retold his story. "He was the biggest influence in my life. . . . I really

Figure 3.2. Monsignor Cassato five hundred dollar bill. Photo courtesy of OLMC Archives.

feel that I have my calling to the church because of him." When I asked him why, he continued, "Because of his leadership. He never said no to anybody. He made a point to get to know who everybody was. Almost every job I've had, I had because of him. . . . Look, he's created vocations." John always enjoyed Cassato's preaching; one day he told me, "My faith is so simple—at Mass a parable or story from the Gospel is what really resonates with me—Cassato preached using parables. He never said no to anyone, he brought Jesus wherever he went. I grew up in these four walls with him." After serving as an altar boy for years along with Phil, he became a Sunday sacristan: "I was with Cassato every Sunday and after Mass we went inside, had breakfast, laughed and bullshitted, then went out for the ten o'clock Mass. Then I don't know how old I was, maybe fourteen or fifteen, [they] asked me if I wanted to work in the money room, then I became part of that crew."

As John told me his story, he asked, "Are you gonna have color in your interview?" "What do you mean?" I asked. "Like: 'I asked this to John while he was running money through the money counter.'" "Yeah, is that good or bad?" I asked him. "Good, I like that," he said laughing, his eyes crinkling and teeth bared, as he reached over to run a stack of bills through the counter.

4

Public Masculinities at the Feast

From the streets, the Dance of the Giglio looks like all muscle, a display of physical masculinity. Spotlighting money work and manual labor as devotional labor demonstrates the many ways men wield artistic, organizational, and financial authority in their contributions to the church and to feast tradition. This backstage work is hidden from public view but is central to the production of the feast and to the production of men who can enact and transmit the skills crucial to this community's longevity, like creativity, resourcefulness, and financial prowess. In the streets during the feast, men are slotted into the roles of lifters, lieutenants, and capos, each playing a part in the broader choreography of the Dance of the Giglio. In public the masculine values of this community look different than in the spaces of planning and production.

During the ritual of the Questua, crews parade through different parts of the neighborhood handing out blessed bread, gathering donations, and spreading the word about the feast. Men face the reality that the neighborhood is full of newcomers as they traverse the streets to invite Williamsburg's old-timers and new residents alike to the feast. For some, this necessitates postures and performances of welcome, an openness to the changed neighborhood and its residents. For others, this is a time to enact an aggressive, even protective physical masculinity. Distributing blessed bread coexists with drinking, revelry, and displays of heterosexuality during the Questua.

During the Line of the March, capos, the men with the most prestige and seniority, are honored on a procession as they are picked up at homes throughout the neighborhood and chaperoned to Giglio Sunday Mass by a band, clergy, and admiring community members. The capos enter the church to rounds of applause and sit in the front pews with their families. During the Line of the March, capos act as upstanding men and bearers of future generations dedicated to the church and the feast. It is important to think about how gender and sexuality are on display during these events. While lifters present a bodily masculinity during the giglio lift and on the Questua, during the Line of the March the capos represent a family-oriented manhood based on the respect of the neighborhood and a long life of service and commitment. While these are very much part of the religious rituals of the feast, they are also gender performances. What is central to these performances of masculinity and manhood at the feast is the heterosexual male body. Heterosexuality, a command of the neighborhood, a commanding physical presence are all central to these public performances of masculinity, and those men who do not fit those standards are marginalized. In addition to exploring the masculinities performed in these two rituals, it is important to ask: where is there space for gay or even celibate, nonconforming men at the feast, and how do they fit into or challenge visions of masculinity produced in public ritual?

To answer these questions we also turn our attention away from the streets of the neighborhood and to the shrine of Our Lady of Mount Carmel, where the only publicly gay men at the feast work and spend their time during the days and nights of the festivities. The distinction between heterosexual and homosexual men maps onto the distinction between spaces coded masculine and feminine. While the giglio and its accompanying rituals are coded male within the community, involvement in the shrine is looked down upon by some of the men. Spatial strategies are central to visions and practices of manhood and masculinity.[1] By focusing on a trio of ritual spaces in feast geography—the Questua, the processional route of the Line of the March, and the parish's shrine—we can see which masculinities are affirmed, constructed, and reinforced in how men are organized, the ritual roles they perform, and how they navigate neighborhood space.

The dance draws crowds of thousands to North Eighth and Havemeyer streets to watch the spectacle of men's laboring bodies lifting the soaring tower, bearing its weight along with the full brass band that stands atop it. The feast is a lifetime commitment for the men of the community. Many begin their involvement in the feast as little boys and rise through the ranks—first as lifters, valued for their physical labor, then as lieutenants, valued for their dedication, knowledge, and service. After decades of participation lieutenants become capos, who are respected as fathers, mentors, community leaders, and integral figures in feast history.

On the morning of Giglio Sunday, men wear their status and role in the community on their bodies. Masculinity and successful displays of authority are contingent on props, stuff, clothing, and setting. With their clothes and accessories, they communicate exactly how much authority they wield and what role they are going to play in the Dance of the Giglio. Everyone is in uniform. The lifters all wear matching T-shirts that mirror the color scheme of the giglio. In 2014 the giglio was painted an ethereal marbled gray, and the T-shirts were also gray—printed on them in purple ink was a line drawing of the giglio and San Paolino soaring above a ship riding choppy waters. Lifters wore purple bandanas tied around their necks like kerchiefs, or around their foreheads to sop up the sweat that would eventually pour down them later. White sneakers and cargo shorts abounded. The matching shirts signified the performance to come, where singular male bodies would unite to form a strong mobile collective. On Giglio Sunday other older men wore slacks, neatly pressed and creased down the leg in shades of white and khaki, with sensible suede loafers and silky dress shirts. Some were daring and flamboyant in their color choices: white linen pants matched with bright blue and pink short-sleeve button-downs, white leather loafers, and dark wayfarer sunglasses. One man wore blood-red slacks, a hibiscus printed shirt, and shock-red loafers. Another man wore royal blue from head to toe. A blue fedora topped his head; even his socks and loafers were shades of light blue and navy. They all walked with canes, not because they needed them but as a symbol of status and authority: thin black canes topped with baby's breath and ribbons in the colors of the Italian flag; brown canes with orbed metal handles; canes that curved like unicorn horns carved of contrasting wood. These men in their more formal outfits with their canes were the capos—the men who orchestrated the giglio lifts and told the lifters how to move and had the power to start and stop the music of the brass band that stood atop the giglio. The last group, the lieutenants, exist between the lifters and the capos in the feast structure. There were nine of them, and some years they wore matching polos with their names embroidered on the chest, their individual identities contrasting the sameness of the lifters' uniforms. Other years they wore white baseball jerseys. As if it was the name of their team, the words "O' Giglio e Paradiso" were embroidered across the front. On the back, in big jersey

Figure 4.1. Giglio and boat meet as lifters lock hands during the Double Lift, with a pair of capos in between, 2015. During the Double Lift the giglio and boat meet in front of the church, and the crews lock hands and bounce the structures, cheering and jumping in vigorous elation. Photo by the author.

letters, were each man's last name and a number indicating the year he was appointed lieutenant.

The lifters work together under the poles of the giglio. They sweat, grit their teeth, bend their knees, and strain their backs. Their masculinity is defined by the capacity of their bodies in motion and their ability to endure the giglio's tonnage. Lieutenants command crews of forty lifters, relay commands from the capo, and ensure the men are moving in unison. A man becomes a lieutenant after ten to fifteen years serving as a lifter and through involvement in the church community. One lieutenant described the job as "the hardest job in the feast. . . . During the lift you have to concentrate on your men, and you know, you get beat up by the capos." Another said, "You got the capos instructing you what to do, God forbid the men do something [wrong]. You get yelled at if the men turn right instead of left." Lieutenants en-

Figure 4.2. Capo, 2015. Photo by the author.

sure each lift goes as the capo wishes and communicate to their team exactly how to move.

The highest honor in the community is the position of number one capo, which a man earns with decades of involvement with the feast as he rises through the ranks of the masculine feast hierarchy. The capo thrusts his cane into the air; with this gesture he commands the lifters to strengthen their legs and to get the giglio up. The power of the capo is epitomized by his swagger before the giglio. Through dancing, marching, yelling orders, and lambasting the lifters to stand up straight or "get it up," the capos exhibit their authority over the performance. The finale of the feast is Old Timer's Day (the last Sunday of the feast), where all the past capos come back, amid much fanfare, to command giglio lifts. These different roles at the feast highlight the importance of thinking about the bearing age and status have on religious masculinities.

Manhood and Masculinity

Gradations in age and life stage matter to ideals of manhood and masculinity. The processes of identifying as a man, acting as such, and achieving that in the eyes of others vary across institutional, spatial, and social settings. The evolving male roles and the different responsibilities and honors bestowed onto each at the feast alert us to the importance of life stage and the study of men's religious practice. There is not a monolithic masculinity. There is not only one kind of male Catholic body at the feast: there are raucous young men and older, respectable fathers, all whose bodies are on display during public events. At the feast we see not just how masculinities vary across social and institutional settings but how hierarchies of masculinity exist within religious communities.

Lifters at the feast perform a physical masculinity that centers on the spectacle of the male body and the synergy of men working together. As capos, older men gain status and respect based on lifelong commitment to the feast and parish and their performance of heterosexuality as fathers and grandfathers: men who can reproduce a new generation that will carry on the feast tradition. These older men represent an aspirational status. The position of capo is exclusive, both earned and formally bestowed. They demand authority and respect that is based not necessarily on their strength or the capacity of their bodies but on their commitment and status as role models. They are fathers, grandfathers, and husbands and are understood to be the driving forces and heroes of the homosocial culture of the feast. While capo is a status held by individual men, more broadly capo is an archetype, a persona, complete with expected performances, props, and choreography. The capos represent the pinnacle of feast manhood, manhood being the stage in the life cycle imbued with authority, respect, honor, and a moral valence. In any community's conception of manhood its most prized ideals, aspirations, and the height of imaginings of men's capabilities congeal. Manhood is often institutionally mandated and granted; not all men reach its apex or are deemed worthy by those able to grant it. Manhood is not only about bodily expression and behavioral practices but also about tradition, authority, values, and morals. Aging and other life stage developments like marriage and fatherhood might decenter the strength, sexual prowess, or aggressiveness typically associated with masculinity in young men.

Sheila Wise, in her research on Black manhood, argues that manhood "denotes a more permanent state of being, arriving at manhood is a process"; it is a "state of being in relation to family, community, and larger society."[2] This is especially useful for thinking about capos, who hold that status long after they serve as number one capo for a two-year term. They bring honor to their families and become prized members of a century-long male lineage, linking the tradition's past and present.

While manhood and masculinity are often used alongside one another as the attributes, roles, and performances of men, historian Gail Bederman cautions us to consider masculinity and manhood in their historical specificity. What is central to Bederman's definitional endeavor is the exclusionary aspect of manhood—manhood is not a male essence; it is not biological or a collection of traits but is rather a "historical ideological process."[3] Manhood has a moral dimension—it designates what is thought to be "noble in a man"; it indicates a worthiness, a self-mastery, a strong character, an earned power.[4] Therefore, not all men can achieve manhood, not all men possess manliness. Masculinity is a category that came into popular use at the turn of the twentieth century and was not exclusionary but rather a "relatively empty and fluid category" that could refer to distinguishing characteristics of men, either good or bad, while manhood was a privileged state and a "standard to live up to, an ideal of male perfectibility to be achieved."[5] Masculinity thus exists in the plural—almost as a post-hyphen: like working-class masculinity, Irish masculinity, or Protestant masculinity.

What is missing from these definitions is the notion of performance, audience, and role maintenance. Men scrutinize each other's behavior; they police the boundaries of manhood, perform for each other, and evaluate each other. The ascent to manhood requires the approval of other men and is enacted in homosocial spaces.[6] While masculinity is often thought of as being constructed in relations of power and domination between men and women, homosocial cultures in particular demonstrate the way masculinity is achieved and performed for other men. Men are often the gatekeepers and assessors of each other's behavior, postures, and reputations. "'What men need is men's approval'" is how scholar of men and masculinities Michael Kimmel framed this.[7] Manhood must be "maintained in the eyes of other men": in the eyes of those with the authority to grant its privileges, guard its pathways, and judge the worthiness of other men.[8] But manhood is not simply about individual relationships and achievements; it is reserved for some and institutionally guarded and promised. Historian Kathleen Brown, in her writing on manhood and slavery, has argued that manhood accrued to white men through their rights to bear arms, literacy, property, and family. These were all institutional arenas, privileges granted by church and state and denied to Black men. Gender is individually and socially performed, but it is important to see how it is also institutionally controlled and mandated—there are barriers to entry and belonging in a broader religious or body politic.[9] Manhood is thus achieved *and* bestowed.

The feast locates men in a historical continuum, as bearers of tradition burdened with the responsibility of passing it on, which is key to understanding the manhood of the capos. Manhood is achieved under the gaze of other men and approved by the church. While lifters express an aggressive, physical masculinity in their homosocial rituals, capo masculinity is about embodying and performing the "state of grace" of manhood; they present themselves as upstanding members of the community and family men loved and fawned over by all.[10]

The Questua

While the central ritual is the Dance of the Giglio, which takes place in the blocks around the church, other rituals take the men of the feast onto the streets of the neighborhood for fundraising and processions. The first of these rituals is the Questua, which means begging in Italian; it is a Saturday morning ritual where crews of lifters walk the streets of South and North Williamsburg and the adjacent Polish neighborhood of Greenpoint to offer blessed bread and let others know the feast has begun.[11] The crews are accompanied by a van full of the blessed loaves of bread, a member of the clergy, police escorts, and a large group of lifters. A brass band announces their presence throughout the neighborhood on the sleepy Saturday morning as they take over the streets and sidewalks to offer the bread for donations of one dollar. The Questua encompasses charity, camaraderie, fundraising, and partying. These are not mutually exclusive, and men understand themselves as serving the church through their participation. Giving blessed bread, smoking cigars, and drinking scotch are part and parcel of religious practice during the Questua. When I told one man in particular the way people have reacted with surprise to my descriptions of the Questua (with its cigar smoking and drinking) with the question "What is Catholic about this?" he responded, deadpan to denote the obvious, "This is literally begging for money for the church."

Each Questua crew has its own style and identity. The Southside crew is more reserved and family-oriented. Both men and women compose that crew. They visit the homes of the remaining Italian Americans in the neighborhood and quickly distribute their loaves to families and neighborhood businesses. On the other hand, the Greenpoint crew, which is all-male, is known for its raucousness, treating the Questua like a roving party. Rather than moving from home to home, the Greenpoint crew leaves its turf, Williamsburg, to venture into the territory of another neighborhood, aiming to raise money from its pious Polish residents. The Greenpoint crew enacts an aggressive neighborhood masculinity during their fundraising efforts, and at times they are antagonistic toward those they consider "hipsters" and newcomers. On their march to Greenpoint they retake the streets of Williamsburg for their party-in-motion, making their presence in the neighborhood known.

The pastor and a deacon walked with the Southside crew, giving it a reputation for being more family-oriented, more inclusive of women, and more tame than the other Questua crews, known for having coolers stocked full of booze and a case of vodka in tow along with their van of bread. The Southside (which colloquially designates the part of the neighborhood on the other side of the Brooklyn-Queens Expressway, which bisects the neighborhood, rather than the streets officially marked "south"), where many parishioners lived and where many local businesses were enthusiastic about donating to the church, was also the most successful of all of the crews. There was a familiarity along the route, where old women waited in their windows and on their stoops expecting bread deliveries, holding rolled-up dollars in their soft, wrinkled hands. The Southside performed the respectability expected when in the sight of a priest. Before they embarked on their morning trip through the neighborhood they huddled behind the church. One of the leaders reminded them, "Let's have fun, everybody smile, that's the most important thing." The Southside crew is to be respectable, friendly, and welcoming, a roving invitation to the feast. For some, it is a chance to usher their children into the traditions of the feast. In 2016 Sal and his wife Jolene walked the Questua with their son in a baby carriage. Earlier that morning we all waited for the Questua to begin in a yard across the street from the church, where it is customary for everyone to gather for a pre-Questua meal and music. The yard belonged to Lucy Smith, who had passed away that year. She was the wife of Jimmy Smith, the first Irish capo, and hosted the breakfast before the Questua every year. This was the first summer she was not sitting under a tricolor umbrella, with her coiffed black hair, surrounded by friends and food. Jolene missed Lucy and said it did not feel the same without her as she fed her son fruit and donuts. As we ate breakfast Sal told me that when he was a baby he learned the word "giglio" before he even learned his dad's name. Sal pointed to the giglio on the corner, asking his son, "What's outside?" Trying to get him to say "giglio," he said it in a baby voice, hoping his son would copy him. Jolene joined in, also repeating "giglio," but the baby was much more interested in donuts than learning this multisyllabic but most important word. As soon as he heard the band play the giglio song he perked up, bouncing excitedly. Even if he could not yet give out bread, he rolled along the route with his parents, an early introduction to what he might very well spend his life doing.

Dan and Matty were both part of the Southside crew and traversed the streets where many Italian American residents still lived. Matty has a smile that perks up the apples of his cheeks and slick hair; there is always evidence of a comb having carefully been run through it. Unlike other men, he married into the feast. He grew up not in Williamsburg but in Upstate New York and married the daughter of a prominent capo, giglio artisan, and parish leader. What many men learned as little boys, Matty learned as an adult, lifting, working in the basement, and traveling to Nola's Festa dei Gigli. In 2019 he became cochairman of the Children's Giglio Committee. Matty is a professional designer and loves photography, and he has put those skills to use in the church by illustrating the 2019 T-shirts and helping with a new giglio design. His love for the feast was newer but prominently on display during the Questua. During the Questua Matty acted as an emissary of the feast and took it in stride when people on the streets ignored his invitations and dodged him.

Dan, a lieutenant and past Turk whom we met in chapter 1, also walked the Questua. He also had a young daughter whom he was teaching to love the feast. He played Pokémon on his phone throughout the route as he doled out bread to Williamsburg's residents. Dan sometimes got frustrated with Williamsburg's new residents, wanting them to be more open to the feast and their message. He reasoned, "I wish everyone was . . . receptive. Just talk to us at least, you don't have to throw money. We look at hipsters and their weird ways, and here we are walking around on a Saturday with bread. We are all weird, just ask why we are walking around in the middle of a Saturday." On the Questua the goal is to get the word out about the feast, but it is also a time to have fun and reconnect with friends. Antics are typical of all the routes. On the Southside big men put quarters into coin-operated horses outside of bodegas, mounting the tiny metal animals and looking laughably large as they rode along to the carnival music. Joe Speruta danced salsa in his Hawaiian shirt as he ducked into the shade of store awnings. Sometimes the crew members got dollars or even fives for the bread, but other times they just pressed it into a passersby's hand, receiving nothing, especially when someone did not speak English or when they said they did not have any cash on them.

The contrast between a roving group of parishioners in matching T-shirts and people brunching at sidewalk cafés and on the decks of new condominiums was striking. At one tall stucco building that towered over the older houses next to it, young women sat on a huge deck overlooking the sidewalk as they drank mimosas out of champagne glasses. Their friends hung over the edge of the balcony capturing pictures and videos of the bread-toting group. Some of the men tossed bread up to the balcony, while others across the street offered bread to men outside of a tattoo shop and passing women in workout gear. While they were welcoming, they also ridiculed those who occupied Williamsburg's cafés and restaurants. The loader, the man who sat in the open door of the van distributing bread, wearing classic dad sunglasses and a big gold chain around his neck, yelled, "Vegan, gluten-free, lactose-free bread!" "Gluten-free, organic, farm-raised, free-range, soy latte!" a duplicitous and satirical advertising call. When one man from the Greenpoint crew told a young woman "C'mon buy some bread, it's gluten free," she angrily responded, "Is it really gluten free?? You can't tell people that!" yelling back at him and taking it personally. That joke obviously became a mainstay on the Questua as men poked fun at newcomers with their capricious dietary restrictions.

Down Metropolitan Avenue, a busy street and bus route, we passed packed brunch places as people looked on smirking and taking pictures with their cell phones. Two young women were so excited about the bread that they asked to take pictures with one of the men and his daughter; they all proudly held out their loaves with big smiles. Later I saw that the woman had posted a picture of the bread on Instagram with a caption about it being a sign of generosity toward the poor and how proud she was of her Italian neighborhood along with heart and flag emojis. In 2019 a podcast host with a large Twitter following posted a "Parade Church Bread Review," comedically rating it 7.2 out of 10 for its warmness and its potential for being spinach dip bread.

On Graham Avenue Matty approached passersby with a big smile on his face. Some people stopped; women in workout gear took off their headphones, but others swerved to avoid him, shook their heads in surprise, and frowned as he approached. He gave away bread to punks in spiked motorcycle jackets with pentagram patches and neck and hand tattoos and to young white men with beards and tight jeans. After seeing two men avoid him and swerve away as if he was a con artist on the street, he told me, "You gotta love everybody, I just give them a smile and tell them to come to North Eighth and Havemeyer." Dan agreed, "You got to be nice, people don't want to be attacked. That's how you get them to show up. A dollar is not what you're doing, this isn't a fundraiser" (although others very much treated it as a fundraiser). Matty talked to a young white woman in leggings, sunglasses, a headband, and a tank top and told her that the feast was going on. "Oh, the Italian feast?" she asked. "Yeah we are going to lift the giglio, you know, the big tower? We would love to see you there, come by." This is the same line he repeated in a hair salon to girls with bleached bangs, who refused the bread. While Matty and Dan are part of the Southside crew, which is presided over by the church pastor, the other crews do not have the same oversight, which necessitates respectability.

While the Questua, according to the community, is a welcome ritual as old as the feast itself, the Greenpoint leg of the Questua, as I observed it in the summer of 2014, was not simply a wholesome ritual of generosity and publicity. Instead, the Greenpoint crew, as they interacted with the young residents of Williamsburg and Greenpoint, often seemed more antagonistic than welcoming. That year the pastor consistently voiced collective anxieties regarding the rapidly changing neighborhood around the church. With property values rising, the built environment changing, and an influx of new tenants and homeowners with the social capital to challenge the existence of the feast and log complaints with the city, the community worried about placating Williamsburg's new residents while also feeling bitter about being perceived as the "leftovers" of the neighborhood's past.

In June 2014 Monsignor Calise addressed the men at a feast meeting, citing concerns about a forty-thousand-dollar deficit in fundraising, the lack of feast posters around the neighborhood, and new challenges the feast and parish would face with the new condominium developments in the blocks around the church. Calise was concerned about the construction sites around the church and new buildings with garages that would bring traffic to the streets and make it difficult for the feast to occupy the road. With the new buildings and construction on the Brooklyn-Queens Expressway (BQE), Calise told the men that it was more important than ever to have the support of the people who live around the neighborhood. He noted that the feast would present a greater "intrusion" as more and more people live in Williamsburg who are not part of the tradition. He explained, "They need to feel welcome and understand what the feast means. . . . We need a longer procession, to make sure we are on both sides of the [BQE], doing our best to make ourselves known. If we are not giving out good information, others are getting bad information." Many of the men were instructed to "be nice" to stay in the good graces of Williamsburg's seemingly powerful new residents. Especially during the Questua, Calise underscored the need to give out brochures that explained the tradition.

During the Questua itself, when the Greenpoint crew members got a little too pushy or too rowdy, they were reminded by apprentice capos, "Be gentle, be nice." They politely sold bread to old Polish women and families, but at other times, disregarding these instructions, and perhaps in spite of them, they interacted antagonistically with newcomers. The crew swaggered down the center of the road as we made our way through the neighborhood. They held red Solo-brand cups full of scotch and all wore cargo shorts and their Questua T-shirts, which announced that the event was "in honor of our deceased members." I walked along with the men with my own watered-down cup of scotch, keeping to the sidewalk and sidelines until I too briefly began to sell bread once we arrived in Greenpoint. Most men clutched a handful of the clear plastic bags that held the round loaves of bread, ready to sell; inside the bag were also yellow cards on thick stock that explained the ritual with the title "Why are we giving out bread today?" The blessed bread is "offered as a sign that you are invited and welcomed to join our great Feast. It is a way of offering a gift and invitation to all."

The group made their way down Jackson Street, with a mix of old multifamily buildings and new condominium developments, and the blaring brass band announced their presence and cut through the sleepy Saturday morning with booming trumpets and drum rolls. Some condominium residents emerged onto their balconies, confusedly watching the crew go down the block. Other residents, with Italian flags displayed on their stair banisters and in their windows, heard the crew coming and waited on their stoops and in their doorways to receive their bread. As the curious condominium residents looked out, the men yelled up, "Bread, special delivery!" and "Eyy, buy some bread!" cajoling people to throw down cash, to go back inside and get some money when they, by patting their bodies, indicated they did not have any cash on them. The people that they yelled up at usually complied, running inside to grab a dollar and throwing it off the balcony. As the bills fluttered down, the men made a scene by throwing the bread up with uneven success. The bags flew through the air, often right to the open hands of the person waiting, but other times the tosses failed and the bagged bread came tumbling back down.

The men repeated the refrain "c'mon it's for charity!" when people did not want to give. We passed by new developments like a four-story long gray building—its surface was not planar but broken by recessed spaces to fit more balconies on its facade. Unlike the small one-lot houses, this new building consumed multiple lots and extended down half the block. One of the older men looked up at the building and told the crew, "When I was a kid this was all factories!" They repeated this sentiment when we stopped at 68 Jackson Street; one of the men mentioned to the group that he used to live there. He pointed at the windows of the three-story building. With each window he identified who used to live in what apartment—"my aunt, my aunt, my uncle" he said, moving his finger across the air, reconstructing a time when his entire family lived in close proximity. As the men made their way through the neighborhood in this homosocial ritual of raucousness, drinking, and fun, they called attention to what had changed and took the opportunity to make themselves heard on the streets, whether through harassing people to throw money from their balconies or with their takeover of the roadway with their brass band.

As some of the younger men stood outside the Catholic War Veterans storefront on Lorimer Street, which acts as a social hub for many of the older men in the neighborhood, a disheveled (read "hipster") young white woman passed by while walking her dog, and she averted her eyes to ignore the men. Some of them began to harangue her, "C'mon, it's for the church!" "Look, the dog likes bread!" Looking uncomfortable, she moved to the edge of the sidewalk and tried to avoid the men. "You don't have a dollar? That's all it takes. I feel sorry for you, I'ma say a prayer for you," one man retorted as she avoided them. Although they peacefully sold to older Latina and Black women who stopped for the bread, when a group sweaty of young white men (read "newcomers") passed by, one of the men scoffed, "Oh you, yeah, how are you, yeah fuck you." Often the men took the opportunity to do charitable acts like giving bread to those who looked homeless or down on their luck, or giving someone extra and instructing them to give the loaf to someone in need. At other times they attempted to attract the attention of women with lines like "Can I interrupt you for a second?" and "Hello sweetheart, how are you? You could smile if you want." On Jackson Street the men noticed a young woman standing on her balcony in a black tube top watering her plants. Fifteen of them gathered, including two police officers, to look up and yell at her, pressing her to buy bread. All of the men grinned and laughed, some waved for her attention, but they never did get a donation from her.

After winding through the residential streets of Williamsburg, we reached the bustling commercial center of Greenpoint: Manhattan Avenue, a wide avenue lined with small businesses, markets, pharmacies, salons, liquor stores, and restaurants, many bearing Polish names. Unlike at the Williamsburg processions, there were no Italian flags in sight.

Many of the men were still drinking, toting Solo cups in one hand and fistfuls of bread bags in the other; the men in the van provided extra bread and extra booze as well as stogies (cigars). Escorted by a police car, the men, the band, and the van took over one lane of traffic on that busy Saturday morning as people walked along the streets, probably running weekend errands and taking walks.

The boisterous homosociality of the Questua put pressure on those men who did not conform to the vision of a heterosexual public masculinity. The crew was accompanied by a young Polish priest (he may have been a seminarian at the time). As the day went on and as it got hotter, his presence became more central to the experience of the Questua. He walked with his long black cassock; it grazed the ground and the sleeves tightly hugged his wrists. The men bothered him about his robes: "Man you must be hot!" "Take that off!" "Yo, we gotta get the priest some shorts." They continued to pester him about it, and multiple men offered to go buy him a change of clothes, even as he refused to take off his garments. Sweat dripped down his pale brow and his eyes squinted in the bright sunlight. He continued to refuse their offers, but he did partake in drinking and smoking with them. The young priest walked down the center of Manhattan Avenue, red cup in hand, in his long swishing robes with a thick cigar between his fingers. When the men entered a neighborhood salon where a capo's wife was getting her hair done, one of the men yelled out to the women in the salon chairs, "Any of you ladies wanna do a priest??" The salon filled with a burst of laughter over the sounds of hairdryers and clippers. The young priest did not comply with physical, aesthetic, or sexual attributes of their masculinity, and they were quick to point out his difference without pause for his official religious authority, even as he tried to fit in with their revelry.

Many men, frustrated with the lack of interest, responses, and donations from the newcomers in the neighborhood, blocked people's paths as they walked down the street, taunting, "If you wanna go through you have to buy bread." Another man asked some of the young white people walking down the street, "You know the festivities going on in the neighborhood?" and turned away when he did not get a response, "They don't care." As many young people in the neighborhood saw the spectacle and whipped out their phones to take pictures, one of the men said, "You want a picture, it's a dollar." One lifter repeated this sentiment, frustrated after hours of walking around with the refrain "One dollar donation, c'mon, one dollar, one dollar." He complained, "They want to take a picture but not donate." One of the men told a young woman who did not have any cash for a donation, "We swipe now," and she believed him, digging around her purse for a card. In 2019 they actually updated and did get credit card readers, but few people on the streets were willing to swipe their cards.

At first I felt apprehensive when some crew members asked me if I was going to sell bread. Eventually I accompanied one young lifter into hair and nail salons and told the women inside that we were raising money for Our Lady of Mount Carmel Church. Many of the business owners opened the cash register, handing us a few dollars, but refused the bread—the lifter, a young guy from Greenpoint, joked that they could make sandwiches with the bread and left the women with a few loaves. A little defeated, as we walked he told me, "Honestly here we are out here but the neighborhood has changed so much, people don't want to buy it." When everyone was exhausted after hours of selling bread, one of the accompanying apprentice capos told the men, "C'mon we have five hundred loaves, we wanna go home. Be gentle, be nice," insisting that they sell all the bread before the "march back to our territory." These Questua men saw themselves as representatives of Williamsburg: "their territory," even though the neighborhood had since changed hands.

The men treated the Questua like a party, a time to be among friends, carry on, and make themselves known. As they went through the territory of others, such as the streets of Manhattan Avenue, they lamented how much the gentrifiers of Brooklyn did not care about the bread, the church, or their mission. While some were visibly frustrated, others took the opportunity to catcall women, mess with people, block their paths, joke about their dietary choices, and complain about newcomers, all while representing themselves as feast men with a large crew of friends, lots of liquor, and lots of spirit—good natured or otherwise. As we see in the many interactions between the men, the people on their condominium balconies, and the newcomers who refused to donate but would like to post to Instagram what seemed like a spectacle, the Greenpoint Questua crew enacted an aggressive neighborhood masculinity.

Rather than fulfilling Calise's instructions to be nice and welcoming, the men took to the streets to claim them as their own. The men had seen the neighborhood change rapidly; they had known times when they would quickly sell out of bread, but now with the new faces and new developments, it was harder to get people to care about the feast. While they were supposed to extend a welcome, they also scornfully critiqued and challenged the changing neighborhood, making themselves visible and audible on the streets. As the feast they knew and love changed, they took to the streets with their cups, their cigars, and their matching T-shirts to proclaim that the feast was here and that they were the lifters of the giglio, although this status did not ensure them respect and generosity from those on the streets.

The Line of the March

The song "O' Giglio 'e Paradiso" is played throughout the giglio lifts and on every procession through the neighborhood, and it is the audible symbol of the feast.[12] The song not only is a theme song for everyone who loves the feast, but also glorifies feast men and provides a compact description of masculinity and manhood within the community. It is so iconic that men have it played at their weddings and funerals. The song, as translated from Italian by Joseph Peluso, honors the lifters and the capos and expresses the value that the community places on each of these male roles, and the traits that the men should embody.

> Each year the work gets harder
> but the committees are up to the task,
> Their faith keeps growing forever,
> for church and saint they never ask.
> They give the feast their hearts,
> these faithful and honest men,
> for Paolino, the Bishop of Nola,
> they do it the best that they can.

> 'Neath the giglio stand all of our lifters,
> young and old, they're from near and from far;
> every year with one thought they're all anxious,
> to lift the giglio and show how strong they are.
> Oh, the leader commanding the giglio

is a worthy man who's loved so dear,
and together all these men of steel
guarantee the success of the year.

When they lift up the giglio,
they make such a beautiful dance,
their leader is [the capo]
the one giving all the commands.
With the assistant capos,
and apprentices learning their trade,
shining like roses aglow
presenting this festive parade.[13]

The lifters, the "men of steel," are eager to prove their strength, while the capo is a "worthy man who's loved so dear." Not only is the capo a commander; he is also a skilled teacher, helping the apprentices learn the trade; they are church men who devote their lives to the parish and the saints. The men who strive to become capos wait for decades, planning their ascent through the hierarchy and the years of faithful service they will give to the feast before being bestowed the honor. A previous capo, Vinnie Occhiuto, told the *Queens Courier*, "Most men, when they start lifting, dream of being a capo. What else in life do you plan thirty-five years for?"[14] It is important to note that becoming a capo is a lifelong endeavor, but men do not romanticize the journey. One man who did not hold a rank, knowing I was writing about the feast, told me, "Are you gonna talk about the tradition and all the bureaucracy and evils in all of this? . . . I think there's evil here, people will cut each other's throats to get a spot." It was true that people speculated about old or sick capos dying, which would allow them to move up the ranks. When many of the men took a trip to Nola in 2017, many of those who held ranks were on the same flight, and some joked that if that plane went down they could shave a few years off their ascent to the position of number one.[15] Despite personal competition and animosities, capos are not just singular men; capo is an aspirational position and status—the love, honor, faithfulness, and honesty of the capo are best performed and presented during the Line of the March, the ritual pickup of the most important men of the feast.

The Line of the March takes the community on a procession throughout the neighborhood as they stop at the homes from which the capos will make their Giglio Sunday debut. The homes on this processional route are decorated with pennant flags, streamers, banners of congratulations, and other feast paraphernalia. The route glorifies Italian American households. They become nodal points on a reimagined map of Williamsburg, momentarily making and representing a whole, legible community out of fragments of blocks, houses, and families.[16] While the processional map represents the whole community, it is the love and respect for the capos that brings people to the streets on this Sunday morning. The capos become the representatives of these Italian American homes. Unlike the Greenpoint Questua, the Line of the March highlights the capos within their domestic spaces and lives.[17]

Although there are many stops on the Line of the March, a few examples will provide us with snapshots of capo manhood as it is publicly enacted in this ritual. On a quiet Sunday morning in 2014, the long processional crowd arrived on Skillman Avenue; the booming trumpets of the band announced the crowd's presence. We all gathered around the four-story home of an apprentice capo. It had a large set of stairs leading to the front door. The vista up the stairs created a dramatic space for an exit. The house was decorated with signs hanging from the fire escape that read "Congratulations Daddy." Signs that read "Congratulations Apprentice Capo O' Giglio e Paradiso" were decorated by a picture of the giglio and an image of San Paolino nestled between the Italian and American flags. Long strips of pennant flags were draped down the facade of the building, so that it stood out amid all others on the block. Italian-flag-colored stars were hung in every window, and streamers were draped down the banisters, enhancing the festive decor of the house. His wife and two oldest daughters had spent days preparing the breakfast that his friends and family shared before he made his grand exit. The family also spent much time shopping for coordinating outfits, so that all the women could match his pink and white outfit. Unlike the Greenpoint Questua, which was a homosocial event, the Line of the March included many women who celebrate the capos; they stood at the base of the stairs clapping and scurrying to take photos.

A regal song played as the door opened and his youngest daughter walked out in a pretty white dress as the crowd "whooped" for her. The band then changed the song and played a cool, sexy theme song, which turned out to be the saxophone instrumental of Jason Derulo's pop hit "Talk Dirty to Me." The capo finally came out, looking smooth at the top of his stairs. He wore a light pink shirt, crisp white slacks, and white loafers. The crowd, especially hearing this song, cheered for him. He held up his hand and fist-pumped along to the music, waving his white handkerchief. In the other hand he held his brown wooden capo's cane, decorated with curly ribbons. Monsignor Calise met him at the foot of the steps as he bowed his head to be blessed with holy water before they embraced in a tight hug as his family proudly clapped and took photos. Monsignor always took so much joy in shaking the aspergillum, a metal rod inserted in a small bucket of holy water that would sprinkle water when shaken. This exit was one of the most memorable because of his sultry song choice and the support of his three daughters, who expressed their pride with their "Congratulations Daddy" sign.

While the men on the Questua presented themselves as having fun and roaming the streets, in this ritual the capos presented themselves as fathers, especially blessed by the priest. Capo manhood is affirmed through public expression of their Catholic identity. The Line of the March is not a ritual of homosociality. It is a time when women are present as spectators, admirers, and loved ones. The apprentice capo's wife waited at the foot of the stairs with his oldest daughters and received him with hugs and kisses. The admiring gaze and audible praise of the community affirm the manhood of the capos and the great honor they bestow on their family and home.

The 2014 Line of the March was unusual as the community faced the impending loss of the beloved capo Phillie Manna, who was terminally ill. Phillie was Joey Aragona's uncle and was capo from 2007 to 2008; many people at the feast reminisced to me about Phillie, as he brought a new life to the feast by introducing the band to Italian folk songs. He was the only man left who still had tangible ties to Italy, with dual citizenship, and he invited men to stay at his house in Nola to visit the original Dance of the Giglio in Italy. The year he was capo, many Nolanis and even the mayor of Nola traveled to Brooklyn to honor him. According to one woman, the year Phillie was capo, "it was different, there was a sense of togetherness" and strength.

The Line of the March stopped at Phillie's house on Devoe Street—a simple white house with a long set of stairs and diagonal vinyl paneling. There were no congratulation signs, no pennant flags, no streamers, just an American flag and an Italian flag hanging over the staircase. Unlike the other houses, where I had a view of the men of honor because the crowd was scattered through the streets, people were densely packed against the front of the house. Many women, men in lifter shirts and purple bandanas, and people both old and young pressed close to the front of the house to see Phillie. I never did catch a glimpse of him but stood within the crowd watching many people blink away tears, their eyes glassy as the band played a medley of songs. Women stood on the two adjacent staircases to catch a glimpse of Phillie, fighting tears through thick mascara.

The men in the crowd were also solemn—they craned their necks to see him or bowed their heads and uneasily shifted their weight. The atmosphere was heavy with sorrow that I could not share because I did not know Phillie. As the band played upbeat songs, some of the men jumped and fist-pumped; others had their cameras and phones raised high above their heads to capture a photo. People waved and clapped and someone tossed a handful of confetti, making the moment feel festive. With each passing song some from the front pushed their way back through the crowd, their heads lowered, seemingly unable to handle the sight anymore. Phillie's wife, who was obscured from my sight by the gathering, relayed a message from Phillie. "Phillie loves everybody. He lived for the feast. He wants to say that the kids are the future, let's take care so that the feast goes on for another hundred years." The scene in front of Phillie's house was heavy with sadness and solemnity as well as celebration. Phillie's was a life lived in love for the feast, and the Line of the March expressed how beloved and respected he was as a capo.

There were limits on how to mourn a capo, and the way Phillie's wife chose to honor him at the feast crossed gendered boundaries. That year the giglio had been outfitted with large tarps that memorialized Phillie, and they dedicated a lift to him. Capos command the giglio by yelling commands to the lifters in a Nolani dialect. As Philip Franco explains in his work on the feast, the commands are "Uaglio!," "Alzate le spalle," "Guingi, Guingi," and "Ai giette!" and roughly translate to the capo instructing, "Boys, listen/pay attention!," "Up on the shoulders," "Steady, steady," and "Drop it!"[18] Each of these commands has a bodily movement that goes along with it. Shoulders are raised higher in preparation for dropping the giglio to the ground, and knees are bent, allowing the giglio to forcefully return to the ground, releasing their burden. That day Phillie's wife approached the mic. Resolutely she said "for my capo" and spoke the commands clearly and forcefully into the mic, unwavering. In her husband's absence she took on the voice of the capo. After the lift, she and her daughters walked away from the feast, dressed in all black with their heads bowed in tearful sadness. Later the women in the shrine talked about Phillie's wife and daughters: "They were hugging and crying together, that was very brave that they came to honor him like that, that's love. . . . I got the chills, I don't think I could ever do something like that." The women agreed that it was a powerful gesture, and I wondered if they meant it was brave just to come to the feast after the death or brave as a woman to take on that role and say the words of the capo.

Although so many were torn up about Phillie's death, some thought the tribute was over the line and challenged the masculine authority of the lift. Some men said things like, "That was dangerous, we are going to have a lot of problems now, with people asking, why wouldn't you let the women lift. They are just looking for it as a glorified thing. They are just looking for a photo op, they are not going to stay under like the guys." Others agreed that her actions "opened a can of worms." Those who critiqued her way of memorializing her husband marked men as physically and temporally committed to the feast in a way they thought women could not be. Dedication to the feast in the form of time, effort, and embodied commitment is coded masculine, obscuring the ways women enable and support men's participation. The talk of "photo op" and looking for a "glorified thing" is not just about different physical capabilities but also about dedication. This is one explicit instance of how exclusion sustains homosocial culture and tradition. In subsequent years that I know of, none of the conflict that they prophesied ever arose.

The capos are responsible for ushering in a new generation of feast men. Fatherhood is constitutive of capo manhood. The capos are fathers and role models, and Phillie's message expressed the importance of inspiring young men and boys to become more involved in the feast to ensure its continuity. Mark, a lieutenant, imagined passing down the tradition to his son. Mark's "proudest moment as a father" was during his son's first children's lift. As he told me the story, his eyes crinkled at the corners. He explained how his son diligently took on the role of lifter: "All the kids are scattered and the band starts playing and he runs over to the pole." Mark acted out his son putting his arm around the pole, preparing to lift without even having to be prompted, demonstrating how he already knew the start of the music meant he needed to get ready for the lift. "Proudest moment as a father," he repeated, his smile wide. He continued, "I told my wife and she said 'proudest moment . . . ? Not when he was born?'" He explained to her that him being born was not him doing something; that was her. "This is him doing something for himself," he clarified. "Proudest moment as a father. I took him home [from the hospital] in a giglio shirt. I kid you not. I found out she was pregnant and I had [the guy] who was making the shirts that year make me up a onesie." He scrolled his phone and pulled up a picture of a little custom giglio onesie.

The feast hierarchy works almost dynastically. Sons inherit their father's or their mentor's love for the feast, and this fuels their drive to become a leader in the community. In Sal's words, "The men that are just lifters didn't have people in their family at a rank. That makes them want to reach that position, that goal. Now we have a bunch of teenagers that want to aspire to be something great." Sal differentiates between the men who are "just lifters" and those who have a lifelong commitment to rise through the ranks, emphasizing how boys are inspired by the men in their families.

The community is especially proud of father-and-son capos as symbols of feast succession. In 2014 the Line of the March processed under the underpass of the BQE to arrive at the Catholic War Veterans storefront. Paste (pronounced "Basti") Vecchione, who was the youngest capo in 1989, and his son, apprentice capo and band leader Danny Vecchione, were exiting from the club. Rather than the typical signs of congratulations, a different display decorated the storefront. There was a large collaged poster that depicted a long ribbon that read "25 years 1989–2014." In the center there was a large oval photograph of the 2013 giglio rising against a bright blue sky. Flanking this image were mirror-image photos of Paste and Danny, Paste when he was capo, Danny as a boy holding a cane and emulating his father, and pictures of him as an adult commanding the giglio alongside images of his father commanding the giglio. This image celebrated a father and son integrated in the tradition. It was not a sign of congratulations but one of commemoration, of generational continuity and male succession that visually depicted how Danny's trajectory mirrored his father's. Following in the respected steps of his father, Danny had achieved manhood in the community. Danny exited the storefront with his two sons amid much applause. Like their father, who had been wearing robin-egg-blue slacks, white shoes, and a pale blue plaid shirt, the boys were also dressed in blue. Danny carried his younger son at his waist, and the older one walked beside him holding his wooden cane that was decorated with a red bow and a superhero toy. Three generations of men were celebrated in this Line of the March stop, and one can only guess that like their father and grandfather, the little boys too will strive to become capos.

Homosociality and Heterosexuality

Although the performance of masculinity by the men on the Questua and the capos' performance of a family-centric glorified manhood are different, heterosexuality is central to both performances. Because women are largely prohibited from participating in certain feast rituals, such as the giglio lift, and feast planning meetings, the feast comes to fruition in largely homosocial spaces. Homosociality has traditionally been defined in the sociological literature as "nonsexual interpersonal interactions," social segregation, and preference for social interaction with members of one's own sex.[19] These definitions extend from Jean Lipman-Blumen's 1976 definition of homosociality as "seeking, enjoyment, and/or preference for the company of the same sex. It is distinguished from 'homosexual' in that it does not necessarily involve an explicitly erotic sexual interaction between members of the same sex."[20] While this definition is predicated on exclusion based on sex and not sexuality, other scholars have probed why the excision of homosexuality or the strict boundary maintenance between the homosexual and the heterosexual is the foundation upon which homosocial spaces thrive.[21]

Men maintain homosocial spaces through practices that build solidarity and inclusion as well as practices of exclusion. John Bartkowski, in his research on the Promise Keeper accountability groups, support groups where men gather to talk through their personal struggles and faith, argues that "dividing practices" manage homosocial interaction and intimacy.[22] Promise Keeper homosociality is deliberately desexualized, and "man-to-man relationships are tempered by mechanisms of social control."[23] It is particularly important to interrogate the boundary work around issues of sexuality at the feast in the case of a gay former capo who, despite a life of service to the feast and parish, was excised from the feast hierarchy after he married his male partner. Feast manhood and masculinity are contingent on the excision of any nonconforming performances. Capo manhood is decidedly morally Catholic and strictly heterosexual.

I first met Anthony when I began working in the shrine of Our Lady of Mount Carmel during the feast. He always worked diligently, darting in and out of the church to set up the goods and relighting and arranging candles, but he was always quiet and kept to himself. Like all the other men, Anthony had forged lifetime connections to the feast. He would accompany his father, who was a lifter, ever since he was about six years old. In the late 1990s he had the honor of being Turk and fondly remembered how he picked out the papal insignia to decorate the sails of the boat and the thrill of riding the boat through the streets. In the summer Anthony and his husband travel to Nola where they stay for the duration of the Festa dei Gigli and walk through the rough cobbled streets of the small town, admiring all the different giglio designs.

As I learned toward the end of the feast 2014, he had run the shrine for decades, but following what some called a "controversy," he had to step down from that role. He had gotten legally married to his long-time partner and invited everyone to the wedding, although many feast people chose not to attend. Because he did not keep his union secret and chose to make it public by inviting the people of the parish and because of the new legal and "official" status of his union, he violated the "don't ask, don't tell" standard of Monsignor Calise. Calise decided that it was no longer appropriate for Anthony to be in charge because there was no way he could pretend he did not know about his sexuality now that he was married. Anthony's party was an announcement to the community, and as one cleric explained, it theologically could no longer be understood as a "transient" lifestyle choice. Rather, gayness was now permanent; he had assumed an indelible gay identity. He was able to continue to help out in the shrine; as one man told me, "He won't leave, he is very devoted." While the Church could turn a blind eye to secret sexual acts with men, it was an affront to the morals of the Church and also an affront to the ideals of masculinity and manhood in the feast community that he enshrined his sexuality and identity.[24]

One of the most special rituals of the feast comes on Old Timer's Day, the last Sunday of the feast, when all the past capos return to command giglio lifts. Like celebrities, the men enter the crowd, down a ribbon-lined walkway, flanked by lieutenants who escort them to the giglio. The crowd is full of the friends and extended family of the capos. Generations of each family are present on this day to honor these men who represent the longevity and vitality of the feast, some even wearing the T-shirts with the capo's name from the year he was number one. Anthony had dedicated his life to the feast and was an upstanding member of the parish, so much so that he rose through the ranks to become an honorary capo in 2005, a title that was taken away from him. An honorary capo is someone who is appointed to the status of capo without necessarily having to become a lieutenant first. Anthony could not partake in Old Timer's Day, and during the festivities, as we watched from the roof of the church, he paced along its surface and complained about being "excommunicated" and treated by some like he had "the plague."

It is important to note that capos have been excluded and excised for sexual improprieties, like adultery. One capo who had an extramarital affair resigned from his position as number one. But in 2014, the year Anthony complained to me about his exclusion, that man had been included on the list of the capos whose names were read out on Old Timer's Day. Although he did not show up, inclusion mattered; it was an incredibly symbolic privilege to be included on the lift list, and Anthony was not. The Catholic Church under Pope Francis has critiqued fluid sexual identity as "often founded on nothing more than a confused concept of freedom in the realm of feelings and wants, or momentary desires provoked by emotional impulses and the will of the individual, as opposed to anything based on the truths of existence."[25] Gay does not fit into "true existence" in the Church's theology of gender and sexuality. As the Church continues to write gay people out of existence as such, on a local level Anthony was being erased from feast history.

Anthony's identity as a gay man essentially disrupted and challenged the heterosexuality implicit in the archetype of the capo as a family man. The Line of the March glorifies capos and domestic space; the capos emerge from homes with their families, their children and grandchildren in tow. This performance tells a story of feast succession and of fatherhood, a performance that Anthony could not give; it may seem unimaginable that he could participate in the Line of the March, emerging under the loving gaze of his husband, rather than a wife and children.[26] He has been committed to working in the shrine for decades but is also confined to the shrine; he does not walk the streets of the neighborhood during the Line of the March or command the lifters before the towering giglio. The shrine is a safe space for him—his work there does not challenge the heterosexual logic of feast manhood. The shrine is coded feminine by many of the men at the feast: men who are involved with the shrine are not "cool"; they are not considered masculine in the same kinds of ways as the lifters are; some think they are essentially doing the women's work of the feast. Lifters and capos do not work in the shrine; they seldom even visit. Unseated from his position as head of the shrine, he continued to tend to the candles, to create a devotional space, to remain loyal to his parish and his faith where he could and in a space where he did not pose any threat to the manhood the community holds dear.

Sometimes as we worked in the rectory together counting the shrine's earnings and de-pinning ribbon money, Anthony would say, "Maybe one of these years I'll get my lift." He was always annoyed that those he was close to did not ameliorate him being left out. He particularly wanted Phil, who served as the emcee on the giglio, to read his name when he announced the list of capos on Old Timer's Day: "They could just announce me as honorary, no one knows me anyway. They're going to leave me out again." Anthony proposed that he could just dress up for Old Timer's Day and show up "no matter what they announce . . . I'm just gonna bring a cane." He just wanted to be there: "It's like pastor emeritus," he explained. Emeritus is a title conferred on someone who has retired or stepped down from a position, but the title continues to honor them for their service. That is what he wanted—honor for his service and dedication to the community.

Anthony finally got a lift in 2016. He got to do the very last lift of the day, commanding the men who were lifting the boat. When I asked him how it went, he shrugged indifferently, "Yeah, I got one lift. It would have been better if the boat were on rollers." He hunched his back over to act out the lifters, already worn out by an entire day of lifting, struggling to get their bodies up. Anthony was disappointed that some of his friends who were capos themselves did not defend his right to get a lift. "I thought my friend would give me a lift and nothing. I get one lift, everyone's friends give their friends six lifts. I don't have friends. . . . But that's church!" he said resignedly. In 2017 as well his name got called for a lift on Old Timer's Day, but it was something of a consolation lift. When someone told him they had recorded it, Anthony said, sarcastically, "You got all five feet of it? They wanted me to move it three feet forward back and to the right, I said listen there are not that many men, they're tired, I'll just move it to the right. I appreciate the lift." Even when he was included, it was often in a limited way, without the recognition, glory, and respect given to other capos. His lifts, when he did get them, were short in distance and at the end of the day, when the crowds are thin and the lifters are weary, with none of the fanfare the other capos received.

In 2018 Anthony finally did get a moment of glory. He told the number one, Gerard, "You can give me the last lift of the night, I will not put it down." But Anthony did not get the last lift; rather Gerard gave him the honor of taking the giglio off the sidewalk, the ceremonial first lift often reserved for the number one. It was during the night lift, when the giglio gets lifted in the cooler temperatures of the evening. That year Anthony had decided that whatever lift he got it would be his last. When he talked about it, he reflected on how he had been involved in this community for forty-six years. It was 1973 when he first lifted at the age of seventeen. Back then, he told me, it was tougher to get under the poles because there were so many lifters; if you wanted to do it as a teenager you would have to sneak under. In 2018, when he commanded the lifters to begin moving the giglio down off the sidewalk, he never commanded them to drop it. Instead Gerard took it over. "Always lifted in my heart, I never put it down," Anthony said, sounding proud and wistful. As he dashed out of the money room to head back to the shrine, he repeated, "Always lifted in my heart," smiling.

As the Italian Americans of Williamsburg hold steadfastly to the feast, there is always concern about the survival of the feast and parish not only because of neighborhood change but also because of inner tensions. What Anthony's excommunication from capo manhood and the masculine hierarchy of the feast highlights is that perhaps one of the problems of the feast is a problem of sexuality and reproduction. The worry "if the feast goes, the parish goes" is best ameliorated by new generations of children and young men who will strive to maintain the tradition, who will follow in the footsteps of their fathers and male role models to become lifters, lieutenants, and capos, who will keep the feast strong and thus ensure the longevity of the parish.

The narrative of the parish's dependence on the feast emphasizes that men ensure the survival of the parish. This echoes the language of the Holy Name Society in the early twentieth century, which emphasized that "the healthy state of religion in a parish . . . could only truly be—judged from the practice of religion by men," and the interdenominational Men and Religion Forward Movement (M&RFM) of 1911–12, which cited churches' dire need for men's work.[27] Unlike movements like the Promise Keepers and M&RFM, which emerged forcefully with a strong revivalistic message and subsequently faded away, this study of the mundane and enduring contributions of men to the life of the feast and parish contradicts the tendency in the scholarship to study men and religion in these "flashpoint moments" and well-publicized national movements.[28] Masculinity and religious practice do not just converge in these moments of revival. The feast and the Dance of the Giglio demonstrate the embodied, relational, and lifelong nature of men's religious practice within the Catholic parish.

The community celebrates men for keeping its tradition afloat as the coordinators and champions of the feast. The hope of one day becoming a capo keeps young men in the community. They attend feast meetings and work day and night crafting the giglio. Here attention to masculinities and manhood highlights gradations in life stage and performances of authority in the feast hierarchy. Capos are not just individual men; capo is also an idea, an imagined archetype, an ideal figure. At the start of the 2017 feast, one man said with wonder in his voice, "You know there are less than one hundred men in the world that have done what [the number one] is gonna do this year. Less than one hundred men," emphasizing the special, exclusive nature of the position. Lifters, like those under the giglio and on the Questua, perform physical prowess and ethnic pride, and their masculinity is about performances of strength, the capacity of the body, and homosociality. Feast manhood, that of the capos, is an aspirational status achieved through devotion to the parish and a life of service to the church and family, but is one that many men will not achieve, although they may strive for it and respect the position.

Homosexuality threatens the devotional physicality of the homosocial ritual. It threatens to take it from the official realm of devotion, sacrifice, and penance into the overt realm of pleasure. The sweaty, straining bodies of the lifters, their arms interlocked in mutual support, the embraces, and the euphoria many feel after a successful day of lifting—pleasure is always already there. Proximity, touch, contact, and mutual support rely on the presumption of a shared heterosexuality. Homosexuality not only challenges the sexual morals of these Catholics but also challenges the community's logics of reproduction. The capo, as archetype, is a man who is honorable, faithful, and beloved and, importantly, is a man who can provide a new source of membership—a new generation of Italian Americans devoted to the feast. The capos serve as male role models but also are the nodal points in the male lineage; stories of old-timers inspiring young men, of fathers bringing their babies to the feast hoping they too will love it and devote their lives to it, ensure that the feast will survive. Heterosexuality is central to the community's vision of a thriving feast.

5

Constructing Catholic Propriety on North Eighth Street

There is a persistent anxiety about continuity at the feast. In the Line of the March and in the lift of the children's giglio we see how gaggles of little lifters and capos with children and grandchildren in tow publicly demonstrate the strength of the community and how that strength is very much contingent on logics of reproduction, generational transmission, and socialization of young Catholics, especially boys, into love and labor for the feast. Italian Americans move through the neighborhood during the Questua and are faced with newcomers with seemingly fickle dietary preferences who seem ignorant about the history and traditions of the very places they move to. In contrast to condo dwellers whom they imagine to be from far-flung places like Oklahoma and Kansas, the men of the feast have a historicity, lineage, and Brooklyn authenticity that they perform and reify yearly. The feast has survived throughout the twentieth century despite the inhospitality of urban renewal and gentrification, and through procession and public ritual these Italian American Catholics continue to claim the streets of Williamsburg as their own, whether or not 11211 is their zip code. No matter how many hours of work they put into the feast or how many lifters are under the giglio, the success of the feast also relies on devotees who are not Italian American to pray novenas, go to Masses, and fill the shrine of Our Lady of Mount Carmel. While the giglio is very much sustained on the shoulders of Italian Americans, devotees of other races and ethnicities also ensure a successful feast. While Italian Americans may be the proprietors of the feast and their ancestors are the ones who have prayed before the olive-skinned statue of OLMC for decades, they are not the only ones who do so today, and for some that reality is troubling. Italian Americans at the feast contend with sharing their saint with Haitian and Haitian American devotees who travel to Williamsburg from other neighborhoods. While this sharing might seem a story of urban diversity and unity under the banner of devotionalism, some experience it as a rupture, an occasion for cataloguing and lamenting declining devotion among Italian Americans. For some it becomes an occasion to observe and critique the practices of other Catholics. While there is triumphalism at the feast, there is also insecurity that manifests in discussions of who is doing devotion correctly.

While the feast is a site where Catholics of different races and ethnicities share devotional space, it is also a site of *intra-Catholic boundary making*. Public performances of devotion are sites of intra-Catholic boundary work, where people judge, construct, and enact *Catholic propriety*. These evaluative judgments often rely on racist constructions and complicate notions of devotional events as unifying and collective spaces where love and reverence for a saint efface ethnic and racial tensions.[1] Although it is true that Italians and Haitians peacefully share space on the crowded streets during processions, shared space does not a collective make. Rather, shared spaces offer simultaneous moments for appreciation and admiration and judgment, surveillance, evaluation, and territoriality. Through everyday talk and boundary-making practices, Italian American Catholics at the feast construct ideas of "good" American Catholic practice and label the practices of ethnic and racial others as simultaneously admirable and superstitious, foreign, and excessive. In conversation, they construct and articulate norms especially around questions of materiality and presence. This is not to say that the practices of Haitian and Italian devotees are necessarily different. Italians partake in the same practices they critique. They read the weather for signs from the Blessed Mother. They too touch, kiss, and speak to statues. For a community in which devotion is centered on work—time put in, years of volunteering, actions quantifiable and concrete—public and bodily expressions of prayer and petition, when enacted by others, seem out of place. Today at the feast the frameworks of community survival and fundraising cloak these practices—the very same practices of late nineteenth- and early twentieth-century ethnic Catholicism—in logics of productivity, resourcefulness, rational planning, and service to the parish. So the practices of these devotees are not different, but the Italian American proprietors of the feast echo tropes of superstition, contagion, and the emotionalism of Black religion that have shaped political discourses on Haitian immigration and historical Catholic discourses on immigrant religiosity as they draw discursive boundaries between themselves and the Haitian American devotees.[2]

Although many of these observations largely took place in 2014 and 2015, in the United States this racist language has become a more overt part of the public political sphere, not only to think about whose religion is "good" but also to evaluate who is worthy to enter the United States and who is worthy of being an American. Racist reactions to Haitian devotees at this parish resonate with broader national constructions of Haitians. There are resonances with President Donald Trump's language about immigrants from Haiti and African countries. In January 2018, in a meeting on an immigration deal, he said, "Why do we need more Haitians? . . . Take them out," months after announcing an end to the Temporary Protected Status that offered protection from deportation to nearly fifty thousand Haitian migrants, who are allowed to live and work in the United States after the devastation of the 2010 earthquake.[3]

* * *

The Feast of Our Lady of Mount Carmel (OLMC) officially begins when Our Lady makes her debut. Five men gingerly carry her out of the church as her loving devotees await with arms full of bouquets, cell phones and selfie sticks raised high, rosaries around their wrists, and scapulars around their necks. In 2014 a brass band set the mood by playing a solemn marching tune as a troupe of clergy processed out the front doors of the church. They all wore creamy vestments woven with sparkling green lilies, clouds, and heavenly images of OLMC. The trumpets grew louder, and as the statue appeared in the doorway, faux rose petals and metallic confetti rained down from the roof, sticking to devotees' bodies in shiny constellations, heightening the magic of the moment. Everyone cheered, and it was official: the feast had begun. After the debut, right before the sky turned sunset pink, devotees walked on a short procession, inaugurating the eleven days of the feast. OLMC's devotees followed her as she floated through the streets of the feast, carried on the shoulders of men. In her golden yellow robes, she seemed to glide past carnival games with their cheap colorful stuffed animals, floating through streets marked with Italian and American flags and framed with bright bubbly flower garlands that formed canopies over the sidewalks.

While the Italian Americans of this parish are the ones who run the feast, the crowd assembled to greet OLMC on that opening night was anything but homogenous. The church added a Creole Mass in 1986—Haitian and Haitian American devotees began commuting from other neighborhoods and have consistently composed a sizable portion of the crowd.[4] They waved jubilantly as Mount Carmel appeared. In public space these groups of devotees cooperate and coexist. On July 16 they process for hours around the neighborhood, rain or shine. They walk with Our Lady's statue (the same one that has been in this church for decades). She stands tall at the back of a float lush with flowers, wearing a brass crown studded with cubic zirconia and fake sapphires and a cape woven of twenty-dollar bills. While Haitian devotees shared this devotion, the procession was spatially segregated. Italian American devotees walked in front of the float with their families and friends. Some walked barefoot in white socks, their feet treading hot concrete. White women, some who were part of the Third Order Lay Carmelites and wore large brown scapulars the size of books over their chests and backs, rode the float on metal folding chairs, fanning themselves in the heat. Around the sides and the back were the women of color. Some held tight to the bars surrounding the statue, intent on remaining physically connected to the float. But it was always clear who owned it. The years I walked the procession men patrolled the float and instructed the Black women not to hold on. Sometimes nicely and sometimes stern and scoldingly they repeated the refrains "Cops said no holding on." "Everyone please step in front of the float, no one behind the floater besides the police, everyone in front, thank you." "Walk in front of us . . . we will follow you. We will bring the Lady to the people." White devotees held on to the sides without comment.

According to the works of religion scholars Robert Orsi and Elizabeth McAlister, Italians and Haitians coexist in mutual devotion at the Feast of OLMC that takes place in East Harlem and perform their ethnic and religious identities alongside one another. Exploring the ethnic and racial tensions between Puerto Ricans and Italians as the demographics of East Harlem changed with migration from the island in the 1940s and 1950s, Orsi argues that Puerto Ricans became a "too proximate other."[5] Because they shared the neighborhood and a similar romance language, they became a territorial threat and a linchpin in a developing narrative of loss and thus were overtly excluded during the feast, as Italian Americans defended their claim to the declining neighborhood.[6] On the other hand, according to Orsi, the remaining Italians in Harlem celebrate Haitian pilgrims as "traditional Catholics," a "miraculous" presence and a true testament to the magnetic power of the church on 115th Street as a sacred site.[7] He argues that they never developed any anxieties about the Haitian devotees because as pilgrims they did not pose a threat to the Italian ownership of the neighborhood. Ideas about shared religiosity and devotion shaped their racial logics as some of his interlocutors insisted "Haitians are not black people," and they discursively set them apart from African Americans because of their command of French and their knowledge of Latin songs.[8] McAlister terms their relationship "symbiotic"; they coexist with clearly delineated roles—"Italians control the shrine church" and "Haitians are consumers at the shrine."[9] In her study, McAlister explores how Haitian pilgrims bring new layers of meaning to the event as transnational actors who use OLMC on 115th Street to recall and simultaneously experience the pilgrimage to Saut d'Eau in Haiti, the site of an apparition in 1849 and pilgrimage site for Notre Dame du Mont Carmel and Vodou *lwa* Ezili Dantò that draws thousands of Haitians from all walks of life each July.[10]

My years among the Italian Americans at the Shrine Church of Our Lady of Mount Carmel in Brooklyn offer a different perspective. For the Italian proprietors of the feast, Haitians are a discursive foil—narrative shorthand for discussions on devotional and demographic decline. Williamsburg, once a manufacturing district home to an Italian enclave, is now one of the trendiest and most expensive neighborhoods in the city. People worry about the fate of the parish and its financial troubles. During the feast they depend on Haitian devotees who travel from other neighborhoods to people pews and sparse processions. In the words of one volunteer, "Thank God for the Haitians or else we would have three people and the saint." But they keep these vital devotees at a distance. Although folklorist Joseph Sciorra characterized the Williamsburg feast as a "parturient environment of acceptance and welcome," I often heard racialized and barbed comments like this: "[The feast day] is the worst, the entire island nation of Haiti swarms this place all at once. I would say 50 percent are devout and 50 percent are superstitious and they need the scapulars to do whatever they do—voodoo or whatever—and they'll tell you that, oh I need two more [and] one for my chicken."[11] The feast may be a site of devotional coexistence, but there is also racism, as it is a site of racializing, territoriality, and boundary making. Italian American organizers and volunteers conversationally construct Haitian devotees as superstitious and excessive in their devotionalism.

Studies of increasing Catholic diversity in the United States have explored changing demographics and the realities of sharing parishes.[12] Often scholars highlight the efforts of exceptional priests, diocesan initiatives, and clerical activists to advocate for immigrants especially within the framework of social justice after the Second Vatican Council. What these studies miss is the urban, spatial tensions of Catholic life. Catholics of different races and ethnicities encounter each other not just in church but also on sidewalks. White ethnic parishes with traditions of public devotions and saints' feasts need to share not only their pews but also their saints. Bishops may advocate for immigrants' rights, but on the ground, in the peripheries of devotional ritual—spaces like rectories, shrines, and sidewalks—ethnic identities continue to structure intra-Catholic prejudices. This chapter offers a view of the impromptu and micro-level interactions through which those Catholics resist unity amid demographic and urban change and how they discursively construct difference in their everyday talk.[13]

It is important to note that critical discussions took place not on procession but in the shrine, in the rectory, and on sidewalks, away from places where we consider the "action to happen." It is this vantage point, the peripheries, from which I was able to access this discursive construction of difference. Thomas Tweed has advocated for ethnographers and scholars of religion to account for their positionality. Positionality has a twofold definition for Tweed—the first being a thorough accounting for the constellation of gender, race, age, and class, professional obligations of the ethnographer, and a full accounting for how they bring and carry these attributes into the field with them. His second definition is more literal. He calls on scholars of religion to account for their vantage point. Using ocular metaphors, Tweed argues that theories "are sightings from sites. They are positioned representations of a changing terrain by an itinerant cartographer."[14] He calls for an accounting of the actual geography of fieldwork, asking ethnographers to locate where they *stand*. He makes clear that he builds his analysis of religious life on "what I can see from where I am. I cannot see everything."[15] While the ritual front stage may offer a view of different devotees sharing space and collectively enacting their love for OLMC, insider spaces offer different possibilities for critique and commentary.

While accounting for vantage point is important, the ocular metaphor is limited. Ethnographic work is about not just seeing but also hearing, overhearing, touching, practicing, and acting. The framework of sightings privileges positioned observation in a way that is limited for understanding the way my ethnographic method was very much embodied. I could not have heard critiques of Haitian and Haitian American devotees had I not been working in the shrine exchanging dollars for statues and rosaries and volunteering to help in the rectory. Working and keeping busy made me privy to and part of insider spaces and conversations that the language of sight does not wholly account for. Because I was in these behind-the-scenes spaces, here I cannot account for both sides of these encounters; instead I analyze the production of difference. In conversations we see how this community grapples with the presence of Catholic others and how they produce ideas about Catholic practice in their everyday talk.

Talk is an important realm of analysis, a "social practice" in which people articulate the implicit and "commonly accepted rules" that "govern" religious practice. An analysis of the talk that goes on in the peripheries of devotional ritual helps us see the way Catholics articulate, rehearse, and create norms of practice, placing themselves within the realm of the "proper" and other Catholics outside of it. Sociologist of religion Robert Wuthnow has argued that paying attention to talk illuminates the ways religious actors articulate and express rules, assumptions, and norms in discourse, often in ways that do not always require "conscious deliberation" and "yet [are] observable in the structure and content of discourse itself."[16] Paying attention to talk allows us to see how norms regarding Catholic practice are constructed, rehearsed, and reinforced and how talk contributes to the creation of insiders and outsiders. These social dynamics and the logics of boundary making might not be readily apprehended in an interview.

* * *

In 1975 the *New York Times* reported that Haitians, after Italians and Hispanics, were the third largest population in the diocese.[17] Haitians and Haitian Americans live in Brooklyn neighborhoods like Flatbush, Flatlands, and Canarsie and in Cambria Heights and Queens Village in Queens. They are vital community members at parishes like Sacred Heart in Canarsie, Saint Jerome in Flatbush, and Saint Teresa of Avila in Crown Heights. The Diocese of Brooklyn, which markets itself as the Diocese of Immigrants, often celebrates the faith of its Haitian Apostolate in the diocese newspaper, the *Tablet*. Every year Catholic Migration Services holds a Shining Stars award ceremony to honor parishioners' contributions to their immigrant communities, where Haitian Americans are often among the diocese's stars. They walk the streets of Brooklyn for Corpus Christi processions and gather in the borough's cathedral to celebrate Saint Joseph as a role model for their community. They celebrate Haitian independence with Masses of thanksgiving where congregants share *joumou*, traditional pumpkin soup, an edible symbol of freedom.[18] During the West Indian Day Parade they march by parish, with banners publicly proclaiming their Catholic faith and parish identity.[19] In Queens parishes they share pews with Colombian, Ecuadorian, and Asian parishioners to celebrate the feast day of Haiti's patroness Notre Dame du Perpetuel Secours (Our Lady of Perpetual Help).[20] During the feast of OLMC Haitians and Haitian Americans travel from other parts of Brooklyn and Queens to walk on processions and attend novenas, Masses, and rosary vigils at feasts like the one in Williamsburg and the one in East Harlem, both historically hosted by Italian Americans.

In the late 1980s OLMC in Brooklyn introduced Creole Mass to the schedule of Masses celebrating OLMC on July 16. One day as we sat in the rectory on gray cushioned chairs that look like they came right out of a staged home, Monsignor Cassato, the pastor who instituted these new Masses told me, "At the first Mass we had maybe forty to fifty people and since, it grew to be the biggest Mass." When I asked him what people thought, he continued,

> There's always the naysayers but when they saw the devotion that's what changed it. They have a tremendous devotion. Our Lady of Mount Carmel and Perpetual Help are the copatrons [of Haiti] so they always have a tremendous devotion. I used to stand out there and bless them with the holy water and they loved it, they used to go crazy, they would grab my

cassock and they were pulling on it and they wanted more holy water. It was a smart thing to do because the feast was always too Italian and we weren't living in an Italian neighborhood anymore. . . . That was the goal, I wanted to bring more international flavor to the feast.

He took credit for starting all the language Masses, adding a Polish Mass and a Spanish Mass to the schedule as well. He told me that although other people might want to take credit for the diversity of Masses, it was all him. Before his tenure they had only the Italian and English Masses.

Racial tensions were high in New York City just as many Haitians were beginning to visit the feast of OLMC. In 1986 in Howard Beach, Queens, a group of white teenagers assaulted, attacked, and chased three Black men, resulting in the death of a man named Michael Griffith. In 1991 the deaths of Gavin Cato and Yankel Rosenbaum set off violence between the Lubavitcher Hasidim and Black and West Indian residents of Crown Heights, as the Black community protested systemic racism and police discrimination.[21] As the borough was undergoing demographic changes, in February 1991, in response to racial tension and violence in the borough, the diocese asked parishes to hold council meetings on race.

The minutes of OLMC's parish meeting reveal that white people in Williamsburg were struggling with the changing demographics of Brooklyn and the presence of Black and Hispanic people in the parish, at the feast, and in the neighborhood. Minutes from the parish council meeting show that a small group of parishioners gathered to vent, to come up with ways to increase racial harmony in the parish, to make it clear that they preferred their neighbors to be Italian, and to debate affirmative action. Although they did not specifically talk about Haitian devotees at the feast, they reflected on parishioner complaints about the increasing number of minorities and Hispanics.[22] They elided overt confrontation of racism, but talked about how they felt "racial tension in the parish," and some reported that "people are standoffish when blacks attend Mass." While some proposed outreach and educational efforts to teach about different cultures in the church, others argued "there is nothing wrong with like people desiring to be together" by citing the "anthropological history of human nature." Like in other neighborhoods in Brooklyn, the language of insularity and wanting to live around one's own ethnic and religious kind and logics about belonging and proximity were tangled with racism.[23] The existence of these notes, these citywide events, and the influx of new devotees speak to tensions and racism that likely existed around the changing faces of the feast, where "physical co-presence" was paired with racist critique.[24] When Haitian devotees began to come to the feast to express their love for OLMC, they did so at a time when change was afoot and racial territoriality was on people's minds.

Evaluating Devotion

Devotional celebrations have often been sites of religious evaluation, where onlookers judge who is and who is not acting as a "good Catholic" and whose devotional affinities verge on superstition. In the early twentieth century Irish Catholics, clergymen, and Protestants and policemen alike were spectators at feast day celebrations. In 1905 a police officer in Williamsburg critiqued feast days, saying, "These saints' days are no good at all—fireworks, music, beer, and fightin'! And that's what these people think is religion."[25] In 1908 Irish and Italian priests from all over Brooklyn signed a letter critiquing Italian feast days, arguing that "street celebrations are a burlesque of the spiritual side of religion."[26] Clergy critiqued Italians as "peculiar" and of "deficient faith" and claimed processions did not constitute "true piety."[27]

These early twentieth-century discourses were not only negative but also double-edged—celebratory, admiring, and condemning. In 1914 clergy wrote in to periodicals like *America: A Catholic Review of the Week* debating whether Italians were good Catholics. Many concluded that although their faith was "childlike"—and perhaps too emotional—they had a deep piety, evidenced by their love for the Madonna. Clerical leaders wrote in praising their "simple and beautiful faith" and the "glowing vivacity," of their devotions, but always noted that their "knowledge in religious matters . . . was not sufficient."[28] Onlookers like Jacob Riis too looked upon Italian devotional practices and characterized them as admirable, yet foreign. In an 1899 piece titled "Feast Days in Little Italy," published in the *Century Illustrated Monthly Magazine*, he wrote of the "religious fervor" of tenement dwellers, describing them as clamoring during processions to throw themselves before the Virgin. His description of a feast in Harlem centered on the tactile and relational exchanges between the devotees and the Virgin—how they clutched their "beads" and stumbled to catch just a "single touch" of the image's garments and "kiss the hem of her robe." He described the crowds with their clothes soaked through with sweat as they carried heavy candles and piled their gold jewelry before the Virgin. Children emerged from the shrines with their hands wrapped in handkerchiefs, the same hands that had touched the Virgin's robes in order to "keep the blessings safe and to make it last."[29] At Saint Donato's feast day Riis saw a man lose a game of cards and throw his boot at the saint's shrine, angrily asking, "Why did you let me lose? I gave you a new candle last week."[30] What Riis found captivating, frenzied, beautiful, and seductive, albeit "other" about feast day celebrations, Catholic critics found to be vulgar, overly theatrical, transactional, empty, and exterior expressions of faith.[31]

Still today the contours of "appropriate" American Catholic practices are articulated in normative and racialized double-edged discourse as spectators look upon the practices of new immigrant Catholics, lauding their devotional energy as beautiful and on the other hand indicting it as emotional, excessive, and frenzied. In Williamsburg, the same people who claim Haitian devotees are superstitious also admire their love for OLMC. Explaining the liveliness of the Creole Mass on feast day, one feast organizer told me, "You've got to see it . . . seven hundred Haitian women show up to Mass. The Haitian Mass is the most beautiful, you can really see their true devotion, it's real. They are packed in there, sweating, crying, kissing the statue, exclaiming Baptist-style. It is really beautiful devotion." This statement is admiring but also constructs an emotional and feminized Black Catholic otherness that echoes the "romantic racialism" through which Catholic missionaries constructed Black Catholics throughout the twentieth century, as Matthew Cressler explores in his study of the growth of Black Catholicism during the Great Migration.[32] Naming these expressions "Baptist-style" marks this exuberance as both racially and religiously other, with roots outside of what he perceives to be Catholic worship styles, despite them being wholly unremarkable in Catholic devotionalism more broadly.

Lay Catholics actively construct the norms of Catholic practice—locating themselves within the fold of the normal and locating others at its margins. At the feast today, Italian Americans echo the early twentieth-century discourses that once placed their traditions outside the boundaries of correct and appropriate Catholic practice. Now in the twenty-first century, these have come full circle, as they shore up their propriety by mobilizing similar discourses. Jay Dolan has argued that the twenty-first century is the era of the "Catholic mosaic," defined by increasing diversity, coexistence, and more openness toward newcomers than characterized the church in its earlier era of immigration.[33] At the feast, we see and hear the limits of that argument. Lay and clerical Catholics alike are active in constructing and articulating intra-Catholic difference, especially around devotionalism. The discourses about superstition and excess that were so pronounced in the early twentieth century are still alive in the everyday talk of Italian American Catholics at the feast.

On July 16, 2015, I stood outside of the church with a priest and a parishioner. It was the feast day, and while devotees walked the procession we had been running errands. The parishioner and the priest lamented the changing feast and neighborhood and complained that now fewer people wait on their front steps and stoops to greet the float. Comparing the Italian turnout to the number of Haitians present, the parishioner complained, "Our people are put to shame, they don't bother taking the day off anymore." This conversational declension narrative quickly turned to an overt critique of Haitian devotees. The priest claimed that some Haitians were a distracting presence during Mass. He said that they sit in the first two pews, near the statue of OLMC that flanks the sanctuary, and described them as "blabbering" with their hands up, talking to the saints and interrupting the feast day Masses. He detailed one episode in which he scolded a woman who was talking to OLMC during Mass. He said, "I told her, 'she's ignoring you, she is listening to her son and when you are speaking to her she is not listening to you. You speak to the mother and ignore her son.'" He told us he confronted a man who was doing the same thing during communion: "I told him, 'I'm going to say a prayer for you, because you don't care about Jesus.'"

In this conversation we see how the Haitian is a flattened character in a trope, either a foil for the lack of devotional dedication among Italian Americans or a representation of far too much devotion. The priest's overt critique of Haitian devotees marked them as inappropriate, disruptive, and theologically misguided. Although he often praised their devotion and admired how beautiful it was when they sang hymns in

French along the processional route, in this conversation he portrayed their devotion as hyper-Marian and almost pathologically so. He was offended that someone would attend Mass and use it as an opportunity to communicate with OLMC rather than partake in communion. In his narrative he draws the lines of "proper" devotional practice: it is quiet and nondisruptive; it is Christ-centered; it is reserved; it is in no way more important than the liturgy; it is temporally bounded to "appropriate" times; and when it fails to meet these standards, it is pathological and ineffective—hence the "she's not listening." So devotion done wrong falls on deaf ears.

This priest's indictment of Haitian practice as misdirected and disrespectful to liturgical norms and Catholic propriety uncannily resonates with early twentieth-century discussions over whether Italians were good Catholics. In the 1914 debate on Italians in the pages of *America*, one writer who dubbed himself "An Old Pastor" wrote that he was disgusted when upon entering an Italian church he found that they did not come to adore or receive the Blessed Sacrament but instead busied themselves at the shrines in the church, prostrating themselves before statues, completely "side tracking . . . the main altar wherein reposed the Saviour of men."[34] In his scolding, the priest at the feast reenacted a centuries-old critique that had once been directed at Italian Catholics as he conversationally fleshed out the norms of appropriate "American" Catholic practice.

Evaluative conversations often took place in the rectory. The rectory was the organizational nucleus of the feast. It was private, accessible only if you were a trusted parishioner or worker and was therefore an insider's space where critique flowed freely. Especially on the feast day, rectory workers were often frustrated from fielding phone calls from Haitian devotees. One year the rectory workers complained among each other that Haitians had been asking, "Why can't we sleep [in the church]?" One of women offered the frustrated group a firm response: "Because we are in the United States!" As I sat in the rectory, helping count the collections for the day, two men talked through how they were going to need extra ushers for the Creole Mass to deal with the crowds. One of the men leaned back in his chair and told me, "Tomorrow is going to be crazy with the Creole. . . . Once you've seen that. . . . Their customs are very strange, they could bathe in that pool [of holy water] back there.

They leave money and notes." He mimicked rolling up a note and told me, "I hope they are petitions and not voodoos."

Other volunteers also worried about the presence of "voodoo" and brought it up in everyday conversation at the feast. One day I was in the shrine talking to a teenage parishioner and Rosie (pseudonym), a volunteer. That day it was Rosie's job to sit next to the statue of OLMC and take offerings. The two complained about the saint statues outside the church being vandalized a few years back. In February 2012 a vandal drew what looked like KISS makeup on a white statue of the Virgin and Child outside the church; messy Sharpie batwings and a misshapen star outlined the eyes on the two figures.[35] It was in this context of statues being stolen and defaced that she began to tell us about the time a statue of OLMC was installed in honor of the church in a small park called Mount Carmel Triangle on Union Avenue, around the corner. "I was the honor guard when they put the statue on Union Ave, I had to protect the statue. The Creoles, you should have seen them, they all wanted to touch the statue." She explained that she had to block them in order to protect it: "I was convinced someone put a voodoo curse on me, I told monsignor, 'you have to bless me!' I was scared." In her narratives, Rosie fashioned herself as a protector of the statue of OLMC, concerned for its well-being and an apt discerner of who approached it with proper motives and postures.

That same week we were sitting in the rectory talking about the proper way to attach the dollars offered to OLMC to the ribbon that was draped around her body. The shrine workers used sharp pins to pierce through multiple bills, securing them to the ribbon, and we threw around a few ideas to make the job less painful and onerous. One man suggested staples, and when I jokingly suggested they could use paper clips to avoid messing up the bills, Rosie said, "No, no paper clips. Those Haitians, they'll just pull it down. Today the statue was too close to the railing. There was a mob, I had to stand between [the statue and the railing] so they don't pull the ribbon down. They can be very vicious."

In the same breath people who put forth critiques hem them with statements like "their devotion to Mount Carmel is incredible, don't get me wrong," "these ladies are so devoted," and "it is beautiful, but they swarm the church." These critiques are racialized and dehumanizing—they construct Haitians as a mass with suspect motives and less-than-respectable religious practices. Late nineteenth- and early twentieth-century critics wrote of Italians with their swarthy complexions, describing them as a "vast army of sinewy and dark-brown men" that were "invading" parishes, and were people that "fed on the luxuries of religion without its substantials."[36] Clergy looked upon Italian feast days and saw everything that was being construed as un-American, foreign, superstitious, and corrupt about Catholicism in the popular imagination and distanced themselves from these practices. Perhaps the Italian Americans see Haitian devotionalism and see mirrored practices, some of their own reflected back in people they consider "others." It is important to note that in their imaginings of Haitians Italian Americans are expressing not just racial anxieties. Talk about Haitians expresses ambivalences about the right relationship to the Blessed Mother and the appropriate relationship to Catholic materiality, things like holy water, scapulars, and statues. They will make comparative statements, saying things like "Italians don't talk to saints," setting strictures on devotional propriety that they themselves often flout. Their comments reflect a concern about tactile practices of presence and relationality—touching, kissing, and speaking to statues become problematic, superstitious practices when they see them mirrored in others. Critique shores up their American Catholic identity and assures them they are doing it "right."

In their comments Italian American priests and parishioners alike imagine "voodoo." Rosie imagined that because of her actions to protect the statue she might have gotten a vengeful hex put on her. The other organizer, in hoping the notes are "petitions not voodoos," imagined the devotional writings of Haitian devotees to be substantively different from petitions, the efficacious requests for intercession that devotees hope will have real effects on the lives of themselves and their loved ones.[37] One elderly woman and loyal devotee always brought snacks and juice for the children in the shrine, but some speculated that she had the capacity to cast spells through mundane channels like fruit juice, called "voodoo juice" by one man. Adam McGee has studied the way "voodoo," spelled as such, is an "imagined religion." As an imagined religion, voodoo is a representation, a "receptacle for anxieties," and a "trope that comments on racial anxieties" that "spring from perceived out-group threat and a sense of the uncanny—the presence of something which is at once familiar yet irrepressibly foreign."[38] McGee importantly points out that Vodou and voodoo are different; the latter is a produced category shaped by popular (mis)conceptions, historically racist discourses, and media. His category is instructive for thinking about how religions and peoples can become tropes and representations, their proximity sparking anxieties and generating ideas and discourses of foreignness.

Italian American suspicions of Haitian devotees reach beyond the realm of the discursive and have spatial consequences and more physical expressions of distancing and territoriality. Watching over the shrine was as important as walking on the procession. One July 16 the shrine was largely empty, save for two workers and a few older Haitian devotees who sat on folding chairs in the shrine. It was a hot day, and the shrine was one of the only places with shade around the church. Although the shrine was empty, shrine workers, who all sat behind tables full of candles, complained about the group of Haitian devotees sitting in the shrine and eating their lunch. They noted, "We are outnumbered" as they discussed what to do about this imposition on their space. One shrine worker was exasperated: "What would Jesus do?" she said, trying to work out and moralize how they would ask the people to leave.

Some privately took issue with the territoriality; they were most vocal in their critiques of the shrine workers behind their backs. It is important to note that there are not simply two categories of people: those who are critical of Haitian devotees and those who defend their right to space in the shrine and admire their devotion. Among women and men alike, both old and young, there is a doubleness to their discourse about Haitian devotees, so critiques of them as superstitious and "swarming" can go hand in hand with defenses of their right to spend time in the shrine sharing a meal. At the feast, commentary about Haitian devotees almost follows scripts. As Wuthnow argued, religious discourse is patterned by social institutions and "implicitly modeled so that practitioners adhere to commonly accepted rules."[39] Some of the same people who bristled at the way the shrine workers reacted to their presence are the same people who were suspicious of them doing "voodoo." In the rectory some who worked closely with the shrine workers critiqued the way they reacted to the Haitian devotees; one said, "I don't get it, they go to church every Sunday to hear the gospel preached, but they'll be like, these fucking people need to get out. . . . One Haitian is rude and they take it out on the whole island. They have different ideas of protocol but they shame us with their generosity and faithfulness."

Anthony, who had worked in the shrine for decades, was particularly frustrated. Anthony spent all day every feast day in the shrine. Throughout the day he carried heavy boxes of candles outside the church and tended to the flames of those lit by devotees. He helped use the shrine's budget to purchase scapulars, religious goods, and candles each year. When he was not in the shrine he sat in the rectory removing the pins from the dollars that had been stitched together on the ribbon draped over the statue of OLMC. Anthony loves baked goods and always shows up to the rectory with a box in tow—brownies, pecan rings, crumb cakes, and apple turnovers are all on offer throughout the days of the feast. Anthony is quiet and sarcastic and always jokingly critiques others for not doing enough manual labor to help out in the shrine. In 2017 I stood with him in the shrine as he watched another worker ignoring a Haitian devotee's request for four extra scapulars. The shrine worker helping her held on to a basket of scapulars and told her she needed to make a donation. "Just give her the extra four scapulars," Anthony mumbled, but she ignored him and said, "Just make a donation." Angry, and questioning how much longer he would work in the shrine, he told me he was "too religious for this."

The day following the episode about the devotees eating in the shrine, Anthony was frustrated. He complained, "They are rude, they are rude. They are trying to chase them out. They are so ruthless, so ruthless. Put that in your thesis, I could tell you stories." This is when Anthony said that without the Haitians it would just be a few people and the saint and a shrine devoid of devotees. As people worried that attendance at Masses had been more sparse than usual, Anthony told the group, "The Haitians are our only hope." One of the rectory workers assured him, "Don't worry they'll come." When the Creole Mass turned out to not be as full as usual, Anthony suggested that they get buses to bring Haitian devotees from other parishes over to the feast.

These instances of territoriality, backstage critique, and statements of dependence capture the way Haitian devotees are desirable because they are reliable Mass attendees and consumers in the shrine. Even if Italian Americans do not show up, feast organizers are sure that Haitian devotees will come to worship, pray, and spend. On the procession an observer may see Haitians and Haitian Americans sharing space with Italian Americans as they all walk with OLMC, all wear scapulars, all sweat under the summer sun, and all attend Mass together. But from the semipublic space of the shrine, I was present for conversations and interactions that were more overtly critical and territorial, where rifts in the idea of shared space and devotion were visible. During these "off hours," when other main events of the feast are taking place, the shrine and the rectory are peripheral feast spaces. They are not the main sites of ritual events but instead are the spaces where organizers and volunteers spend most of their time, and spaces where they ostensibly have ownership and authority. Shrine workers mark themselves as threatened and outnumbered and imagine their spaces as impinged upon by outsiders. In these instances of territoriality we see the limits of coexistence at the feast. That day in the shrine Haitians were not filling the role of pious devotees in the pews of the church or on the long hot processional walk. Rather, they were relaxing, taking a break, hanging out, essentially doing the same thing as the shrine workers at that time.

In the rectory we see the flip side of the discourse about Haitian devotees at the feast and how that critique and dependence intertwine. Although some shrine workers may reject the "idle" bodies of Haitian devotees outside of the main ritual events of the feast, others understand the feast as critically dependent on the Haitian devotees who visit from other parts of Brooklyn. Anthony captured this idea of dependence when he said, "The Haitians are our only hope." At the feast there are products to be sold and profits to be made. Reflected in this conversation is a concern for numbers: numbers in the form of people to walk on processions and to visit OLMC in the shrine, and numbers in the form of money. Talk of money, spending, and profits in the shrine happens alongside talk of the Haitians: they come, they people the shrine, Masses, and processions, and they spend money on candles and give offerings to the ribbon. There is always a discourse of alterity. Even when some praise Haitians for their generosity and dedication, it comes with a statement about their "different ideas of protocol," language, and assumptions about how they may be poor but are rich in faith and generosity, or conversations about their extraordinary devotion.

Implicit and explicit in these conversations is a declension narrative about the feast. When Anthony counts "three people and the saint" and when shrine workers complain about sparse processions, they are constructing a past where they were not outnumbered but plentiful. When they worry if the Haitians will come to Mass or if the shrine will recoup back its thousands invested in candles, rosaries, and scapulars, they are constructing a declension narrative about a feast past, one with big profits that benefitted the church. When they make statements about the Haitians "putting them to shame," or when they say they are outnumbered, they are constructing a past where their collective devotion as a community and parish was stronger.

One last instance of intra-Catholic boundary making is particularly salient to close with. In 2015 I was working in the shrine when a priest from another parish, dressed in a striped polo and khaki shorts, entered the shrine to greet OLMC's deacon. He looked around and said, "As an Irishman, this all strikes me as very out there," as he raised his arms to indicate all the hubbub. Just a few days later, during the Creole Mass, I sat in the shrine with a volunteer. Talking about the Creole Mass and its music, she too made a comparative statement: "We are Catholics that are very sedated. They are. . . ." She threw up her arms and waved them, indicating exuberance and praise. Gestures did the work of comparison and critique. This juxtaposition speaks to the public devotional performances as historical sites of comparison and spectatorship, sites to articulate ethnically and racially inflected ideas about other Catholics. The priest's statement echoes late nineteenth- and early twentieth-century ideas that Italians exceeded the boundaries of proper Catholic practice. The shrine worker re-echoes these discourses—comparatively constructing Italian American Catholics as sedate, "normal" perhaps, compared to Haitian devotees. In this scene there are layers of self-definition by which Catholics construct what is appropriate practice vis-à-vis a proximate, but also Catholic, ethnic/racial other.

Haitians in the everyday discourse of the feast become something between an imagined population and a real people.[40] In these side comments and conversational critiques, "the Haitians" become a layered trope not only for racial anxieties but also for producing ideas about devotional decorum and a plot point in declension narratives about the feast and parish. The Feast of OLMC offers a site to study the tensions around increasing diversity, lay resistance to multiculturalism, and how discursive and physical boundaries structure interactions between Catholics. Italians and Haitians share Brooklyn's summer streets to express their devotion. But as clerics did in the early twentieth century, defining what was "good" Catholicism vis-à-vis Italian immigrants, in contemporary Williamsburg this kind of comparative project is still at work in the presence of a proximate other with a shared devotion. Especially in a diversifying Church and urban landscape, the concept of Catholic propriety helps us think about intra-Catholic boundary making and the tenacity of racialized discourses of superstition and exclusionary ideas of "good" American Catholic practice. Catholic propriety helps us see how lay Catholics are active in constructing norms and articulating and enforcing "appropriate" practice and how they resist unity, continuing a cycle of critique and exclusion.

6

Religion and Gentrification in the Twenty-First-Century City

In June 2019 the Shrine Church of Our Lady of Mount Carmel made headlines. "An Old Brooklyn Church Seeks New Muscle to Save a Tradition" and "Who Will Save the Tower of Giglio Tradition?" *CBS New York* and the *Wall Street Journal* blared, broadcasting how the church was recruiting new lifters for the giglio in places like gyms, fraternal organizations, and NYPD and FDNY. These places were likely where they would find white ethnic men: "Irish or Polish" men "engaged with their faith."[1] The articles and stories explained, "Through gentrification—or yuppie-a-zation, as some call it—the number of traditional Italian families in the area is dwindling, creating a dearth of able-bodied strongmen and a changing culture."[2] There was collective indignation among parishioners and feast organizers. Text messages and social media were alighted with responses to the news. Their main protest? These stories not only made them seem desperate but also made it seem like they were dying or, worse, dead. Those were the words repeated in critiques of the press: "dying," "desperate," and "dead." A dying tradition meant not just irrelevance and the end of a festival but a gutted church and lost generations. The community promptly issued a response, in a format that has now become classic, a Notes app screenshot, and declared, "Let us be very clear: the feast is here to stay. The feast will go on this year and for many years to come. . . . Our feast has survived world wars, the building of the [Brooklyn-Queens Expressway], and many other good and bad changes in the neighborhood. It will continue to do so for decades into the future." What the press saw as the last-gasp attempt not to be drowned in the demographic and architectural changes of gentrification, they saw as proactive steps that reflected their staunch ethic of survival. The stakes are always life-and-death in talk of the parish and the feast. With the feast it is important to see that practices usually slotted as "popular" or supplemental to "official" and liturgical forms of

Catholicism now do the work of sustaining a parish; we have seen how money is central to ideas of futurity and survival. OLMC is a case study in how the fear of death and desire for survival resonates throughout a community and how men are imagined as those who secure the future of the church.

Increasingly churches are closing throughout North America, especially among mainline congregations and Catholic parishes. In the Northeast and Midwest, Catholic parishes, especially those established by and for white immigrant populations in the nineteenth century, have closed due to declining numbers of parishioners and rates of attendance and affiliation, as well as parish consolidations and a scarcity of priests.[3] Descendants of Polish, German, Irish, and Italian immigrants have increasingly moved out of the cities and into the suburbs. This "urban exodus" and white flight is well represented in the scholarship on Catholic parishes and suburbanization in the United States.[4] According to *America: The Jesuit Review*, over the past four decades the number of parishes has decreased in twenty-five states, including "more than 1,000 in New York and Pennsylvania alone." The landscape of Catholicism is shifting to the South and the West. The question of survival that is ever present in the Northeast and at OLMC mirrors broader trends.[5] On one hand Williamsburg is representative of these national scale changes. On the other the transformations in Williamsburg are much more radical and the persistence of this Italian American Catholic community defies these trends. Looking at the question of parish survival from Williamsburg offers fruitful directions for the study of urban parishes and congregations more broadly. It places architecture, development, and gentrification at the center of threats to the longevity of religious communities. In contemporary cities pastors and parishioners alike worry about new buildings, zoning, and property taxes. When looking to understand city parishes and their seemingly precarious futures, attention to these broader urban realities is as important as discussion of rates of affiliation and Mass attendance.

Throughout the twentieth century the community has had its church buildings demolished; it has weathered the construction of a highway that split the neighborhood in two; and today it exists in an ultra-gentrified neighborhood defined not by ethnic enclaves but by luxury development. In many ways the history of OLMC is a microcosm of the history of development and city planning in New York City. The church has been caught in the crosshairs of modernization and development in Brooklyn since the 1940s when Robert Moses, who was chair of the Committee on Slum Clearance and chairman of the Triborough Bridge and Tunnel Authority, implemented his modern vision of a high-speed interconnected city by building a vast network of highways. The land OLMC stood on was seized by the city, and the church was demolished and rebuilt a few blocks away to make way for the BQE. In 2005 under the tenure of Mayor Michael Bloomberg (2002–13), Williamsburg became the site of the largest rezoning plan in the city's history, encompassing nearly two hundred blocks. As a result, the once industrial neighborhood became some of the most sought-after real estate for luxury building.

Williamsburg captures, in miniature, broader twentieth- and twenty-first-century trends of deindustrialization, urban renewal and the decline of the white ethnic enclave, gentrification and the revitalization of cities, and neoliberal politics. These trends are strikingly readable on its built environment. Williamsburg today is an amalgam of old homes, faux-brick condos (attempting to look organic and contextual), and tall glass towers. Rezoning drastically transformed the real estate landscape of the neighborhood, redefined who could live there, and made the high-value property particularly coveted by developers. In 2000 the median sales price of a home in Williamsburg was $378,344, but by 2014 it was $806,000.[6] The most recent real estate figures, from 2019, put the median sales price for a home at $999,999; census figures put it at $1,005,600.[7] In 2004 average rent was $1,276, but throughout 2019 the average rent for a one-bedroom hovered over $3,000.[8] From 2004 to 2019 the price per square foot in the neighborhood soared from $269 to $1,109.[9] Developers created units for "upper income single or couple" households and invited new educated residents to move into the neighborhood.[10] The feast, with its mobile devotional structures and its fair, rides, and processions, moves through this changed Williamsburg each summer.

Some have likened Williamsburg to another neighborhood that epitomizes dramatic, artist-led gentrification: SoHo—the neighborhood below Houston Street in Lower Manhattan that today is a premier shopping district.[11] The narratives men tell about the neighborhood are both wistful and bitter, which I would argue is the peculiar affect a New Yorker has toward their neighborhood. Nicky, who is now in his seventies, grew up on Roebling Street in a "cold water flat," a house without steam heat, moved out of the neighborhood to Las Vegas after 9/11, but returns each summer to work in the shrine. He too remembered the neighborhood of the past. "When I left, this neighborhood was still intact. . . . It was a good neighborhood. On Saturday the pie people came, bleach people, a truck would come to fix umbrellas, there was a shoe maker around the corner. My mother had a butcher and a regular grocery store. There were no supermarkets in this neighborhood, that is very recent." But now, he said, "On Bedford [Avenue], you can't walk on a Friday, Saturday or Sunday, it's the new SoHo, you can't walk."

By calling Williamsburg the "new SoHo," he fell into a long line of people who have seen urban change as a "three-step process" in which "industry moves out, artists move in, upper-income professionals push artists out," and neighborhoods are transformed into retail playgrounds and crowded corridors, with more places to shop than live.[12] What he did with this comparison was show how Williamsburg went from scorned and marginal to coveted: "I could never as a teen get a taxi to take me to Williamsburg. Before I had to sit in the cab and refuse to pay. From Roebling [Street] to Kent [Avenue] they refused to stop. I never said I was from Williamsburg, I always said Greenpoint or the Metropolitan Area."

New millennial Brooklyn residents, who moved to New York City from places like Florida, Texas, Michigan, and Upstate New York, describe Williamsburg as "claustrophobic" with people, stores, and restaurants, bursting at the seams in a neighborhood never designed to be a shopping corridor. Another described it to me as "Instagram IRL [in real life]": aesthetically consumable and "a safe space for tourists to get a manufactured Brooklyn experience." Even as they acknowledge they are "part of the problem" of gentrification, they still know Williamsburg has choice dive bars.[13] Williamsburg's cityscape and its residents changed around OLMC in a matter of years, and the church is now hedged in by new buildings and construction sites. Yet the parish remains tenacious.

For some gentrification requires a simple definition: the transformation of working-class, industrial areas, or even a "vacant" part of a city into a hub of middle-class consumption and residence.[14] Surely this fits in the case of Williamsburg, as it went from a manufacturing area to a playground of leisure. For others, gentrification refers to the economic, social, and cultural process by which "private capital and individual homeowners and renters reinvest in fiscally neglected neighborhoods."[15] As artists and creatives rehabilitate factories, homes, and lofts, they gradually transform a neighborhood, making it more "hospitable" to retail and investment. Often a neighborhood becomes more "investable" and "desirable" as longtime residents, often people of color, and poor or working-class communities are displaced. This process can also be understood as a retaliative taking back of areas abandoned in white flight or a retaking of the city by the elite.[16] Where there was once white flight from Brooklyn, there is now white flock *to* Brooklyn.

The state too has had a hand in gentrification through rezoning and urban planning. While gentrification can be piecemeal, occurring one loft or converted factory at a time, in New York especially it has become state policy, as government officials created and put into effect a comprehensive "luxury vision" for New York City. This vision would not only change the cityscape but make the city competitive on national and global scales.[17] Some term this "hyper-gentrification": not a gradual process driven by a search for affordability on the part of the "creative class," but the aggressive work of developers and corporations that influence neighborhood rezoning on a mass scale.[18] In the lifetimes of many of the young men in this book, Williamsburg has experienced these stages or waves of gentrification: from artist bohemia to premier site for luxury condos and hotels.[19]

While it is easy to see issues of race and class most brightly when looking at the outcomes of gentrification—the processes of displacement, public policies antagonistic toward the urban poor, the effects of soaring real estate prices on working-class communities, and the decline of manufacturing—bringing religion into discussions of gentrification also highlights the gendered logics of gentrification and the gendered logics by which communities work to secure their survival in a city increasingly built for leisure, tourism, and the creative class. The giglio is an assertion of a particular kind of masculine history of Williamsburg; it remembers and reenacts a neighborhood that was not a destination or landscape built for boutiques and cafés. The gentrified landscape is a feminized landscape: sanitized, safer, more hospitable to consumption and thus frivolity. White newcomers, of all genders, who are seemingly more concerned with eating and shopping than family and faith are feminized in these logics. While there are masculinities to be analyzed in the spaces of real estate investment and development, the giglio offers a spectacle of a white ethnic masculinity imagined to be collectively efficacious, hardy, and authentic.

When success is correlated with the number of strong male bodies lifting the giglio, it imagines that strong men can resist the macro, structural processes of gentrification. As one organizer said, "The health of this feast is based on how many lifters we have. . . . Like a business: a business looks at net profit or whatever, and we have to look at how many lifters we have. If we have our permits and lifters we have health." Gentrification hastened and rose from deindustrialization, in its both state-led and more sporadic forms, a process destabilizing to white American men.[20] The narratives at the feast, and the rituals and spaces it provides, empower men to recapitulate and enshrine a Williamsburg that no longer exists. It provides a place where men are not the victims of structural, economic changes and places men at the very center of survival. Through their efforts they help their church live and preserve (no matter how momentarily) the ethnic history and character of this corner of Williamsburg.

What is missing from narratives about public policy, planning, and gentrification in Brooklyn is religion. Religious actors are strikingly absent from discussions of gentrification and urbanism.[21] Urbanists seldom explore the persistent nature of religious institutions and practices in the built environment of gentrified neighborhoods. The works that do explore religion and gentrification see gentrification and development as responding to and hastening secularization and work with a circumscribed definition of religion as what happens within church buildings. They focus largely on the closing/sale/redevelopment of religious buildings and correlate that with decline in belief.[22] As Williamsburg transformed from a working-class enclave and industrial landscape to a haven for artists and alternatives and to a site of government and developer-led hyper-gentrification, it became a cool place to shop and drink and a luxury place to live, all while remaining a place important for Italian American Catholics. In exploring how New York City became a destination rather than a place of origins, and in casting tight-knit religious and ethnic communities (urban villagers à la Herbert Gans) as a thing of the past, irrelevant in the neoliberal city, scholars simultaneously perpetuate that idea of New York. These frameworks often erase the very ways people from places like Brooklyn hold on to their neighborhood identities, their churches, and their ethnic identities in spite of and in conversation with larger trends of urban redevelopment and gentrification. While many often think of urban renewal and gentrification as processes that destroy social networks and communities, placing a religious institution like a Catholic parish at the center of inquiry complicates those processes. While parishes have indeed closed in Williamsburg because of white flight and declining rates of participation, OLMC has survived.

"Disrupting" Neighbors and Surviving Urban Renewal

Brooklyn, traditionally known as the borough of churches for its many steeples contrasting its low-rise industrial and residential buildings, is increasingly seeing churches converted into condominiums. One of those churches was the Church of Saint Vincent de Paul at 163 North Sixth Street, just a few blocks away from OLMC. In December 2011 it was sold to developers for a staggering $13.7 million.[23] What once may have been home to a duplex parish, where Italians worshipped in the basement before they had a church of their own, is now the Spire Lofts, full of duplexes that house wealthy entrepreneurs and start-up founders—the talent Mayor Bloomberg's zoning sought to attract. These new developments boasted of salvaged wood, vaulted ceilings, and "condos blessed with stained glass windows." In the former Saint Vincent de Paul, for rents ranging from $4,625 to $6,800, residents can "live on hallowed ground."[24] Many other churches in Brooklyn have met the same fate of becoming "stunning lofts": their pews carted out so that young professionals can glide in to buildings with cheeky names like The Abbey and The Sanctuary. This kind of development represents the latest stage of neighborhood change. But far before OLMC was threatened by luxury condos, it was a populous ethnic parish threatened by the highways of urban renewal. Throughout the twentieth century and into the twenty-first there is a longer history of urban policies that were antagonistic to this church's survival—those very conditions shaped a community committed to thriving in this section of Williamsburg.

The Church of Our Lady of Mount Carmel was established in 1887 by Father Peter Saponara (1846–1926) as the first Italian national parish in the neighborhood. Before Brooklyn was annexed to the City of New York in 1898, Williamsburg had been annexed by the City of Brooklyn in 1855 and, along with Greenpoint and Bushwick, became part of Brooklyn's Eastern District.[25] It was characterized by journalists as one of the "lowliest districts": "dark," poor, crime-ridden, where Italians lived "isolated from their English speaking neighbors."[26] It was composed mostly of Italian immigrants who owned businesses like fruit stands and barbershops and were "sadly destitute of church conveniences."[27] Estimates put the number of Italians in this part of the Eastern District at two to four thousand, and this large population had no church to call their own.[28] According to one source, Italians in the neighborhood worshipped in an Episcopal church on North Fifth Street before the arrival of the pioneering Saponara.[29]

The story of OLMC, like that of many other Italian parishes, begins in the dearth of space that Italian immigrants could call home in the diocese. Italians, without churches of their own, were relegated to the subterranean spaces of German and Irish parishes, termed basement churches or "duplex parishes" by scholars.[30] Before they had a church of their own, Saponara gathered with Italians in the basement of Saint Vincent de Paul Church on North Sixth Street and in the Church of the Annunciation, the Lithuanian parish on Havemeyer Street, as well as Most Holy Trinity Church on Montrose Avenue, the first German parish in the diocese.[31] In a very New York death, after serving OLMC for thirty-nine years, Peter Saponara fell ill and dropped dead in the middle of Grand Central Station in 1926.[32]

As the number of Italian Catholics soared and communicants swelled to over fifteen thousand by 1912, the parish needed a new church. The original 1887 building on North Eighth Street and Union Avenue, painted to look like brick, was replaced by a grand Romanesque building. It was the pride of parishioners as they fundraised for the construction. The majestic building, completed in 1930, was set back from the sidewalk with a plaza reminiscent of those in Italy. It had a hundred-foot-tall campanile and thickly hooded arched windows and stained glass.[33] Lewis Mumford, esteemed architecture critic for the *New Yorker*, called the design a most "interesting piece of eclectic architecture." It could seat over a thousand people.[34] Parishioners would have looked upon a twenty-two-foot-tall Italian Renaissance–style fresco of Saint Simon being bestowed the brown scapular. Sometimes art deco fabric and a plaster altar backdrop obscured the fresco, giving it the gilded feel of an ornate theater, a theater in which saints looked down on you from above. All of the pride the parishioners took in their new beautiful edifice must have made the coming blow even harder to bear.

As early as 1929, as the grand new Our Lady of Mount Carmel Church was being built, the city was considering building a highway that would run right through its land.[35] By 1945 an engineer was warning the diocese that "the City is progressing the improvement very fast and I am afraid that our friend, Commissioner Moses, is going to try and have the City take title to the property."[36] In 1948 demolitions began in Williamsburg in preparation for the construction of the elevated highway that would run along Meeker Avenue. When the city seized the land, the beloved Romanesque church was torn down, not even twenty years after it was built. In its place was part of the Brooklyn-Queens Expressway, a six-lane highway that would aid industry and business by shortening transportation times.[37] Moses's $137 million 11.7-mile highway bisected Williamsburg. According to Nicole Marwell, "The structure slashed through the heart of the neighborhood, destroying the vibrant business district on Broadway and bisecting the cohesive community of Orthodox Jews, Italians, Poles, Slavs, and Russians."[38]

While affluent neighborhoods like Brooklyn Heights were able to fight plans to run the expressway through the neighborhood to prevent the destruction of historic brownstones (resulting in the cantilevered expressway under the Brooklyn Promenade), in Williamsburg residents and parishioners could not resist the construction.[39] After its building was dismantled, the parish relocated to North Eighth and Havemeyer streets. Its new building, a practical orange brick structure with a school, gym, and bowling alley, did not match the splendor of the demolished church. The dismantling of the majestic new edifice seldom shows up in any accounts of the creation of the BQE and Moses's impact on the landscape of Brooklyn. While the community cycled through three buildings and experienced the upheaval of urban renewal, the feast remained a mainstay on the church calendar.

Today the 133-year-old parish of OLMC, albeit in a different building, and the 117-year-old tradition of the feast chafe against a new landscape. New residents make calls to the rectory and to 311—the city's hotline— and take to social media with their complaints. The feast may exist to the chagrin of the new condo dwellers but enjoys municipal favor and the cooperation of the mayor's office, NYPD, and FDNY. But that was not always the case. The feast of the past chafed against local standards of propriety and infuriated residents and church and city officials alike.

In 1908 the *Brooklyn Daily Eagle* published an article that proclaimed, "Priests Unite to Stop Religious Fireworks/Italian Saint-Days, with Red Fire on Streets, Are Not Favored." It described a movement to stop the excesses of feast day celebrations among the Italians of Brooklyn, with pastors from twenty-seven parishes signing it, including the pastor of OLMC, Peter Saponara. They argued that street celebrations and displays like fireworks, street shrines, altars, and the stringing of lights were a "burlesque of the spiritual side of religion" and not in "accord with the liturgical instruction of the Church." These "flagrant abuses [were] perpetuated in all the Italian colonies under the semblance of religion." The priests pledged, in the interest of "true religion, morality and the peace and security of the community," not to help anyone get permits for fireworks, musical bands, lights, or altars. Not only were they perverting "true religion," with practices "entirely alien to the true spirit of Catholicism," but they were also a general annoyance.[40] A South Brooklyn resident wrote in to the newspaper and called for an end to the "abominable nuisance" that are Italian celebrations, a law "prohibiting these people from annoying a whole neighborhood" and pleaded with the paper, "Anything you can do for a suffering people will be greatly appreciated." The letter was signed TAXPAYER.[41]

Throughout the city the Bureau of Combustibles, the police department, and the Church were frenzied about curbing the use of fireworks in Italian celebrations, citing loss of life and limbs. In 1906 letters to the editor appeared in the *Brooklyn Daily Eagle* complaining about the "medieval barbarous nuisance" of the celebrations and their fireworks; they called the displays "senseless nightly bang-bang-bangs," nerve-racking, and "silly and unnecessary."[42] In 1907, in a strikingly long article, the paper reported that the fireworks at a saints' day in South Brooklyn disrupted the circus animals that were in town, especially terrifying a two-thousand-pound baby elephant named Toby. Toby would not perform and became aggressive with his handlers because an Italian community nearby was "honoring some saint" with music and the "whiz of rockets." That same year the Bureau of Combustibles and the fire marshal cut down the period during which fireworks could be sold to two weeks at the end of June and made their explosion illegal without permits in order to stem this "custom in vogue in Italian quarters."[43] In 1902 there was a riot at the Feast of Our Lady of Mount Carmel when police charged a crowd, clubbing attendees with their nightsticks. When Captain Short, from the Bedford Avenue Police Station, notified celebrants that they could not use fireworks or gas pipe bombs unless they displayed a permit, some defied these orders. At nine o'clock they exploded fireworks and a fight ensued between Italians and the police.[44] This was not the first violent encounter on a saint's feast day.[45] The *New York Tribune* wrote that in 1888 there was a "small riot at the Church of Our Lady of Mount Carmel where two police officers were wounded with stilettos."[46]

These incidents offer early evidence of how the feast and saints' celebrations chafed against clerical notions of devotion and were understood as "disruptions" in the neighborhood. The parish hosted the Feast of Our Lady of Mount Carmel, but its celebratory landscape, lights, pyrotechnic displays, and music exceeded municipal and Church expectations of order. In the 1950s, after locating to its new building, the community defiantly celebrated its feast and used it as an opportunity to fundraise to build its school. Acrobatic daredevils performed high-pole balancing acts on the roof of the church, 125 feet above the ground, a big bazaar filled the church yard, and people danced in the streets.[47]

Today, the parish's robust street feast, with its days of music, carnival rides, food, and noisy processions, clashes with a revamped Williamsburg and its new residents. Italian American Catholics who were once residents of Williamsburg now live in Queens, Long Island, and Staten Island—but they return to the neighborhood for meetings, Masses, and the feast. Some still do live in the neighborhood, proud to call 11211 their zip code. At the feast people buy bumper stickers that say, "No matter my address, my heart lives in Williamsburg." Yet this is not a story of the death of a tradition or the death of a community.

Figure 6.1. The statue of Our Lady of Mount Carmel under a canopy and dense crowd of onlookers and devotees, circa 1939. Photo courtesy of OLMC Archives.

This is not about the romance and tensions of ethnic enclaves, a history that is already well told.[48] At OLMC pastors and parishioners alike often say the feast is the reason the church was rebuilt, attributing parish survival to devotional tradition. In the words of one former pastor, "The feast is the heart and the soul of this parish; not only does it keep it going financially, but it really defines what Our Lady of Mount Carmel is as a community." The feast is often synecdoche with men: lifters, the men who command the giglio, the men who build and paint the giglio, the men who fundraise and seek sponsors and donors, and the men who carry and tow the saints in procession. The feast helps the parish achieve financial stability, attract and retain new generations of Catholics, and stay relevant in Brooklyn's changing landscape.

Gentrification in Williamsburg

In a city and neighborhood rebranded by government officials hoping to attract investment, business, and talent, new young white residents in search of urban authenticity and retail and brands who commodify the very idea of New York, the church has the option to mourn a changed neighborhood and watch itself die or to rebrand itself and reinvigorate its members. In my time at OLMC parish leadership took both those roads. One pastor consistently elegized the neighborhood and pointed to bike lanes, parking garages, and condos as harbingers of destruction. Narratives of an encroaching built environment plus an institution financially languishing bred hopelessness and fear at OLMC. They strategized ways to maintain their community and devotional traditions. In a neighborhood where an infusion of real estate capital completely transformed its architecture over a decade, its remaining parishes too need to focus on the bottom line. As this parish was caught in the destruction of urban renewal, it was also caught in the throes of two different waves of gentrification in Williamsburg.

In June 1992 *New York Magazine*'s cover featured an alluring nighttime scene. A group of friends gathered at an outdoor table, eating and drinking by streetlight. Behind them, behemoth against the night sky, was the Williamsburg Bridge, its geometry in silhouette. "The New Bohemia: Over the Bridge to Williamsburg" it read. When it opened in 1903, linking Brooklyn and the Lower East Side of Manhattan, the bridge brought Jewish, Italian, Irish, and Eastern European immigrants into Brooklyn from Manhattan's "slums." It was a gateway to new jobs then and allowed for the formation of ethnic enclaves in the different parts of the neighborhood. In the 1990s it represented a gateway to speakeasies, secret parties, and Polish taverns. It was imagined as an industrial playground, an escape from already gentrified neighborhoods like SoHo and the East Village. In imagining Williamsburg as a place frozen in time, with its factories and working-class grit, the so-called bohemians constructed it as more *interesting* than Manhattan.[49]

An interior spread depicted a muscular artist wearing only cutoff denim shorts and work boots, painting a huge abstract canvas in the open air, behind him a defunct pier. The Manhattan skyscrapers in the distance were a mere backdrop, decentered in this vision of an artistic oasis across the river. One poet described Williamsburg as "the land that time forgot."[50] New residents, who lived in converted lofts, loved its "spooky" waterfront with its terrain of factories and "barren, overrun, industrial qualities." They frequented warehouse parties and art galleries that began opening in the neighborhood starting in 1987, a time when it was the only neighborhood experiencing net gains in manufacturing jobs. Williamsburg had the romance and grit they desired.[51] They rented two-bedroom apartments, overlooking the river and the Twin Towers, for $425 to $450 and imagined themselves more subcultural than "Manhattanites."[52]

Throughout its history Williamsburg had been the site of manufacturing plants for furniture, mustard, spices, buttons, sugar, beer, tortillas, and garments.[53] Until the mid-2000s, it was one of two of the most industrial neighborhoods in New York City, with 56 percent of its land zoned for manufacturing. Williamsburg seemed a postindustrial playground even before industry had really died there. Geographers have argued the city's policy makers, responding to the influx of artists, the gentrification of the neighborhood, and the desire to brand New York as a luxury city, created rezoning initiatives and policies that neglected and "actively contributed" to the decline of manufacturing in the neighborhood, in favor of the development of luxury condominiums.[54]

Market-led gentrification, led by artists and creatives, primed the neighborhood for state-led gentrification, and Williamsburg went from bohemian to the "epicenter of cool."[55] Urban sociologist Sharon Zukin has argued that Williamsburg is the neighborhood that made Brooklyn cool. In a formulaic way, a working-class ethnic neighborhood rife with factories becomes a playground of cultural consumption, boutiques, and then chain stores, first through the influx of artists, creatives, and cultural entrepreneurs who transform derelict buildings and manufacturing spaces into lofts and galleries. This kind of gentrification happened in the "absence of investment by either the private sector developers or [the] government."[56]

As the city struggled financially in the 1960s and 1970s, it shut down its port and closed the Brooklyn Navy Yard, which impacted factories in the borough.[57] The city, on the brink of bankruptcy, suffered a fiscal crisis in 1975 that led to disinvestment, a "withdrawal of public services," and layoffs of public employees that threatened municipal unions and led to cutbacks in funding of education and transportation.[58] The city government supported initiatives to grow finance, insurance, and real estate sectors, quickening deindustrialization in the borough.[59] That same year the city declared the peak of white flight, using the language of a crisis to describe the demographic changes. New York City commissioner of human rights Eleanor Holmes Norton "publicly predicted a 'Dim Future for City if White Exodus Continues'" in the *Daily News*, citing statistics that between 1970 and 1973 the city had lost four hundred thousand white residents, an 8.3 percent decrease. Coterminous with this "exodus" were even larger increases in the Black and Latino populations of the city.[60] But in areas like Greenpoint-Williamsburg, areas that were Polish, Italian, and Jewish, residents limited access to housing, and used surveillance and segregated religious institutions, like national/white ethnic parishes as "informal strategies to resist the growth of neighbors of color." According to urban sociologists Jerome Krase and Judith DeSena, for Greenpoint and parts of Williamsburg, "these tactics were successful and maintained largely white, working class communities."[61]

When artists moved to Williamsburg in the 1980s and 1990s, they began to transform its cultural landscape and cachet and its retail landscape. According to Zukin, "Growth in new entrepreneurial retail activity surged after 1995, with an increase in 'creative' residents and an accompanying increase in media reviews of the area's new restaurants, art galleries, and bars."[62] This entrepreneurialism, which results in new cafés, boutiques, and specialty retail, is a process that has been called "boutiquing," a feature of postindustrial change in which local retail shops that serve residents' needs (butchers, bodegas, hardware stores, etc.) are replaced by stores offering niche goods for more "mobile clientele," often due to rising rents.[63] This was the Williamsburg writers dubbed bohemian.

But "bohemian" as a category surely does not have purchase for the millennials, young professionals, and tourists who occupy Williamsburg's streets today. The neighborhood is now home to media companies, start-ups, and design firms and is perhaps more synonymous with "innovation" than with art.[64] Williamsburg, like other sites that were once "outposts of difference," like Saint Marks Place in Manhattan's East Village, recently got its own brand-new office building, a huge new complex that spans an entire square block. At 25 Kent, the developer promises rooftop decks and terraces and an "old-world charm": "red brick masonry meets blackened steel for an industrial aesthetic." In what seems almost like a caricature of development lingo, the building itself promises to breed innovation, offering "15-foot ceilings so you can keep thinking big" and "Every Amenity Imaginable," even lockers and showers. A corporate dream, Williamsburg is now marketed as the perfect live-work-play terrain for today's "thinkers, makers, and doers."[65] The label Bohemian, with its DIY quality and its chic Euro-allure, is largely irrelevant as a descriptor for today's Williamsburg, a luxury-cool neighborhood that is much more business than bohemia.

The urban imaginary changed when Michael Bloomberg was elected mayor of New York. In his three terms from 2002 to 2013, Bloomberg effectively led a campaign to rebrand New York as a "magnet for people with dreams."[66] He argued that more so than any place on earth, New York has been a place where people have found celebrity, success, and prestige. New York was rebranded as a hub for cosmopolitanism, a global center of commerce, diversity, and innovation.[67] This was not a gritty New York or artsy New York; this was New York: the center of global flows of capital, investment, and people.

Urbanists have placed Bloomberg on par with Robert Moses as an urban visionary, whose "grand, sweeping imagining of New York City" had profound effects on its built environment and policy that privileged postindustrial elites over the middle and working classes.[68] For Moses, to create was also to destroy, and neighborhoods marked as slums, unfit for a new modern city, were razed for the construction of these large-scale projects.[69] Bloomberg's vision of the city was translated into development policy that favored large-scale rezoning efforts, the creation of luxury and high-quality housing, recreational amenities like parks, and the development of waterfront areas.[70] Urbanists knew the 2005 plan would remake Brooklyn's skyline and transform the scale of the neighborhood. Jane Jacobs, an activist and urbanist who adamantly and successfully opposed Robert Moses's urban renewal policies, critiqued the "destructive consequences, packaged very sneakily with visually tiresome, unimaginative and imitative luxury project towers" of the mayor's plan. She pleaded with the City Council and the administration to respect the community's proposals, but the 2005 zoning plan ignored these plans to preserve Williamsburg's "low density, mixed income, and mixed-use character."[71]

The once industrial and then bohemian neighborhood became some of the most sought-after real estate for luxury building. Far from the decaying and burning city of the 1970s, New York in the 2000s experienced a construction boom that especially catered to those who could afford to live in gleaming waterfront condominiums and those with middle-class or alternative consumer tastes.[72] Often, those moving into these new developments and gentrified neighborhoods were not New York natives. Increasingly under Mayor Bloomberg, New York was represented as a "place of arrival," "a place one comes to, rather than a place where one is born and raised." Brooklyn especially has become the ultimate "place people come *to*, not a place they come *from*," because it has been developed and marketed to feel uniquely authentic: historically rich, diverse, and gritty in aesthetic and consumable ways.[73] In a city that is only 43 to 46 percent white, Williamsburg is far more homogenous at 74 percent white, with a population that is younger and more educated than that of the city as a whole.[74] While those who are young, white, and college educated may not yet be able to afford the luxury condos going up in Brooklyn, they do find neighborhoods that seem to be "outposts of difference" and places that cater to their alternative consumption practices: whether that be trendy restaurants, vintage clothing, dive bars and concert venues, or cafés that offer oat milk.[75]

I first met Williamsburg as a teenager. My friends and I would hop on the L train at Manhattan's Union Square and get off at Bedford Avenue, the central retail corridor in Williamsburg. For us, even as New Yorkers, Williamsburg was a destination, a place to get vegan ice cream, to visit the Salvation Army to buy plaid miniskirts and satin pumps from the 1980s and vintage boots that would ruin our feet. In the mid-2000s, right before the zoning plan really started to transform the built environment, Williamsburg still seemed like a wasteland between vintage shops. To me, through teenage eyes, Williamsburg was aspirational, the terrain of cool guys in leather jackets and girls with baby bangs. I was a mid-aughts mourner when a tiny vegan bakery on Bedford Avenue shut down—I actually shed tears. I was but one person in a long line of people who mourned the changes to these Brooklyn streets, even though I technically was not from them.

In Williamsburg bars, making small talk over retro beers, it is rare to meet anyone who is born in New York City. I can attest to being the odd one out when I say I was born and raised in the city. People from Oklahoma and the United Kingdom alike have told me, "That's so weird!" These are exactly the people the parish has worried about. In 2014 a priest lamented, "The people living in the neighborhood, their parents, grandparents, great-grandparents are in Kentucky, France, Sweden, Norway, and now they're in Brooklyn. . . . People coming from Kentucky, Europe, and Vermont, need brochures, they don't know the artistry or the decades of history that the giglio represents."

The Neighborhood's Prophets of Doom

On July 16, 2015, I stood outside the church with the pastor, Monsignor Calise, as he inspected the orange brick on the side of the building. Shaking his head, he said, "This building was not meant to last. Everyone around here is biting the dust and we are still here." Parishioners and pastors alike tell a story about the church as one that defied the odds and survived even as the neighborhood changed around them, and they cite the feast as its mechanism of survival.

In 1945, when the diocese learned that the city was seizing the land where the Church of Our Lady of Mount Carmel sat, there were proposals to liquidate the parish rather than relocate it and to allow the other Italian national and territorial parishes in the vicinity to absorb OLMC's parishioners. There was the idea to relocate it north of Meeker Avenue, but it would impinge on Saint Francis of Paola, another Italian national parish that opened in the adjacent neighborhood of Greenpoint in 1918. Another suggestion was for it to combine with Saint Francis of Paola and still adequately serve the Italian population. Another idea was that the other parishes in Williamsburg, including the Lithuanian parish, Annunciation, and the territorial parishes in the neighborhood like Saint Vincent de Paul on North Sixth Street, could "absorb the present generation of Italians" and the diocese could place Italian-speaking priests in these parishes "to take care of the older people [and] overcome a practical criticism which could be made of this arrangement."[76] Although there is no evidence in the archive that the diocese chose to rebuild OLMC because of the feast, today, and perhaps ironically, Saint Vincent de Paul no longer exists, and Annunciation of the Blessed Virgin Mary merged with OLMC. What Calise said rings very true; everyone really was biting the dust, and OLMC was the survivor in a changed Williamsburg.

When I first met Monsignor Calise, pastor of OLMC from 2008 to 2016, he was wearing shorts and a polo shirt. He is a lanky, smiling man, who was welcoming when I explained that I wanted to write about the feast. Monsignor Calise loves "money bag" pasta from Patrizia's in South Williamsburg. One day we shared dinner in the rectory and he generously encouraged me to fill my plate from Tupperware brimming with homemade biscotti, spicy eggplant, and baked ziti. He was passionate about Alcoholics Anonymous ministry. He practiced deadpan humor, liked to play pranks, and was always quick to offer donuts, ice cream, and snacks during the late feast nights in the rectory. During processions he carried around a silver bucket and little orbed scepter (an aspersorium and aspergillum), which he would fill with holy water for blessings. His blessings were not a delicate sprinkle but a playful and mischievous soaking. One day as we stood outside in the rain, Monsignor Calise laughed joyfully as he soaked me with holy water, splashing it across my face and hair. Sometimes Monsignor Calise was bright and playful, and other times, especially in feast meetings, he looked weary. At that very first feast meeting I attended in 2014, Monsignor Calise looked at the body of men gathered and told them, "The feast is a lot more than money, without the feast, the parish would not survive another two years."

Monsignor Calise did not present a hopeful future to the men who gathered at the meetings in the lower hall. Feast meetings were about the minutiae of planning a devotional event; in his addresses to the body of feast organizers, Monsignor Calise too talked about minutiae of the more urban sort. He used his platform at meetings to talk about changes to Williamsburg's built environment, new features of the neighborhood that he interpreted as threatening the feast. At one meeting in March 2015, Calise looked fatigued; he wore his coat through the meeting and tried to quell an argument between the men that was taking place over a proposed fundraiser. Calise encouraged honesty and communication and told everyone they should not be wasting efforts fighting among each other when a bigger threat loomed outside the doors of the church. "The ultimate goal is a successful feast. My main concern is if you go up to the roof and look out in every direction you see more construction. Look up and down, more trees, more stop signs. . . . It's not a changing neighborhood, it's a changed neighborhood." At the next meeting he sat slumped at the table in the front of the room and documented the changes right outside the doors that might impact the permits the city gives for street closures around the church.

> This year's theme is creativity. As we look around us there are more changes. [Houses] are no longer going to be there . . . There is a lot more going on on Havemeyer, and we have to keep our eyes and ears open so that we could be more creative. It might be harder in the future to get permits for the cross street and side streets. Now the Metropolitan Avenue Bridge is going to be closed some nights, and that is going to be a traffic nightmare. In the future there may be more limited permits. . . . We need more creative use of space.
>
> We are going to have to do more, and invite more people, with less space. It is going to command lots of thinking outside of "this is how it's always been done." Where there used to be houses with one-car driveways, there are now parking garages that can't stay closed for eleven straight nights. We are going to have to adapt so that we don't lose the essence of the feast. So this year's catchwords are creativity and cooperation.

He was tired of hearing people complain about how the feast had changed; he insisted that they could not look to the past and how things used to be but must look to the future. They needed to open up and invite Williamsburg's new residents to participate and compromise for the survival of their tradition. "The changes have already started taking place and will affect the longevity of the church if we don't think outside the box of what is feasible. If we do, there will be many more years of the feast; if we don't we are committing suicide." His pronouncements did not go over well with all the men gathered every week. After the meeting they grumbled, "He makes me want to kill myself," and "Yes, His Happiness. So doom and gloom. Me and San Paolino are going to take a swan dive off the giglio."

While Calise saw outreach and neighborhood relations as a priority, others saw the challenge of instilling a love for the feast in subsequent generations as their most important obstacle. Their narratives of change and decline center on the dwindling numbers of children and lifters who participate in the feast. When I asked John, a feast organizer, about neighborhood change and whether he saw it as a threat to the feast, he shrugged it off. He said that they have to approach the feast with a "concern for preservation" and articulated another declension narrative: "Naysayers have said the feast will close for the past twenty years: you'll lift the giglio on a Sunday and that's it. In 2014, the streets are still packed, and we are still offering a product. We still have the feast going strong. Passing it down to the next generation is the biggest risk. This used to be a breeding ground for kids, now they're not involved. I don't know if my kid will want this. I saw the old-timers—they raised me. I grew up inside this church. Will it be instinctually instilled?"

In 2016 a son of the parish, Deacon Philip Franco, stood before the packed sanctuary to deliver his Giglio Sunday homily and articulated the community's ethic of survival. He knew the weight of this responsibility as he was the first deacon in the history of the feast to preach this homily and one of the only men baptized at OLMC to preach there. In his characteristic way he cracked jokes about his stature and needing a milk crate to see over the podium and treated his opening remarks as a stand-up routine. Although he seemed to have a lightness that comes with the familiarity of being home, I know Phil was nervous about this grand honor. Phil told the people gathered that day that they needed to "ring the bells" and persistently broadcast their love for the church and the feast and invite people no matter what changed around them. Quoting Saint Pope John XXIII, he cautioned, "We must disagree with the prophets of gloom who are always forecasting disaster as though the end of the world were at hand." In his homily Phil traced the history of Italians in Williamsburg and told a story of endurance: "Today, they're not knocking down buildings with the BQE, they are putting them up. We've got buildings going up all over the place. But they could build condos to the sky, they'll never be bigger than this feast. They'll never be bigger than this parish. . . . Together we have survived, and together we will survive."

Lifeblood of the Parish

As I said earlier this community is intransigent, resistant even, in the face of gentrification. They negotiate neighborhood change in public rituals, but also in religious narratives and storytelling. From the pulpit, members of this Italian American community, whether they reside locally or not, are reminded that they are the past and will be the future of this church and the neighborhood. Whereas news articles and histories alike render them increasingly irrelevant, they staunchly insist their community is not dying but remains vital because the feast is the "lifeblood of the parish," a refrain Calise and others often used.

Lifeblood is the substance and vital force that helps something live. It is what ensures sustainability and resilience. The metaphor of lifeblood is essentially a biological one, helping frame something as if it were a living thing: a body that lives and survives and dies. Lifeblood is what helps keep a metaphorical organism, be it a community or a tradition, *alive*. Blood has historically had many valences and symbolic meanings. Most literally, blood courses through the body. In the Middle Ages the idea and discourse of blood became a way of organizing "kin-based identities," an idea that helped those identities transcend the ephemerality of life and death.[77] Blood became a symbolic way to reify hierarchies and social organization and legitimate access to power. Tracing agnatic blood lines, agnatic being that which flows from a king, monarch, or other single point of male power, was a means of tracing connections to male ancestors through male lines. Blood connected generations and organized "privileges, obligations, and rights."[78]

In the nineteenth century the idea of blood was meaningful on a new scale in the political imaginary for thinking about nation, race, and ethnicity, but still maintained its connections to ideas about bilateral kinship extending from a mother and father. Later, in the early twentieth century, with its discourse of genetics, heredity, and evolutionary biology, and in eugenic projects about race and nation, "the assumption continued that blood confers an unchanging identity, based in nature and essential to the definition of self."[79] Descent, survival, identity, inherited traits, male lineage, succession, and power are all encoded in the symbol and discourse of blood.

People at the feast, especially in recounting the strength and insolubility of their ties to the church and the tradition, often use the language of blood. "It's in my blood" is a common refrain. They use the language of blood when they talk about their hopes that their children keep up the tradition. Blood is not only the language of succession and genetics but also a biological language of insularity. Imagining the parish as belonging to those who are bound to it by blood also is a hope for it to remain Italian American, not ceding to effete newcomers or allowing the tradition to be taken over by racial others. In employing the metaphor of the lifeblood of the parish, I am using Monsignor Calise's words as a lens to think about what this community, amid change, understands as most important to its parish and tradition. For some space and territory threaten the community. In documenting and indexing those changes parishioners and pastors assert that adaptation to a new Williamsburg is essential to survival. Others see it differently. Rather than being concerned with what lies beyond the walls of the parish, they are concerned with bringing children, and especially young men, into the fold so that they may love and perpetuate the feast. For some what matter most are generational ties and family and passing on a persistent devotion to the saints.

But blood has yet another valence. According to Caroline Walker Bynum, in the fifteenth century there were debates about whether or not blood was the core of human nature. Despite crucifixion not being a particularly bloody death, devotional images of Christ became "increasingly bloody," especially in late medieval northern Germany.[80] Droplets and swollen globules sprung forth from his wounds as paintings and statues became "awash in blood." New devotions to Christ's wounded heart and side wound became increasingly popular, as devotees looked upon images and meditated on each fleck of blood using them to "calculate the prayers they owed for their own sins or those of their loved ones suffering in purgatory."[81] Mystics bled from their mouths after taking communion. In this period between the thirteenth and fifteenth centuries there was a "frenzy" for "blood piety." Miraculous hosts also bled and pilgrims flocked to visit the stained and hemorrhaging relics; they were indestructible, surviving fire and disaster. Theologians debated if Christ left any bodily matter behind, fingernails, hair, blood drops, or if it was all assumed, his body incorruptible and whole in heaven. Franciscans and Dominicans debated the vitality of blood. According to Franciscans blood was a sign of the death of Christ; on the other hand, Dominicans considered blood to be alive, "shed yet living."[82] According to Bynum, "However counterintuitive it may seem, the eruption of blood was a miracle announcing the indestructibility of God."[83]

Blood was a sign of presence and vitality; even separated from Christ's body it was still alive and present. Bynum sums up this paradox at the center of blood devotion beautifully when she writes, "Red and pulsating while poured out and left behind, blood could signal both Christ dying and Christ alive. . . . The dense web of blood symbolism may be summarized by saying that, in it, blood is life and death, continuity and separation, immutability and violation."[84] This is all to say that in the Catholic tradition, relevant now and in the Middle Ages, discourses and symbols of blood pointed to the paradox of change and changelessness, corruptibility and continuity. I hear echoes of this theology in twenty-first-century Brooklyn, in priests' words "the more things change, the more they remain the same" and "everyone around us is biting the dust and we are still here." The feast community is a community fragmented, not territorially bound but still paradoxically whole. Williamsburg changes, and yet much of the feast remains the same. The feast, as the lifeblood of the parish, also resists decomposition: decomposition of the sort imposed by neighborhood change. To call the feast the lifeblood of the parish is to understand its mechanisms of survival; it is to understand persistence, narratives of triumph and resistance to the fragmentation and decay so often hastened by gentrification.

The feast is the lifeblood of the parish—this was asserted over and over. Throughout my research I waded into the component parts of the feast, its inner workings, its back stages, and the actual agents and processes of this symbiotic dynamic between the feast and parish. While the language of biology and blood is always on the lips of community members, what underlie those more symbolic discourses are men and money.

Epilogue

Ethnography is fickle. The basement has been cleansed of most of its refuse. There are no broken statues littering shelves, no tangled wires or piles of old paint cans. There are fewer eyes peering out from the dark recesses and corners. Everything is very . . . orderly. Everything is very contained. The entire operation has moved from the very front of the basement, where one first walks down the small ramp into the space, to the very back of the room, out of sight and out of mind. The two San Paolino statues, the ones people fondly called "the brothers," are hidden in a nook under a huge metal duct. The large rolling wooden waves of the boat too sit under that duct next to ceramic statues of choir singers, their little mouths frozen open in song. What used to be a maze is now open space. Large swaths of floor are visible. It looks more like an actual basement, an orderly collection of tools and workspace, not a place layered with the sediments of decades of craft and construction. The heads do remain. The stony Christ Child, the shiny lacquered mannequin head that belonged to an angel, the slumbering head of Our Lady of Mount Carmel (OLMC), and a gilt bishop's miter sit propped up on a rusty pipe along the back wall. The giglio pieces are now hidden behind big doors. The decades-old metal boxes from the money room, those caked literally and metaphorically with history, are gone as well. Although basement detritus and boxes seem like small changes, these changes were huge to some, a signal that their new pastor was "challenging every single tradition and everything we've been doing." The new pastor shut down complaints, critiquing the men for "living in the past."

I recount these changes not to lament them but to note that ethnography probes the ephemeral. Relationships, material spaces, and practices are not stable. The basement as I entered it in 2015 was very different from what it would have been like in the 2000s or the 1980s. When I began fieldwork the old money room with its graffitied walls and hidden location had just been whitewashed. By 2019 the money room had moved three times, from a nice conference room to a tight spare room in the rectory to a narrow windowless maintenance room in the gym, so that the money crew sat alongside bags of basketballs behind a metal grate. In 2019 we shot hoops in the dark between deliveries of money boxes and collection baskets. So this book has captured this place at this time and the ways people form relationships to tradition, move through the church, and make meaning of the many things they do within its walls and on the streets surrounding it.

Whereas people felt worried about the survival and financial future of their parish, that all changed in the months leading up to the 2017 feast. People thought that they were entering a new era of publicity and prosperity because the church was getting a new pastor whose powerful connections and fundraising ability would change things. No longer would the church be cash-strapped, no longer would they hit record lows for the Century Board. Before the pastor was welcomed into the community people speculated, "You know, he knows everybody, he works bringing all the money into the Church, with the Catholic Charities. Now it's going to be all about publicity." Others chattered, "I guarantee you we will need a new Century Board with all the money is he going to have coming in, I guarantee you he is going to fill it up. He will bring in a lot . . . and really help our parish." One man told me, "The only way I can put it is that this is a little country resort and now it's gonna be like the Atlantic City boardwalk. I don't know if it's going to be good for us or not, we will see. But things are going to be different."

The new pastor renovated the church interior, and what once was a dim space with walls and ceilings painted in shades of light blue and cream now is a brightly lit space with mint green walls. The barrel vaulting of the ceiling has been painted a reflective gold. The sanctuary walls surrounding the altar that were once wood are now clad in deep jungle green and white marble. Most striking of all, green lights were hidden in the walls behind the altar, framing the altar and the crucifix in a neon green glow. People joked that he chose green lights because green is the color of money. The initial hope people had about their new pastor quickly turned to critique during the renovation and the feast.

During the 2017 feast, OLMC's shrine was moved to the church steps. According to some the shrine had been in the gated space adjacent to the church and under a tent for sixty years, but in 2017 it seemed foot traffic, visibility, and money mattered more than tradition. OLMC would no longer stand elevated and protected in front of a stone niche but would be right in front of the church, surrounded by metal platforms that held the candles and framed with an arch of glowing lights affixed to the brick wall of the church. Many feared she would be damaged in the "bedlam" of the feast day. At the foot of the stairs was a brand-new merchandise booth that sold things like rosaries but also Italian flags and all kinds of things printed with the flag and maps of Italy: T-shirts, dish towels, suspenders, shopping totes, and baby onesies, also centered in order to bring more foot traffic and increase sales. Most shocking of all to some shrine workers, there was now an ATM machine inside the former shrine. One said, "Are you going to write . . . that we don't consider this the shrine? Sacred space has been desecrated with an ATM." By 2019 everything was back in the newly renovated shrine, but some had a problem with orders to carry around a collection basket during the feast day procession, bristling that an acquisitive spirit dampened the devotional occasion.

While money and devotion were never separate, changes like moving the shrine, putting corporate sponsorships on feast T-shirts (lifter's shirts had a Cross County Savings Bank logo on the sleeve), and installing the green lights made people some uncomfortable. One man was frustrated during the feast and told me, "This is a parish, these are parishioners, this is not a business." Although business practices and priorities have been part and parcel of the feast since the giglio first came under the jurisdiction of the parish, the overt prioritization of money over relationships, tradition, and the sacrality of beloved objects like the statue seemed to cross an invisible line. The critiques highlighted the ways there were "appropriate" and "inappropriate" ways to do money at the feast (just as there were appropriate and inappropriate ways to do devotion), and people saw those standards being violated. While the pursuit of money is sanctified through discourses of keeping the parish alive, some of these new measures seemed like sacrificing tradition in exchange for money for money's sake.

Some even thought features like the pastor's award, which both Mark and John won during my research, would change. In the basement some comically speculated that the award would now go to the "highest bidder" and that soon there would be a "for rent" sign over the church calling for sponsors. These were jokes, but ultimately they spoke to their fears that the parish would fundamentally lose its identity and stray from the way things have always been done. In a tradition that is balanced between the past and the present, there is always a tense and tenuous connection between temporal frames. Any change seems unsettling and can be read as a harbinger that they are losing grip on the way "things have always been done," which itself is a constructed idea. Nostalgia for the past, whether centered on leaders, material objects, the neighborhood landscape, worries about pastors' priorities, or changes on scales both big and small, seems perennial in this community.

These concerns about change are mitigated by the stability of positions of honor reserved for men at the feast. A new generation with hopes of ascending these ranks offers the community the promise of survival. In the summer of 2019 Joe Mascia and I sat in a room in the rectory, and he sunk into a navy arm chair. He was freshly shaven; the only trace of the thick beard he had grown to be Turk was that the skin around the bottom of his face was stubbled and light, contrasting with the summer tan of his cheeks. In the corner stood a cardboard cutout of Pope Francis, the Holy Father looming with a grin as Joe and I talked. Just a few days prior he had the grand honor of being Turk on Giglio Sunday, what he described as "a day I'm truly never going to forget, and it truly is one of, or the best day of my life thus far," still coming down from the elation. That day, in just the shorts and T-shirt that had been soaked with sweat from the three-plus hours he walked the neighborhood on the procession for OLMC, Joe was his regular self, not a character, just everyday Joe: the social media manager for the feast and parish.

The night before playing Turk he woke early from excitement, and little by little he put on the custom outfit that would transform him into the figure. His turban perfectly swirled in the front like a soft-serve cone dotted with big jewels. His T-shirt was adorned with a sunburst of gold rhinestones. He wore a long gold and maroon robe, printed like an elaborate Persian rug. A red vest with gold piping, golden pants, and even sneakers that had been spray-painted gold completed the look. While Joe was inside with family, bracing himself for the day to come, outside people all wearing T-shirts with his name on them milled about, waiting for his debut. Neil, the 2018 Turk, came in to wish Joe good luck, and when he saw him he playfully chided, "Who shot the sofa?" jokingly likening his outfit to upholstery before taking Joe into a big hug. As a crowd gathered outside and he waited in the hallway, Joe felt like time was moving syrupy slow. The band outside played a song from Nola, the very song that he had lifted to in Nola his first time there. As soon as he heard it, under the poles in Nola, he knew that if one day he was Turk that song must be played. He negotiated with friends in Nola, "obviously through Google Translate," to get the sheet music for the song so the giglio band in Brooklyn could learn it. When Joe climbed into the boat, fully stocked with confetti poppers, he looked out onto the feast and thought, "This is legitimate . . . this is my time." Riding atop the crowd, on the shoulders of lifters, Joe waved his sword, sprayed the crowd with confetti, and texted us photos of his view: "Living a dream" he captioned them. During the Double Lift, the climax of the Dance of the Giglio, when the boat and the giglio meet in front of the church and the crews come together at the center, joining hands, jumping, celebrating, and bouncing the structures, Joe threw carnations into the crowd. He pumped his sword with one hand. The handle he was holding on to inside the boat broke off, so as the boat bounced he had to keep his balance. He reenacted it for me, looking like he was riding a mechanical bull. That moment when the giglio and the boat met was emotional for Joe: "The history behind what I represent, fact or fiction, we're not sure, but we know what I was representing, and it was truly unbelievable."

What might be surprising is that Joe only recently officially became a Catholic. The son of a Jewish mother and an Italian Catholic father, he made the decision to become Catholic as an adult. Although he had been coming to the feast with his grandmother since he was a baby, he was not an official part of the Church until his late twenties. Yet he dreamed of being Turk as a child and came to the feast almost every year for the thirty-one years of his life. For a while he took a break from lifting; a combination of interpersonal tensions and family reasons kept him distant from the feast. Then one day, he said, "something told me, I don't know what it was, that I have to be back. And sure enough, I went back as a lifter that year. It was just like, I was gone for so many years, and something told me, something inside of me said, 'I've gotta be there that day.' And the rest was history. It's just one of those things that you can't explain, something inside of me said, 'you've gotta be there.'" The sail on his boat was symbolic of these life-changing events: his baptism and his trip to Nola. In the center was a cross, representing him becoming Catholic, surrounded by eight lilies, one for each of the gigli in Nola. While Joe did not explicitly say this, it seemed that he was hinting that that "thing" was God, that the call to come back to the feast was also a call to faith. Joe always knew he wanted to be a Catholic, but lagged on taking the official step and necessary classes and getting baptized.

> What really gave me that kick was because I started seeing the other side of this feast . . . the religious side of it. When you're a kid you really don't understand the religious side of it. . . . I want[ed] to be able to participate in the Masses, pray, and really get the full idea of what this feast really is. . . . That was honestly the best decision of my life. You know, I may not be great Catholic, I may not go to church every Sunday, but I go as much as I can. . . . This feast really drove me to make that decision. [It] gave me that boost to say "You know what? I see the religious aspect and I want to be a part of the religious aspect that goes along with it." Ever since then the feast really changed for me.

When I asked him if he had his own definition of what it meant to be a good Catholic, he said, "You know obviously I pray almost every day. I don't feel like—yes it's very important to go to church—but I don't think it's a necessity to be a great Catholic. As long as you say your prayers, you do good for others, that kind of stuff [and] you're not a complete idiot. And I give a lot to the parish, to the church." He emphasized the importance of volunteering his time for the church, and said, "It may not be monetary, but you're giving your time, which in turn is saving the church money, because they don't need to pay someone to do the jobs I'm doing. So I feel like all that combined makes you a good Catholic." When he reflected on the work he does for the parish, he made it clear that he is involved "365 days a year": "I may not necessarily be physically here but I am working for the parish," broadcasting Masses and running the website. He still dreams of being a capo, just as much today as he did when he was a little boy. When I asked him what that meant for him, he said, "It's just something you dream about from a baby, being able to control that giglio, taking it off the sidewalk."

To get there, Joe continues to do anything and everything he can for the parish. "You've got to give your time, you've got to earn your spot to get up there. You've got to put in almost thirty years to get to that spot. And in those thirty years, you've got to work for the parish." Becoming capo, and "getting that stick," as Joe puts it referring to the cane each capo wields, "it's like you've worked your entire life . . . it is almost like getting the highest educational degree you can get, or the best job in the world you can get, or winning the lottery. That's really everything that can compare to it because you're investing your life into it, to making sure this feast continues and you get that stick, and you're in charge . . . that's what it truly means to me."

What the feast provides men, in addition to a religious community, connections to real and imagined ancestors, and a group of friends, is status, power, and meaningful labor. The men of the feast work jobs ranging from advertising professionals to union elevator technicians, employees of the office of emergency management, IT professionals, principals, teachers, drivers and deliverymen, sanitation workers, service workers, and business owners. Occupational status has little to do with how men ascend the feast hierarchy. When a man dresses as Turk and exits a house to the cheers of a crowd, or when he raises his cane and sees his command materialize on the stern faces of the lifters and in the mobility of that massive tower, it is a moment of potent power and glory. Some have complained to me that the men of today are not as physically capable of lifting the giglio as their fathers and grandfathers. One feast leader who is a school principal pointed to men who were teachers and managers and told me, "The guys now are like us, you have a degree, you're a teacher not a dock worker. You're not pouring asphalt." The connotation here is that the men today, who are teenagers, or those who work in offices are not as physically capable as the lifters in the past whose jobs centered on manual labor.

No matter how they make their living, the community at OLMC offers a chance to make meaningful connections to other men and a clear path to the top for those willing to work for it. Joe likens money, education, employment—the usual arenas for the making of masculinity—to becoming number one. These comparisons demonstrate how the feast and parish promise young men a route to manhood. Even if they never achieve the kinds of successes Joe listed—riches, promotions, and degrees—being number one is the aspiration, the pinnacle of male potentiality in the community. Even if there is broader uncertainty and instability in routes to upward mobility, the feast community still offers the promise of mobility, a promise that if you show up at the church, if you give hours, months, and years of your life, if you can point to your labor, you will be celebrated. The combination of devotion, work, and fatherhood means that men not only can win the respect of an entire community but also can be active in the perpetuation and survival of that very community. They can make history. The feast promises belonging and glory. It promises meaningful labor. The possibility of being a self-made man is very much alive at the feast. In this particularly church-made version, the idea stands that with "talents, discipline, and dedicated hard work" *for the parish*, they can achieve the apex of manhood.[1] Even though interpersonal issues can disrupt the certainty of the formula of work and time that produces men fit to be capos at the feast, the route to manhood in this community is stable despite any and all of the instability within the Church or the city more broadly.

The more time I spent with these Catholic men, the more they showed me how their devotional labor mattered. While an ethnographic study does not have the kind of hypotheses and experiments of a scientific study, all of the promotions in 2019 offered empirical evidence for my inductive assertion that work and devotion are inseparable at OLMC. When I first met Joe he did not run the website and was not in charge of anything at the feast. He had just returned from years of being an outsider in the community. But by summer 2019 he was riding the proverbial waves of Havemeyer Street. Thousands of eyes were on him, and that elation was intoxicating. When I first met Neil he was a just a lifter, albeit a lifter in love with the feast. When I first met Joey he too was a lifter. In that short time each of these men worked in their own ways, using and honing their own skills to give to their parish. They showed up for meetings, they worked behind the scenes, they traveled and painted and posted. They saw this as all part and parcel of their devotion. In the six years I have known him, Neil worked in the basement when many young men refused to. He became the chairman of the Children's Giglio Committee, overseeing the recruitment of over one hundred children to lift. He then became Turk and that very same year became a father. In 2019 he became a lieutenant—the kid who had been lifting since he was twelve, who had no family members involved with the feast, worked his way up over the course of eighteen years. Joey, whose uncle was a beloved capo, the little boy who traveled to Nola and saw gigli floating outside of his window, became not only a Turk in Brooklyn, but a Turk in Nola as well. In 2019 Joey also became a lieutenant, and although soft-spoken and was given the nickname Whispers by his friends, Joey commanded men much his senior during the Dance of the Giglio that summer. When I first began this project, I had no idea that these would be the men to ascend the hierarchy, that their devotion would so readily produce results and promotions. Within some other framework, Neil, Joey, Joe, Mark, and the others might not be fit for a study of Catholic devotion. Perhaps their relationships and practices would be slotted under the category of camaraderie or considered the stuff of symbolic ethnicity, not the "real" emotional or intimate stuff of devotion, narrowly conceived. But these men are a new generation enthralled with the promise of community, honor, and respect. These are men who are passionately Catholic in their own way. As the city changes around the parish, and as the parish changes from within, the promise that the feast offers to men makes it such that there will be generations of men in the basement; they will bounce San Paolino down the center aisle of the church and bring OLMC through the neighborhood; they will grow beards and dress up; they will feel the sore shoulders and exhaustion of lifting; they will continue to return to Williamsburg. As Joe said, "It's devotion."

ACKNOWLEDGMENTS

I am in my feelings as I think about everyone who made this book possible. I am overcome with stories I want to tell, but this genre calls for restraint. Just know all those memories are swirling around my head and there is so much more I want to say.

I am grateful for the intellectual community and friends I found at Princeton. First, my graduate advisor Judith Weisenfeld, whose mentorship is a kind of magic I will always be grateful for. Jessica Delgado helped me wrangle my thoughts and theorize. Seth Perry challenged me to think deeply about methodology. Wallace Best helped me tell compelling stories. I am thankful for the Center for the Study of Religion, which provided fellowship support for this research, my Religion and Public Life seminar colleagues, Robert Wuthnow's encouragement and keen eye, and Jenny Wiley Legath's support and comedy. Other ethnographers imparted their skills and knowledge: at Columbia, Courtney Bender offered a space to learn and reflect on ethnographic methods alongside my colleagues, Liz Dolfi and Andrew Jungclaus. The Religion in the Americas workshop at Princeton shaped my scholarship, and Beth Stroud, Leslie Ribovich, Vaughn Booker, Rachel Gross, Eden Consenstein, Kristine Wright, Madeline Gambino, Kijan Maxam, and Eziaku Nwokocha left imprints on this work.

I am grateful for my time in the Eternal City with the salted caramel gelato crew: Kelsey Moss and Maria Cecilia Ulrickson, and the inspiring collection of scholars of La Patrona Collective. I am thankful for the great minds who read chapters and made this work stronger: Andrew Walker-Cornetta is especially dear to me—he is my friend and champion. Special thanks to Ahmad Green-Hayes, whose friendship and support is unmatched, and Hillary Kaell, who has been an inspiration and a mentor. I had the best conversation partners in Bob Orsi, Gillian Frank, Elaine Peña, Matthew Cressler, Amanullah de Sondy, Anthony Petro, Rachel Lindsey, and Sarah Imhoff; and respondents who provided generous feedback: Brett Hoover and S. Brent-Plate. Joseph Cohen at the Diocese of Brooklyn archives graciously assisted me in exploring parish history. The Religion Department at Kalamazoo College has given me a home, and I am grateful to have shared this process with my friend Taylor Petrey. My students at K energized me. I tried to write a book they would want to read. Thank you to NYU Press, the North American Religions series editors, and Jennifer Hammer for their enthusiasm and support, and the anonymous reviewers for their generosity and for helping me present this story in even more powerful ways.

The ideas for this book started at Vassar College, and I thank the Religion and Sociology departments, especially Jonathon Kahn, Marc Epstein, Christopher White, Michael Walsh, William Hoynes, Robert McAulay, Seungsook Moon, who introduced me to the study of masculinities, and Diane Harriford, whose words sent me to grad school. The late Andrew Tallon taught me to think about space, and his genius is forever with me.

This book would not have been possible without Heba Gowayed and Nicholas Occhiuto, who introduced me to Philip Franco of OLMC. Phil welcomed me into his parish and his world, and I am eternally grateful for his friendship. I thank everyone at OLMC, especially the basement and money crews, for their welcome, for allowing me into their lives and spaces, for the laughs, and for the friendship.

My mom read all my words and waited up for me after long nights at the feast; I try to match her strength every day. Lastly, James Estrada, my mind twin, my love, who lived and breathed this book.

NOTES

INTRODUCTION

1 For more on the giglio as "feast machine," see Katia Ballacchino's work on the feast in Nola: Ballacchino, "Embodying Devotion, Embodying Passion"; Ballacchino, "Is Watching the Feast Making the Feast?"; and Ballacchino, *Etnografia di una Passione*. See also Posen, Sciorra, and Cooper, "Brooklyn's Dancing Tower"; and Sciorra, *Built with Faith*.

2 Catholic studies scholars have argued that priests "tend to be shadowy figures in diocesan archives" and that they need to be more fully fleshed out as persons. See Tentler, "Evidence and Historical Confidence." Others, like Michael Pasquier and John Seitz, have explored and are exploring the emotional worlds of priests, as missionaries and in dioceses. See Pasquier, *Fathers on the Frontier*; and Seitz, "Lives of Priests." This turn in the scholarship has yet to fully analyze or explore the making of clerical masculinities. Seitz argues that "if we are to understand American Catholicism" we need to understand the "tight networks of camaraderie and insularity among clerics." Here I do that work but argue we need to also understand how the Church offers those networks of camaraderie to lay men.

3 Moore, "Friendship and the Cultivation of Religious Sensibilities," 440, 444. Moore argues that the importance of friendship in religious life is "remarkably easy to miss," but it is in these relationships that religion is "apprehended" and "rendered real."

4 Hall, *Lived Religion in America*.

5 "Catechism of the Catholic Church—Sacramentals" (n.d.), www.vatican.va; United States Conference of Catholic Bishops, "Popular Devotional Practices: Basic Questions and Answers" (November 12, 2003), www.usccb.org.

6 On devotionalism and memory see Kaell, "Place Making and People Gathering."

7 Orsi, "What Did Women Think?," 70, 68; Tentler, "On the Margins." In a review of literature on American Catholicism, Tentler sums up this focus on women's devotion and its connection to domestic life: "In virtually every ethnic group, women were central to the devotional life—a situation that prevailed well into the twentieth century. Not only did they dominate the ranks of supplicants, but feminine images and feminine language also permeated the devotional world itself. . . . The devotional life might place women briefly at liturgical center stage, but it was also, via the emphasis on mediators, a powerful source of legitimization

for a hierarchical church." For more on domestic piety, see McDannell, *Christian Home in Victorian America* and Taves, *Household of Faith*.

8 Orsi, *Madonna of 115th Street*, 11.

9 Greer, *Mohawk Saint*; Kane, *Sister Thorn and Catholic Mysticism*; Kane, "'She Offered Herself Up'"; Laycock, *Seer of Bayside*; McCartin, "Sacred Heart of Jesus"; Morgan, "Rhetoric of the Heart." See also Burton, *Holy Tears, Holy Blood*.

10 Blazer, *Playing for God*; Brown, *Mama Lola*; Butler, *Women in the Church of God in Christ*; Byrne, *O God of Players*; Casselberry, *Labor of Faith*; Cummings, *New Women of the Old Faith*; Frederick, *Between Sundays*; Griffith, *God's Daughters*; Matovina, *Guadalupe and Her Faithful*; Nabhan-Warren, *Virgin of El Barrio*; Orsi, *Madonna of 115th Street*; Orsi, *Thank You, St. Jude*; Treviño, *Church in the Barrio*.

11 Kelly and Kelly, "Our Lady of Perpetual Help"; Kane, "Marian Devotion since 1940."

12 Canstañeda-Liles, *Our Lady of Everyday Life*.

13 In "Lives of Priests," Seitz points out the dichotomy in scholarship between the Church and "the people," arguing that priests are "vanishing middle men" in this formula (20).

14 At the opening of *Thank You, St. Jude*, Orsi paints a compelling picture of Jude's national shrine in Chicago, where he is the patron saint of the Chicago police force. Men have taken to the streets in uniform in triumphant and collective processions around the shrine. Men in blue have been the public face of this devotion. Men in black, namely priests and seminarians, also have promoted devotion to Jude. Devotion to the saints is often "under the authority" of men but sustained by a sea of women, their prayers, petitions, and spiritual labor often invisible and behind the scenes (x). Orsi argues that there is a "gendered discrepancy between the 'front and back regions'" of "most Catholic popular piety." Men are often the public faces of churches, shrines, and their auxiliaries, and "it has been women's support, love, and loyalty . . . behind the onstage prominence of male celebrities, marching policemen, and clerical authorities" that has buttressed devotion to saints like Jude (xi).

15 Orsi, *Madonna of 115th Street*, 9; Chinnici, "Catholic Community at Prayer," 66.

16 Scholars have found notable disparities between the "work ethics" of women and men in religious communities both Catholic and Protestant. While men have historically been understood to do "real" religious work, the stuff of church history—preaching, institution building, publicly representing their congregations and organizations—over the past decades scholars have been exploring women's labor, how they "lead from the background" in their church so men can "be on top." See Casselberry, *Labor of Faith*.

17 Pew Research Center, "The Gender Gap in Religion Around the World," March 22, 2016, www.pewforum.org; Pew Research Center, "Gender Differences in Worship Attendance Vary across Religious Groups," March 22, 2016, www.pewforum.org.

18 Kimmel, *Manhood in America*, 252.

19 Kimmel, *Manhood in America*, 252.

20 Promise Keepers, "Promise Keepers Launches New Era of Men's Ministry" (May 8, 2019), http://promisekeepers.org.

21 Thanks to Andrew Walker-Cornetta for this language.

22 Connell and Messerschmidt, "Hegemonic Masculinity," 836; Imhoff, *Masculinity and the Making of American Judaism*, 6.

23 Davis, "Sociology, Theory, and the Feminist Sociological Canon," 3; Butler, "Performative Acts and Gender Constitution," 519.

24 Schrock and Schwalbe, "Men, Masculinity, and Manhood Acts," 280–81.

25 See the most recent document of the Congregation for Catholic Education, "Male and Female He Created Them: Towards a Path of Dialogue on the Question of *Gender* Theory in Education" (February 2, 2019), www.vatican.va.

26 For two examples of queer Catholics' devotion (whether accepted by the Church or not), see Alcedo, "Sacred Camp"; Chesnut, *Devoted to Death*; Machado, "Santa Muerte."

27 Bird, "Welcome to the Men's Club," 122; Connell, *Masculinities*.

28 These thoughts came from interacting with and responding to Escalante, "Playful Masculinity."

29 Devotional labor is Elaine Peña's concept. See Peña, *Performing Piety*.

30 Some works that have demonstrated the fruitfulness of backstage work include Bielo, *Ark Encounter*; Bielo, *Words upon the Word*; Peña, *Performing Piety*; Pérez, *Religion in the Kitchen*; Sklar, *Dancing with the Virgin*. For an analysis of vestments and the back stages of preparing for worship service by clergy, see Richter, "From Backstage to Front."

31 See Ballacchino, "Unity Makes"; Mitchell, "Performances of Masculinity"; Mitchell, "Ritual Structure and Ritual Agency"; Hughes, "God-Bearers on Pilgrimage to Tepeyac"; Driessen and Jansen, "Staging Hyper-Masculinity"; Driessen, "Male Sociability and Rituals of Masculinity."

32 Downey, Dalidowicz, and Mason, "Apprenticeship as Method." The authors argue that "one of the great challenges to ethnographic fieldwork is the simple problem that 'non-participating observer' is not an appropriate role in some social settings" (186).

33 On observant participation, see Mears, "Ethnography as Precarious Work"; Wacquant, *Body and Soul*; Skinner, "Leading Questions and Body Memories," 111.

34 On the idea of competence in crossing gendered boundaries in ethnography, see Hunt, "Development of Rapport."

35 Pascoe, *Dude, You're a Fag*, 192.

36 Brown, *Mama Lola*, 12, 14.

37 Woodward, "Hanging Out and Hanging About," 544.

38 Samudra, "Memory in Our Body," 668. See also Lande, "Breathing like a Soldier," 98.

39 Mauss, "Techniques of the Body." Also see the chapter "Becoming Catholic" in Cressler, *Authentically Black and Truly Catholic*.

40 Samudra, "Memory in Our Body," 668, 665.

41 Wacquant, *Body and Soul*, viii; Samudra, "Memory in Our Body," 666.

42 Nabhan-Warren, "Embodied Research and Writing"; Peña, *Performing Piety*; Pérez, "Cooking for the Gods"; Pérez, *Religion in the Kitchen*; Sklar, *Dancing with the Virgin*.

43 For more on reciprocity and obligation in the apprenticeship model of ethnography, see Downey, Dalidowicz, and Mason, "Apprenticeship as Method," 185.

44 Wacquant, "Habitus as Topic and Tool"; Bender, *Heaven's Kitchen*; Nabhan-Warren, "Embodied Research and Writing"; Nabhan-Warren, "Working toward an Inclusive Narrative."

45 Wacquant, "Carnal Connections," 466.

46 Mears, "Ethnography as Precarious Work," 21.

47 Soyer, "Off the Corner," 460. Woodward, "Hanging Out and Hanging About," 538.

48 Hunt, "Development of Rapport," 286.

49 Hunt, "Development of Rapport," 290.

50 Primeggia and Primeggia, "Every Year, the Feast"; Primeggia and Varacalli, "Sacred and Profane."

51 Franco, "Traditional Italian Festa"; Gibino, "Facciamo Una Festa"; Posen, Sciorra, and Cooper, "Brooklyn's Dancing Tower"; Sciorra, *Built with Faith*; Sciorra, "Religious Processions in Italian Williamsburg"; Sciorra, "'O' Giglio e Paradiso"; Sciorra, "We Go Where the Italians Live"; Posen, "Storing Contexts." An exception to this is Claire Sponsler's *Ritual Imports*, in which she explores the giglio as a reinvented tradition that draws upon the "premodern past to meet the needs of the present." She argues that it is a performance of ethnic continuity and unity and manual labor and that the context of demographic shifts in Williamsburg and histories of Italian immigration make the Brooklyn Dance of the Giglio quite different from the ritual in Nola. See Sponsler, *Ritual Imports*, 121.

52 Anthropologists have noted that "relationships based on apprenticeship may be circumscribed by the context of practice, and a community of practice may dissolve in the intervals between" meetings and performances and "commenting upon their family lives, occupations or domestic worlds may be much more difficult." See Downey, Dalidowicz, and Mason, "Apprenticeship as Method," 187.

53 See Luzzatto, *Padre Pio*.

54 Recent reports confirm this story and especially explore the role of ultra-Orthodox Jewish men in real estate development in Brooklyn and now in Jersey City, New Jersey. See Joseph Berger, "Uneasy Welcome as Ultra-Orthodox Jews Extend beyond New York," *New York Times*, August 2, 2017, www.nytimes.com; Michelle Cohen, "With $2.5 Billion in Brooklyn Real Estate, Hasidic Investors Are a Formidable Gentrification Driver," *6sqft*, August 26, 2016, www.6sqft.com.

55 Rotella, *October Cities*, 26. Rotella distinguishes between cities of facts and cities of feeling. Cities of feeling are "shaped by the flow of language, images and ideas," cities of fact "by the flow of capital, materials, and people." Although we mark cities as pre and post, Rotella reminds us that landscapes overlap and that overlap is

perceptible in the built environment and narrative and memory. Religion offers a rich site for the making of those narratives, for the immersion and molding of the city of feeling.

56 Domino Park, "Artifacts" (n.d.), www.dominopark.com.

57 Robert Orsi, in *History and Presence*, argues that "as modernity evolved, the gods were revered from the media of their representation which became signs and symbols, not embodied presences" (249). Orsi proposes that scholars acknowledge "the gods as interlocutors and provocateurs" rather than evacuating these presences from their writing and academic language. In this vein, statues, prayer cards, texts, images could be understood as "media of presence" (251). Amy Whitehead's work on statues and relationality highlighted to me that to call Our Lady of Mount Carmel "her" or "she" is to acknowledge, not to efface, the potentiality of presence. To limit my ethnographic voice to calling statues "it" is to unnaturally draw a discursive boundary between me and my interlocutors, one that did not exist as such while I was in the field. So here, OLMC may be Our Lady, may be Mount Carmel, may be the Blessed Mother, may be "she," and may be "the statue," which is all to say that my interlocutors had varying ways of referring to the devotional objects, presences, and things that surrounded them at the feast and in the church. Orsi, *History and Presence*; Whitehead, *Religious Statues and Personhood*. See also Finch, "Rehabilitating Materiality."

58 "Department of Finance: Brooklyn Tax Photos," NYC Municipal Archives Collections, www.nycma.lunaimaging.com.

59 Goldin and Lubell, *Never Built New York*, 16, 18.

60 For literary analysis of the ghostly and the spectral in fiction about gentrification in Brooklyn, see Peacock, "Those the Dead Left Behind."

61 See Clites, "Soul Murder."

62 Jack Ruhl and Diane Ruhl, "NCR Research: Costs of Sex Abuse Crisis to US Church Underestimated," *National Catholic Reporter*, November 2, 2015, www.ncronline.org; "Editorial: The Deep, Lasting Financial Cost of Sex Abuse," *National Catholic Reporter*, November 2, 2015, www.ncronline.org; Vinnie Rotondaro, "Researchers Find Drop in Giving in Areas Hit by Sex Abuse Scandal," *National Catholic Reporter*, November 2, 2015, www.ncronline.org; Ian Lovett, "Catholic Church Offers Cash to Settle Abuse Claims—With a Catch," *Wall Street Journal*, July 11, 2019, www.wsj.com.

63 Sharon Otterman, "Brooklyn Diocese Is Part of $27.5 Million Settlement in 4 Sex Abuse Cases," *New York Times*, September 18, 2018, www.nytimes.com; "Brooklyn's List Covers Diocese's 166 Years, Has 108 Credible Abuse Claims," *National Catholic Reporter*, February 19, 2019, www.ncronline.org; Sharon Otterman, "Brooklyn Diocese Seeks to Compensate Sex Abuse Victims," *New York Times*, June 22, 2017, www.nytimes.com; "List of Diocesan Clergy for Whom the Diocese Received Allegations of Sexual Misconduct with a Minor," *Diocese of Brooklyn* (n.d.), www.dioceseofbrooklyn.org.

64 For more on ritual, play, and masculinity in another context, see McAlister, *Rara!*

CHAPTER 1. TURKS, TATTOOS, AND THE MASCULINE BODY OF
THE FEAST

1 Feast Meeting Minutes Booklet, Our Lady of Mount Carmel (OLMC) Archives, 1959.
2 Jennifer Nalewicki, "Tattooing Was Illegal in New York City until 1997," *Smithsonian*, February 28, 2017, www.smithsonianmag.com.
3 In "Virgin of Guadalupe Tattoos," Arturo Chávez explores tattoos and the entanglement of devotion and relationships between men.
4 Simmel, "Adornment," 339.
5 Pew Research Center, "Millennials: Confident. Connected. Open to Change," February 24, 2010, www.pewsocialtrends.org.
6 Kosut, "Artification of Tattoo," 143.
7 Woodstock, "Tattoo Therapy," 785.
8 DeMello, *Bodies of Inscription*, 162–66; Sigmon, "Gospel According to Her"; Snooks, "Enshrined in Flesh."
9 Jensen, Flory, and Miller, "Marked for Jesus," 27, 28.
10 Kosut, "Tattoo Narratives," 90; Woodstock, "Tattoo Therapy," 781.
11 Koch and Roberts, "Protestant Ethic and the Religious Tattoo"; Jensen, Flory, and Miller, "Marked for Jesus," 28.
12 According to Pew, "Most adults with tattoos, whether young or old, don't display them for all the world to see. When asked if their tattoos are usually visible, the vast majority (72%) say that they are not. This is true for Millennials and their older counterparts. Among those with at least one tattoo, 70% of Millennials and 73% of those ages 30 and older say their tattoos are not usually visible." See Pew Research Center, "Millennials."
13 Maldonado-Estrada, "Tattoos as Sacramentals."
14 Sciorra, "'O' Giglio e Paradiso,'" 20.
15 Tattoos then become adornments. "When the clans unite to live a common life and to assist at the religious ceremonies together, then he must adorn himself . . . now those who perform as officiants . . . always have designs representing the totem on their bodies." Durkheim, *Elementary Forms of the Religious Life*, 117–18.
16 McDannell, *Material Christianity*, 19; "Catechism of the Catholic Church—Sacramentals."
17 Maldonado-Estrada, "Tattoos as Sacramentals."
18 McDannell, *Material Christianity*, 19–22.
19 Copsey, "Simon Stock and the Scapular Vision," 653.
20 Saint Paulinus was born around 353 as Meropius Pontius Paulinus into a wealthy landowning family in Aquitaine (Bordeaux, France) and was a prolific poet and writer. In the fourth century Paulinus's family was wealthy and influential in the imperial Roman government, and he followed suit by becoming a Roman consul in 379 and the governor of Campania a few years later. Paulinus traveled to Spain, where he met his wife Theresa, and he was baptized in 389 before

returning to Campania in 395. Together they forsook their riches and noble status to live ascetic lives in Cimitile, where the popular Saint Felix was buried. Saint Ambrose celebrated Paulinus and his wife for abandoning their possessions and their estates and leaving their homes behind in order to retreat to Nola to serve the poor and God. Paulinus became the Bishop of Nola in 409. When Paulinus became the governor of the region he was introduced to the cult of Saint Felix and the miracles that peasants attributed to him. Various scholars have argued that Paulinus was sympathetic to the popular religiosity of peasants and a promoter of the cult of Saint Felix. Paulinus worked to make Cimitile an important pilgrimage destination by building a new church with open courtyards and water installations on the site as well as a hospice, monastery, and lodging facilities for pilgrims and a road to Saint Felix's tomb. According to Dennis Trout, Paulinus was instrumental in "fashioning a Christian context for the continuation of certain sacrificial and votive practices that were firmly embedded in the logic of the Italian countryside," helping to create "synthesis" between rural peasant practices of animal sacrifice and the local devotion to Saint Felix and Christian worship. For more on the historical Paulinus, see Brown, *Cult of the Saints*; Butler, "Lives of the Saints"; Coster, "Christianity and the Invasions"; van den Hoek and Herrmann, "Paulinus of Nola"; Trout, "Christianizing the Nolan Countryside."

21 "Gregory the Great Dialogues (1911)," Tertullian Project, www.tertullian.org.

22 Merrills and Miles, *Vandals*, 114.

23 "Gregory the Great Dialogues, Book 3 (1911)," Tertullian Project, www.tertullian.org.

24 During Paulinus's lifetime, the Goths under King Alaric invaded Nola shortly after he became bishop in 409. Scholars have argued that there were other bishops of Nola, Paulinus II and Paulinus III, and that it was one of these subsequent Paulinuses that gave himself in exchange for the widow's son and that with time his story was superimposed onto the hagiography of Saint Paulinus. Charles Henry Coster has argued that the story was so "typical of [Paulinus's] teaching and practice that one cannot bring oneself to characterize it as essentially untrue." Coster, "Christianity and the Invasions," 153.

25 "Feast History," OLMC Feast (2020), www.olmcfeast.com.

26 My translation, quoted in Avella, *Annali della Festa dei Gigli*, 36.

27 Quoted by Ceparano, "*Gigli* of Nola," 134.

28 Avella, *Annali della Festa dei Gigli*, 67.

29 Bisaha, *Creating East and West*, 69.

30 Bisaha, *Creating East and West*, 71.

31 Snyder, "Bodies of Water," 6; Davis, *Naples and Napoleon*, 22.

32 Kuran-Burçoğlu, "Image of the Turk."

33 Jezernik, *Imagining "the Turk,"* 38, 39.

34 Jasienski, "Savage Magnificence," 180, 183, 174; Jirousek, "Ottoman Influences in Western Dress"; Jirousek, *Ottoman Dress and Design in the West.*

35 Goetz, "Oriental Types," 56.

36 Sponsler, *Ritual Imports*, 116.
37 On the turban and profiling, see Puar, *Terrorist Assemblages*.
38 Said, *Orientalism*.
39 Baltimore, "Ashman's Aladdin Archive," 210.
40 Morgan, *Images at Work*, 51.
41 Anthropologist Katia Ballacchino refers to the gigli as feast machines. Ballacchino, "Embodying Devotion, Embodying Passion."
42 This paragraph is adapted from Maldonado-Estrada, "Loving Saint Paulinus."
43 This is based on geographer Shompa Lahiri's argument that "urban memory is archived in the body." See Lahiri, "Remembering the City."
44 Mitchell, "Catholic Body?," 211, 212.
45 Cressler, *Authentically Black and Truly Catholic*, 81, 73.
46 Franco, "Traditional Italian Festa," 106.
47 Feast Meeting Minutes, May 26, 1959, OLMC Archives.
48 Larry B. Stammer and William Montalbano, "Vatican OKs Use of Girls as Altar Servers," *Los Angeles Times*, April 14, 1994, www.latimes.com; "Library: Vatican Communication on Female Altar Servers" (March 15, 1994), www.catholicculture.org; "Instruction Redemptionis Sacramentum (On Certain Matters to Be Observed or to Be Avoided Regarding the Most Holy Eucharist)" (April 23, 2004), www.vatican.va; David Gonzalez, "Endorsing Growing Practice, Vatican Approves Altar Girls," *New York Times*, April 15, 1994, www.nytimes.com.
49 Michael O'Loughlin, "The Altar Girls Debate: Do They Kill Vocations, or Feel Valued?," *Crux*, February 4, 2015, www.cruxnow.com
50 David Gibson, "Cardinal Raymond Burke: 'Feminized' Church and Altar Girls Caused Priest Shortage," *National Catholic Reporter*, January 7, 2015, www.ncronline.org.
51 Letter reprinted in Shrine Church of Our Lady of Mount Carmel bulletin, July 9, 2017.

CHAPTER 2. MANUAL LABOR AND THE ARTISTRY OF DEVOTION IN THE BASEMENT

1 Swift, "Robot Saints," 61.
2 On fabrication, see Meyer, "How Pictures Matter," 167. Elizabeth Pérez's work on Lucumí is essential for thinking about the material and embodied processes through which food and cooked sacrificed animals become "food for the gods" and the sensory processes through which people become habituated into a religious community. Pérez, *Religion in the Kitchen*; Pérez, "Cooking for the Gods."
3 Bruno Latour, *On the Modern Cult of the Factish Gods*, cited in Meyer, "How Pictures Matter," 167.
4 On decay, see Kendall, "Things Fall Apart." On fragility, see Promey, "Chalkware, Plaster, Plaster of Paris."
5 O'Neill, "Beyond Broken."

6 Peña, *Performing Piety.*

7 Peña, *Performing Piety*, 130.

8 Goffman, *Presentation of Self*, 24.

9 Goffman, *Presentation of Self*, 106. For another analysis of religion that uses Goffman's theory, see Joosse, "Presentation of the Charismatic Self"; Richter, "From Backstage to Front."

10 Goffman, *Presentation of Self*, 112.

11 In *Words upon the Word*, James Bielo explores Bible study groups, which often occurred in rooms outside of worship spaces. He argues that for evangelicals Bible study is a central site of knowledge production, where men and women negotiate and reinforce biblical hermeneutics and rehearse and evaluate discourses of witnessing. It is in these moments of "just sitting around talking" and acts of gathering that evangelicals "make religiosity happen." Bielo argues that the Bible study is a site of "backstage witnessing" where evangelicals work to become proficient in witnessing, to hone and tune their verbal, discursive, and rhetorical skills to "plant seeds" and win souls. Using Goffmanian and linguistic analysis, he looks at the "preparatory discourses of evangelical lives" rather than the finished, polished and persuasive product of witnessing. Bielo, *Words upon the Word.*

12 Pérez, "Cooking for the Gods," 667. Cressler's writing on conversion as an embodied process is useful for thinking about the Catholic context. See Cressler, *Authentically Black and Truly Catholic*; see also Mitchell, "Catholic Body?" On sensory and embodied education and Catholic children, see Ridgely, *When I Was a Child.*

13 Trout, *Paulinus of Nola.*

14 In her writing on Saint John the Baptist and national identity in Quebec, Geneviève Zubrzycki uses the notion of "discursive conditioning" to think about how communal narratives are constructed around Saint John. When Saint John's head broke off during a procession, amid political tensions over the identity of Quebec, the media constructed the event as a "willful murder" and a "beheading" that marked the "death of French Canada." This narrative was conditioned discursively by the biblical murder and beheading of John the Baptist. This framework is helpful for thinking about the ways participants in Williamsburg read events for evidence of OLMC's disapproval. Zubrzycki, "Aesthetic Revolt," 466. In *No Closure*, John Seitz explores a similar incident at Our Lady of Mount Carmel Church in Boston. A beloved statue of OLMC fell on the floor and was damaged, and some parishioners interpreted it as a sign or miracle, thinking perhaps that she had "jumped" in reaction to the church's closure. Seitz, *No Closure*, 131–33.

15 For example, see Savastano, "Changing St. Gerard's Clothes"; Hughes, "Niño Jesús Doctor"; Hughes, "Cradling the Sacred."

16 Whitehead, *Religious Statues and Personhood*, 4–5.

17 Whitehead, *Religious Statues and Personhood.*

18 Whitehead, *Religious Statues and Personhood*, 130.

19 Meyer, "How Pictures Matter," 168.

20 See Kendall, "Things Fall Apart," for more on the official processes and "sophisticated" workshops in Korea, Vietnam, and Myanmar where statues and images are produced and the protocols that ensure objects become "active" and "ensouled."

21 Lipman-Blumen, "Toward a Homosocial Theory of Sex Roles," 16; Bird, "Welcome to the Men's Club"; Ramirez, "Masculinity in the Workplace," 102; Thurnell-Read, "What Happens on Tour."

22 McDannell, *Material Christianity*, 8.

23 When McDannell argues that "when religious objects gain power through their association with the authority of religious institutions, that process is defined and administered by men [and] when objects are enlivened through the power of relationships, that process is frequently mediated by women," we continue to understand materiality and devotion along the binary of clerical men / lay women. McDannell, *Material Christianity*, 138.

24 Fine and de Soucey, "Joking Cultures," 1.

25 Fine, "One of the Boys," 138; Plester, "'Take It Like a Man!,'" 539.

26 Fine, "One of the Boys." Scholars of masculinity in studies of work sites, nightlife, and male friendship often focus on how competitiveness and performances and discussions of sexual prowess structure relationships between men in homosocial spaces. For example, see Bird, "Welcome to the Men's Club"; Grazian, "Girl Hunt"; and Iacuone, "'Real Men Are Tough Guys.'"

27 Collinson, "'Engineering Humour,'" 188–89.

28 Lumsden, "'Don't Ask a Woman,'" 498. For other accounts of women ethnographers and reflections on gender and fieldwork, see Soyer, "Off the Corner," 460; See also Pierce, "Lawyers, Lethal Weapons, and Ethnographic Authority"; Gurney, "Not One of the Guys." In subcultural communities centered on skills usually associated with men, like drag racing, women ethnographers struggle against sexism. Lumsden found that in order to proceed with research she had to do taxing emotional labor to deal with the dislike she developed for her subjects. See also Sallee and Harris, "Gender Performance."

29 Pérez, "Cooking for the Gods," 680.

30 These ideas about competence, gender, and rapport are inspired by Hunt, "Development of Rapport," 283.

CHAPTER 3. MAKING MONEY, KEEPING THE PARISH ALIVE

1 Mundey, Davidson, and Herzog, "Making Money Sacred," 306.

2 Mundey, Davidson, and Herzog, "Making Money Sacred," 315.

3 Smith, Emerson, and Snell, *Passing the Plate*, 127–31.

4 Viviana Zelizer notes that although the "physical homogeneity of modern currency is indisputable," money is socially practiced and thus differentiated by social acts and through different processes and contexts. Zelizer, *Social Meaning of Money*.

5 Mundey, Davidson, and Herzog, "Making Money Sacred," 306.

6 Mundey, Davidson, and Herzog, "Making Money Sacred," 306.

7 Hufford, "Ste. Anne de Beaupré."

8 Mundey, Davidson, and Herzog, "Making Money Sacred," 306; Belk and Wallendorf, "Sacred Meanings of Money."

9 Bederman, "'Women Have Had Charge,'" 432.

10 Bederman, "'Women Have Had Charge,'" 446.

11 Bederman, "'Women Have Had Charge,'" 440.

12 Bederman, "'Women Have Had Charge,'" 446.

13 Gleason, "Going after Souls," 13, also quoted in Bederman, "'Women Have Had Charge,'" 448.

14 Bederman, "'Women Have Had Charge,'" 448.

15 Wenger, "Federation Men."

16 Wenger, "Federation Men," 379–81.

17 Wenger, "Federation Men," 388–89.

18 Wenger, "Federation Men," 392–93.

19 Feast Meeting Minutes, June 16, 1959, OLMC Archives.

20 Feast Meeting Minutes, June 23, 1959, OLMC Archives.

21 Feast Meeting Minutes, June 21, 1960, OLMC Archives.

22 Feast Meeting Minutes, June 6, 1961, OLMC Archives.

23 Feast Meeting Minutes, May 19, 1959, OLMC Archives.

24 Feast Meeting Minutes, March 24, 1959, OLMC Archives.

25 Feast Meeting Minutes, March 24, 1959, May 24, 1960, OLMC Archives.

26 Sciorra, *Built with Faith*, 170.

27 Dolan, *American Catholic Experience*, 382.

28 Dolan, *American Catholic Experience*, 382.

29 Orsi, *Thank You, St. Jude*, 15, 16.

30 Feast Meeting Minutes, April 29, 1958, OLMC Archives.

31 Feast Meeting Minutes, April 29, 1958, OLMC Archives.

32 Feast Meeting Minutes, March 14, 1957, April 23, 1957, OLMC Archives.

33 "Candlelight to Usher in Carmel Fete," newspaper clipping tucked in 1958 Feast Meeting Minutes, OLMC Archives.

34 Feast Meeting Minutes, February 19, 1958, OLMC Archives.

35 Joseph Peluso remembers Mario Bosone as "pretty much a money guy" and told me about these business ventures.

36 Personal correspondence with John, April 11, 2018.

CHAPTER 4. PUBLIC MASCULINITIES AT THE FEAST

1 My focus on "spatial strategies" is informed by Paula Lupkin's book *Manhood Factories*, which analyzes YMCA buildings as sites for the creation of moral, "properly socialized" men. Lupkin argues that the built environment is often taken for granted in gender studies and creates a model for the study of space and gender identity (xvii). By using buildings to ground her inquiry, Lupkin explores how men navigated, inhabited, and used buildings to achieve manhood.

2   Wise, "Redefining Black Masculinity and Manhood," 6; and Brown, "'Strength of the Lion.'"

3   Bederman, *Manliness and Civilization*, 6.

4   Bederman, *Manliness and Civilization*, 12.

5   Bederman, *Manliness and Civilization*, 27.

6   Wise, "Redefining Black Masculinity and Manhood," 16; Kimmel, *Manhood in America*.

7   Kimmel, *Manhood in America*, 5.

8   Sussman, *Masculine Identities*, 2.

9   Brown, "'Strength of the Lion,'" 179.

10 Kriegel, *On Men and Manhood*.

11 For a different perspective on the Questua, see Gravot, "Re-membering Community."

12 Sciorra, "'O' Giglio e Paradiso.'"

13 Lyrics are excerpted from the English adaptation by Joseph F. Peluso, "The Lily of Heaven (O'Giglio 'e Paradiso)" (2006). Original Italian lyrics are by Pasquale Ferrara.

14 Toni Cimino, "The Capo Who Leads the 'Giglio' Lift," *Queens Courier*, June 28, 2011, www.queenscourier.com.

15 It is important to note that some capos leave or are excluded from the community because of improprieties and especially when they disrespect the number one or push the limits of the lifters' bodies and attempt to do particularly difficult or long lifts. One year there was a particularly brutal heat wave, and the number one mandated that all lifts be short and that there be no "number twos," a move where the lifters drop the giglio and immediately pick it back up again. One capo had the lifters perform a number two and a full 360-degree turn of the giglio, disobeying the number one capo and pushing the lifters' bodies to the limit in the heat. In subsequent years he did not receive lifts and did not participate in the feast.

16 For more on processions in Williamsburg, see Sciorra, "We Go Where the Italians Live."

17 Not all capos exit from homes that belong to them because many have moved; they use the homes of friends and relatives but host a breakfast for their loved ones in the yards of the homes in preparation for Giglio Sunday.

18 Franco, "Traditional Italian Festa," 63.

19 Bird, "Welcome to the Men's Club," 121.

20 Lipman-Blumen, "Toward a Homosocial Theory of Sex Roles," 16; also quoted in Britton, "Homophobia and Homosociality," 425. The definition also distinguished homosocial from homosexual—separating the social and sexual, or "explicitly erotic sexual interaction between members of the same sex." Scholars such as John Gustav-Wrathall, in *Take the Young Stranger by the Hand*, have since challenged the strict divide between the social and the sexual; social and erotic-homosocial spaces are not necessarily and must not necessarily be cleansed of or closed to homosexuality.

21 Bird, "Welcome to the Men's Club," 121.

22 Bartkowski, "Breaking Walls, Raising Fences," 44.

23 Bartkowski, "Breaking Walls, Raising Fences."

24 Foucault, *History of Sexuality*; Halperin, "Forgetting Foucault." See Erzen, *Straight to Jesus*, on acts and identity in the lives of Christian men in the ex-gay community.

25 Congregation for Catholic Education, "Male and Female He Created Them."

26 Capos who are separated or whose wives are not present receive much less fanfare.

27 Bederman, "'Women Have Had Charge'"; McCowin, "'For Faith and for Freedom,'" 155.

28 Bartkowski discusses the idea of flashpoint moments in *Promise Keepers*.

CHAPTER 5. CONSTRUCTING CATHOLIC PROPRIETY ON NORTH EIGHTH STREET

1 Sciorra, "We Go Where the Italians Live," 334.

2 Fouron, "Race, Blood, Disease and Citizenship"; Hebblethwaite, "Scapegoating of Haitian Vodou Religion"; McAlister, "From Slave Revolt to a Blood Pact with Satan." For a longer history of these discourses, see Gordon, "'Midnight Scenes and Orgies.'"

3 Julie Hirschfeld Davis, Sheryl Gay Stolberg, and Thomas Kaplan, "Trump Alarms Lawmakers with Disparaging Words for Haiti and Africa," *New York Times*, January 11, 2018; USCIS, "Temporary Protected Status Designated Country: Haiti" (November 1, 2019), www.uscis.gov; Miriam Jordan, "Trump Administration Ends Temporary Protection for Haitians," *New York Times*, November 20, 2017; Jaqueline Charles, "Haitian Quake Victims in the U.S. Will Lose Deportation Protection in 2019," *Miami Herald*, November 20, 2017, www.miamiherald.com; D'Vera Cohn, Jeffrey Passel, and Kristen Bialik, "Many Immigrants with Temporary Protected Status Face Uncertain Future in U.S.," *Fact Tank*, November 27, 2019, www.pewresearch.org; Ibram X. Kendi, "The Day 'Shithole' Entered the Presidential Lexicon," *Atlantic*, January 13, 2019, www.theatlantic.com.

4 Sciorra, *Built with Faith*, 180.

5 Orsi, "Religious Boundaries of an Inbetween People," 332.

6 Orsi, "Religious Boundaries of an Inbetween People," 330.

7 Orsi, "Religious Boundaries of an Inbetween People," 333.

8 Orsi, "Religious Boundaries of an Inbetween People."

9 McAlister, "Madonna of 115th Street Revisited," 151–52. Where Orsi's Italian interlocutors seemed unaware or in denial of the importance of Our Lady of Mount Carmel to Vodou practitioners, McAlister reads the practices of Haitian pilgrims as operating within a bireligious system in which Catholicism and Vodou exist on a spectrum. As Haitians express devotion to Our Lady of Mount Carmel, they simultaneously honor Ezili Danto, the *lwa* that "walks a path" with Mount Carmel. McAlister argues that Vodou is very much present but obscured by shared Catholic idioms.

10 McAlister, "Madonna of 115th Street Revisited," 136. In Haiti, devotees make the pilgrimage to Saut d'Eau, or Sodo, the waterfall that formed following an earthquake in 1842 in Ville Bonheur, a small mountain town outside of Port-au-Prince. According to oral tradition, in July 1849 a farmer saw in a palm tree an apparition of the Virgin Mary, Viej Mirak, wearing a mantle and a crown in a tree near the waterfall. According to Elizabeth McAlister, the palm grove, called Nan Palm, is where "the Virgin dwells with her counterpart Ezili Danto, the powerful African goddess." Scholars have understood the pilgrimage as a multivalent site, of devotion to Our Lady of Mount Carmel and the *lwa* Ezili Danto, and an important Marian pilgrimage undertaken by *katolik fran*, or frank Catholics who do not also practice Vodou and by Vodou practitioners alike. See McAlister, "Madonna of 115th Street Revisited"; Laguerre, "Haïtian Pilgrimage to O.L. of Saut d'Eau." For more on Haitian religion, see Rey and Stepick, *Crossing the Water and Keeping the Faith*.

11 See Sciorra, "We Go Where the Italians Live," 334. In his study of Italian American processions in Williamsburg, Sciorra agrees with Orsi that feasts for Our Lady of Mount Carmel are marked by inclusion and tolerance for the Haitian devotees who began to visit them in the 1980s, citing the inclusion of a Creole Mass in 1986 and peacefully shared processional space.

12 Bruce, *Parish and Place*; Hoover, *Shared Parish*; Garces-Foley, "From the Melting Pot to the Multicultural Table"; Casavantes Bradford, "'Let the Cuban Community Aid Its Haitian Brothers.'" On ethnic succession in parishes, see Jackson, "After the Exodus" and Kanter, "Making Mexican Parishes."

13 Wuthnow, "Taking Talk Seriously," 7.

14 Tweed, *Crossing and Dwelling*, 13.

15 Tweed, "On Moving Across," 257.

16 Wuthnow, "Taking Talk Seriously," 7.

17 David Vidal, "7 Priests from Haiti Bridge a Cultural Gap in Brooklyn," *New York Times*, July 23, 1975.

18 Ed Wilkinson, "These Are the Stars of Diocese of Immigrants," *Tablet*, October 14, 2015, www.thetablet.org; Marie Elena Giossi, "St. Joseph Honored as Role Model to Haitians," *Tablet*, March 25, 2015, www.thetablet.org.

19 Marie Elena Giossi, "Church Puts Faith in West Indian Carnival," *Tablet*, September 9, 2015, www.thetablet.org; Ed Wilkinson, "West Indian Parade Began with Mass in Crown Heights," *Tablet*, September 7, 2016, www.thetablet.org; Antonina Zielinska, "Faith on Parade at West Indian Carnival (with Slideshow)," *Tablet*, September 3, 2014, www.thetablet.org; Antonina Zielinska, "Festive Faith— Diocesan Contingent Participates in West Indian Festival in Crown Heights," *Tablet*, September 5, 2012, www.thetablet.org.

20 Marie Elena Giossi, "Elmhurst Haitians Continue Tradition of Home," *Tablet*, June 29, 2016, www.thetablet.org.

21 Goldschmidt, *Race and Religion*.

22 "Minutes of Our Lady of Mount Carmel Parish Hearing on Racism," February 13, 1991, OLMC Archives. The Southside of Williamsburg became home to increasing numbers of Puerto Ricans in the 1950s as people migrated from the island. They called their part of the neighborhood Los Sures. On the Southside the word "South," Sur in Spanish, precedes the number of each street, for example South First or Sur Uno. Puerto Ricans largely lived between South First and South Eleventh streets according to Nicole Marwell. For more on the Southside and its Hasidic Puerto Rican and Latino population and their role in the neighborhood housing movement, see Marwell, *Bargaining for Brooklyn*, 40.

23 Goldschmidt, *Race and Religion*, 118.

24 Goldschmidt, *Race and Religion*, 117.

25 Mangano, "Italian Tent Work in Brooklyn."

26 "Priests Unite to Stop Religious Fireworks," *Brooklyn Daily Eagle*, September 14, 1908.

27 Herbert Hadley, "Religious Conditions in Italy," *America* 12, no. 3 (October 31, 1914).

28 "Letters to the Editor," *America* 12, no. 7 (November 28, 1914): 168.

29 Jacob Riis, "Feast Days in Little Italy," *Century Illustrated Monthly Magazine* 58, no. 4 (August 1899): 499.

30 Riis, "Feast Days in Little Italy," 494.

31 Vecoli, "Prelates and Peasants," 234; Vecoli, *Cult and Occult in Italian-American Culture*; Tolino, "Solving the Italian Problem"; "The American Bishops and the 'Italian Problem,'" *Center for Migration Studies Special Issues* 16 (2002).

32 Cressler, *Authentically Black and Truly Catholic*. Cressler draws upon Evans, *Burden of Black Religion*.

33 Dolan, *In Search of an American Catholicism*, 222–23.

34 "Letters to the Editor," *America* 12, no. 10 (December 19, 1914).

35 Aaron Short, "Defaced! Sacred Statue 'KISS'ed,'" *Bay News*, February 9–15, 2012.

36 Bernard Lynch, "The Italians in New York," *Catholic World* 47 (April–September 1888): 69, 70. In "Prelates and Peasants," Vecoli discusses how this probably was written by Bernard's brother Thomas Lynch, pastor of Transfiguration Parish on Mott Street in the Lower East Side.

37 According to Robert Orsi in *Thank You, St. Jude*, if petitions can be understood as "manipulative magic," then they are the "manipulative magic of human relationships" made through intimate relations between devotees and the saints they approach as powerful friends (12).

38 McGee, "Haitian Vodou and Voodoo," 233, 239; McGee, "Imagined Voodoo."

39 Wuthnow, "Taking Talk Seriously," 7.

40 Thanks to Judith Weisenfeld for this apt description.

CHAPTER 6. RELIGION AND GENTRIFICATION IN THE
TWENTY-FIRST-CENTURY CITY

1 Katie Honan, "An Old Brooklyn Church Seeks New Muscle to Save a Tradition," *Wall Street Journal*, June 10, 2019, www.wsj.com.

2 "Wanted: Able-Bodied Men Willing to Help Continue a Long-Running Italian Tradition in Williamsburg," *CBS New York*, June 13, 2019, www.newyork.cbslocal. com; "Who Will Save the Tower of Giglio Tradition?," *CBS New York*, June 13, 2019, www.newyork.cbslocal.com.

3 "National Trust: One-Third of Canada's Churches to Close within 10 Years," *Crux*, March 29, 2019, www.cruxnow.com; "Why It Matters 9,000 Churches and Religious Spaces Will Close over Next 10 Years," *CBC News*, May 27, 2019, www. cbc.ca; "Fewer Parishioners, Less Money Has Tampa Bay Churches Selling Off Property," *Tampa Bay Times*, June 17, 2019, www.tampabay.com; "Diocese of Pittsburgh Closing Four Church Buildings in Washington Co.," *CBS Pittsburgh*, February 2, 2019, www.pittsburgh.cbslocal.com; "Parishes without Pastors Decline, but Only Because More Churches Have Closed," *America Magazine*, June 14, 2019, www.americamagazine.org; "Two U.S. Churches: One Is Closing Down Parishes, the Other Is Standing-Room Only," *America Magazine*, April 19, 2019, www.americamagazine.org.

4 See Gamm, *Urban Exodus*; McGreevy, *Parish Boundaries*; McMahon, *What Parish Are You From?*; Neary, "Black-Belt Catholic Space"; Rieder, *Canarsie*. On suburbanization, see McDannell, *Spirit of Vatican II*. On ethnic succession, see Jackson, "After the Exodus."

5 Seitz, *No Closure*.

6 Krase and DeSena, *Race, Class, and Gentrification in Brooklyn*, 21.

7 "Williamsburg Real Estate Market Overview," Trulia, www.trulia.com; "Census Profile: NYC-Brooklyn Community District 1—Greenpoint & Williamsburg PUMA, NY," *Census Reporter*, www.censusreporter.org.

8 "Brooklyn Rental Market Report," MNS Real Estate, www.mns.com.

9 Roxana Baiceanu, "Gentrified Brooklyn Neighborhoods See Home Prices per Square Foot Shooting Up," *Property Shark*, December 27, 2012, www.propertyshark.com; "Real Estate Market Trends for Williamsburg," Trulia, www.trulia.com.

10 Edward Bloustein School of Planning and Public Policy, "Gentrification and Rezoning in Williamsburg-Greenpoint," 5.

11 Shkuda, *Lofts of SoHo*, 2–3, 10.

12 Shkuda, *Lofts of SoHo*, 3.

13 Thanks to Garrett Hall, Hannah Sterrs, R. J. Sonbeek, and Isaac Daniels for these reflections.

14 Lees, Slater, and Wyly, *Gentrification*, xv.

15 Perez, *Near Northwest Side Story*, 139.

16 Smith, *New Urban Frontier*; Brown-Saracino, *Gentrification Debates*, 52.

17 Moss, *Vanishing New York*, 37. See also DeSena and Krase, "Brooklyn Revisited."

18 Moss, *Vanishing New York*, 37.

19 Hackworth and Smith, "Changing State of Gentrification."

20 See Allen, *Rise Up, O Men of God*; White, *Lost in the USA*. See also Linkon, "Men without Work"; Walkerdine and Jimenez, *Gender, Work and Community*.

21 Richard Cimino has argued that "Williamsburg-Greenpoint and the subsequent re-location of the area's long-time residents has not dissipated religious life as much as segmented it as congregations seek to fill and exploit various niches to meet religious needs and reaffirm their identities." Cimino, "Neighborhoods, Niches, and Networks."

22 See Ley and Martin, "Gentrification as Secularization"; Mian, "'Prophets-for-Profits'"; Hackworth and Gullikson, "Giving New Meaning to Religious Conversion."

23 Aaron Short, "No Separation of Church and Estate! W'burg Chapel to Convert to Housing," *Brooklyn Paper*, January 14, 2012, www.brooklynpaper.com; Dave Hogarty, "Vows of Poverty Frowned Upon at Rectory-Turned-Rentals," *Curbed NY*, September 14, 2012, www.ny.curbed.com; Aaron Short, "House of God Saved for Housing," *Brooklyn Paper*, January 20–26, 2012, www.brooklynpaper.com; Rick Hampson, "Our Lady of Revenue: NYC Churches on the Market," *USA Today*, February 27, 2015, www.usatoday.com.

24 "Losing Our Religion," *Curbed NY*, October 20, 2014, www.ny.curbed.com; Sara Polsky, "16 Religious Buildings Converted in Co-ops and Condos," *Curbed NY*, October 25, 2012, www.ny.curbed.com; Zoe Rosenberg, "Mapping 26 NYC Houses of Worship Replaced by Condos," *Curbed NY*, May 29, 2014, www.ny.curbed.com.

25 Krase and DeSena, *Race, Class, and Gentrification in Brooklyn*, 17–18.

26 "A Church in Little Italy," *Brooklyn Daily Eagle*, April 19, 1896. For more on race and gender and the construction of blackness and criminality vis-à-vis European immigrants in this period, see Hartman, *Wayward Lives, Beautiful Experiments*; Muhammad, *Condemnation of Blackness*.

27 "Pastors and People," *Brooklyn Daily Eagle*, July 17, 1887.

28 "A Church in Little Italy," *Brooklyn Daily Eagle*, April 19, 1896; "Priest's 25th Anniversary," *Brooklyn Daily Eagle*, October 4, 1899.

29 "Catholic News," *Brooklyn Daily Eagle*, November 23, 1912.

30 Tomasi, *Piety and Power*; Matovina, "National Parish and Americanization"; and "American Catholicism Aids the Immigrant," *Center for Migration Studies Special Issues* 1, no. 1 (January 1, 1975).

31 Diocese of Brooklyn, "Chronological List of Brooklyn Parishes 1822–2008," http://dioceseofbrooklyn.org.

32 "Priest Drops Dead in Grand Central," *Brooklyn Daily Eagle*, August 1, 1926.

33 In March 1933 architects Hume, French & Lefante displayed photographs of the church at the Architectural League of New York. Mumford and Wojtowicz, *Sidewalk Critic*, 96.

34 "Catholics to Lay Cornerstone for New Church," *Brooklyn Daily Eagle*, September 21, 1929.

35 "$75,000,000 Highway Backed by Engineer," *New York Times*, April 25, 1931.

36 Correspondence from William F. Daley to Bishop's Office, December 10, 1945, Diocese of Brooklyn, Bishop's Office Parish Correspondence Files, box 12 OLL 1834, Brooklyn Our Lady of Mount Carmel.

37 "Father Giorgio Triangle," NYC Parks (n.d.), www.nycgovparks.org.

38 Marwell, *Bargaining for Brooklyn*, 38.

39 For more on Brooklyn Heights and organizing to resist the Brooklyn-Queens Expressway, see Osman, *Invention of Brownstone Brooklyn*; Christopher Gray, "Brooklyn Heights Promenade, Streetscapes—Brought to Us by the B.Q.E.," *New York Times*, January 12, 2012. According to Nicole Marwell, because Williamsburg was the narrowest section of North Brooklyn, closest to both Manhattan and Queens, it was "an indispensable fulcrum for [Moses's] planned Brooklyn Queens Expressway." For more on Williamsburg's other ethnic communities, see Marwell, *Bargaining for Brooklyn*; Schneider, *Police Power and Race Riots*.

40 For more on noise complaints and distinction between "good" and "bad" religion, see Weiner, *Religion Out Loud*.

41 "Priests Unite to Stop Religious Fireworks," *Brooklyn Daily Eagle*, September 14, 1908; "Italian Celebrations: Two Protests Against Bomb Explosions—Houses Shaken and Nerves Racked," *Brooklyn Daily Eagle*, June 15, 1906.

42 "The Glorious Fourth and Its Limitations," *Brooklyn Daily Eagle*, June 15, 1907; "Italian Celebrations," *Brooklyn Daily Eagle*, June 15, 1906; "Prompt Work Stopped, a Possible Panic," *Brooklyn Daily Eagle*, June 14, 1907.

43 "The Glorious Fourth and Its Limitations," *Brooklyn Daily Eagle*, June 15, 1907.

44 "Police Quelled Riot with Nightsticks," *Brooklyn Daily Eagle*, July 17, 1902.

45 "Feast Turned into Fight," *Brooklyn Daily Eagle*, August 6, 1899.

46 "Affairs in Brooklyn," *New York Tribune (1866–1899)*, August 6, 1890.

47 "Daredevil Dancers Face Death High in Sky at Church Fair," *Brooklyn Daily Eagle*, July 13, 1954.

48 See Orsi, *Madonna of 115th Street*; Orsi, "Religious Boundaries of an Inbetween People"; Gans, *Urban Villagers*; Whyte, *Street Corner Society*; Ferraiuolo, *Religious Festive Practices in Boston's North End*; Ferraiuolo, "Boston's North End"; and De Marco, "Boston's Italian Enclave."

49 Gooch, "New Bohemia," 31; Anasi, *Last Bohemia*.

50 Gooch, "New Bohemia," 28.

51 Curran and Hanson, "Getting Globalized," 467.

52 Gooch, "New Bohemia," 28.

53 Franz, *Gentrification in Neighbourhood Development*, 114; Gooch, "New Bohemia"; Zukin, *Naked City*; Curran and Hanson, "Getting Globalized," 472; Curran, "'From the Frying Pan to the Oven.'"

54 Curran, "Gentrification and the Nature of Work," 1247; Curran and Hanson, "Getting Globalized," 462.

55 Zukin et al., "New Retail Capital."

56 Zukin, *Naked City*, 37.

57 Zukin et al., "New Retail Capital," 53.

58 Harvey, "Neo-liberalism as Creative Destruction," 150; Zukin et al., "New Retail Capital," 53; Harvey, "From Managerialism to Entrepreneurialism"; Krase and DeSena, *Race, Class, and Gentrification in Brooklyn*.

59 Curran and Hanson, "Getting Globalized," 465.

60 Krase and DeSena, *Race, Class, and Gentrification in Brooklyn*, 83.

61 DeSena and Krase, "Brooklyn Revisited," 8; DeSena, *Protecting One's Turf*. For more on Catholics resisting African Americans moving into their neighborhoods, see McGreevy, *Parish Boundaries*.

62 Zukin et al., "New Retail Capital," 58.

63 Zukin et al., "New Retail Capital," 48.

64 Hymowitz, *New Brooklyn*, 70.

65 "Retail," "The Building," and "Neighborhood," 25 Kent (n.d.), www.twentyfivekent.com.

66 Brash, "Ghost in the Machine," 138.

67 Brash, "Ghost in the Machine," 140.

68 Brash, "Ghost in the Machine," 143.

69 See Caro, *Power Broker*; New York Preservation Archive Project, "Robert Moses," *Preservation History Database* (2016), www.nypap.org; Gratz, *Battle for Gotham*; Ballon and Jackson, *Robert Moses and the Modern City*; Christin, *Robert Moses*; Larson, *Building Like Moses with Jacobs in Mind*; Schwartz, *New York Approach*; Wallock, "Myth of the Master Builder."

70 Brash, "Ghost in the Machine"; Brash, *Bloomberg's New York*.

71 Jane Jacobs, "Letter to Mayor Bloomberg and the City Council," *Brooklyn Rail*, May 2005, www.brooklynrail.org. For more on Jane Jacobs and urbanism, see Jacobs, *Death and Life of Great American Cities*; Laurence, *Becoming Jane Jacobs*. For more on Jacobs and the rezoning plan in Brooklyn, see Krase and DeSena, *Race, Class, and Gentrification in Brooklyn*, 85; Stabrowski, "New-Build Gentrification," 794; Rauscher and Momtaz, *Brooklyn's Bushwick*, 99.

72 Zukin, *Naked City*, 60.

73 Zukin, *Naked City*.

74 US Census Bureau, "American Community Survey 5-Year Estimates: Census Reporter Profile Page for NYC-Brooklyn Community District 1—Greenpoint & Williamsburg PUMA, NY" (2017), www.censusreporter.org; US Census Bureau, "Race American Community Survey 1-Year Estimates" (2017), www.censusreporter.org; "Planning-Population-Decennial Census-Census 2010-DCP" (n.d.), www.nyc.gov; US Census Bureau, "U.S. Census Bureau Quick-Facts: New York City, New York" (n.d.), www.census.gov.

75 Zukin, "Consuming Authenticity."

76 "Correspondence from William F. Daley to Bishop's Office," Diocese of Brooklyn Archives.

77 Sabean and Teuscher, "Introduction," 17.
78 Sabean, "Descent and Alliance," 144.
79 Johnson et al., *Blood and Kinship*, 17.
80 Bynum, *Wonderful Blood*, 1.
81 Bynum, *Wonderful Blood*, 3.
82 Bynum, *Wonderful Blood*, 125.
83 Bynum, *Wonderful Blood*, 136–37.
84 Bynum, *Wonderful Blood*, 165, 136.

EPILOGUE
1 Kimmel, *Angry White Men*, 16–17.

BIBLIOGRAPHY

Alba, Richard D. "The Twilight of Ethnicity among Americans of European Ancestry: The Case of Italians." *Ethnic and Racial Studies* 8, no. 1 (January 1, 1985): 134–58.

Alba, Richard, Albert J. Raboteau, and Josh DeWind. *Immigration and Religion in America: Comparative and Historical Perspectives*. New York: New York University Press, 2009.

Alcedo, Patrick. "Sacred Camp: Transgendering Faith in a Philippine Festival." *Journal of Southeast Asian Studies* 38, no. 1 (February 2007): 107–32.

Allen, Judith A. "Men Interminably in Crisis? Historians on Masculinity, Sexual Boundaries, and Manhood." *Radical History Review* 82, no. 1 (2002): 191–207.

Allen, L. Dean. *Rise Up, O Men of God: The Men and Religion Forward Movement and Promise Keepers*. Macon, GA: Mercer University Press, 2002.

Ammerman, Nancy T. "Finding Religion in Everyday Life." *Sociology of Religion* 75, no. 2 (June 1, 2014): 189–207.

Anasi, Robert. *The Last Bohemia: Scenes from the Life of Williamsburg, Brooklyn*. New York: Farrar, Straus and Giroux, 2012.

Appleby, R. Scott, and Kathleen Sprows Cummings. *Catholics in the American Century: Recasting Narratives of U.S. History*. Ithaca, NY: Cornell University Press, 2012.

Avella, Leonardo. *Annali della Festa dei Gigli (1500–1950)*. Naples: Istituto Grafico Editoriale Italiano, 1989.

Bachelard, Gaston. *The Poetics of Space*. Boston: Beacon, 1994.

Ballacchino, Katia. "Embodying Devotion, Embodying Passion: The Italian Tradition of the Festa Dei Gigli in Nola." In *Encounters of Body and Soul in Contemporary Religious Practices*, edited by Anna Fedele and Ruy Llera Blanes, 43–66. New York: Berghahn Books, 2011.

———. *Etnografia di una Passione: I Gigli di Nola tra Patrimonializzazione ai Tempi dell'UNESCO*. Rome: Armando Editore, 2015.

———. "Is Watching the Feast Making the Feast? Visual Language and Practice in an Ethnography." *Anthrovision Vaneasa*, no. 1.2 (August 1, 2013).

———. "Unity Makes . . . Intangible Heritage: Italy and Network Nomination." In *Heritage Regimes and the State*, 2nd ed., ed. Regina Bendix, Aditya Eggert, and Arnika Peselmann, 121–41. Göttingen: Universitätsverlag Göttingen, 2013.

Ballon, Hilary, and Kenneth T. Jackson. *Robert Moses and the Modern City: The Transformation of New York*. New York: Norton, 2007.

Baltimore, Sam. "Ashman's Aladdin Archive: Queer Orientalism in the Disney Renaissance." In *The Disney Musical on Stage and Screen: Critical Approaches from "Snow White" to "Frozen,"* edited by George Rodosthenous, 205–20. London: Bloomsbury, 2017.

Barth, Fredrik. *Ethnic Groups and Boundaries: The Social Organization of Culture Difference.* Long Grove, IL: Waveland, 1998.

Bartholomaeus, Clare, and Anna Tarrant. "Masculinities at the Margins of 'Middle Adulthood': What a Consideration of Young Age and Old Age Offers Masculinities Theorizing." *Men and Masculinities* 19, no. 4 (October 1, 2016): 351–69.

Bartkowski, John. "Breaking Walls, Raising Fences: Masculinity, Intimacy, and Accountability among the Promise Keepers." *Sociology of Religion* 61, no. 1 (April 1, 2000): 33–53.

———. *Promise Keepers: Servants, Soldiers and Godly Men.* New Brunswick, NJ: Rutgers University Press, 2004.

Bederman, Gail. *Manliness and Civilization: A Cultural History of Gender and Race in the United States, 1880–1917.* Chicago: University of Chicago Press, 2008.

———. "'The Women Have Had Charge of the Church Work Long Enough': The Men and Religion Forward Movement of 1911–1912 and the Masculinization of Middle-Class." *American Quarterly* 41, no. 3 (September 1, 1989): 432–65.

Beliso-De Jesus, Aisha. *Electric Santería: Racial and Sexual Assemblages of Transnational Religion.* New York: Columbia University Press, 2015.

Belk, Russell W., and Melanie Wallendorf. "The Sacred Meanings of Money." *Journal of Economic Psychology* 11, no. 1 (March 1, 1990): 35–67.

Bell, Catherine. *Ritual Theory, Ritual Practice.* New York: Oxford University Press, 1992.

Bender, Courtney. *Heaven's Kitchen: Living Religion at God's Love We Deliver.* Chicago: University of Chicago Press, 2003.

———. "Review Essay: Past Practices—Ethnography and American Religion." *Religion and American Culture* 21, no. 2 (2011): 259–76.

Bielo, James S. *Ark Encounter: The Making of a Creationist Theme Park.* New York: New York University Press, 2018.

———. "Materializing the Bible: Ethnographic Methods for the Consumption Process." *Practical Matters Journal* 9 (2016).

———. *Words upon the Word: An Ethnography of Evangelical Group Bible Study.* New York: New York University Press, 2009.

Bird, Sharon R. "Welcome to the Men's Club: Homosociality and the Maintenance of Hegemonic Masculinity." *Gender and Society* 10, no. 2 (1996): 120–32.

Bisaha, Nancy. *Creating East and West: Renaissance Humanists and the Ottoman Turks.* Philadelphia: University of Pennsylvania Press, 2010.

Blazer, Annie. *Playing for God: Evangelical Women and the Unintended Consequences of Sports Ministry.* New York: New York University Press, 2015.

Bourdieu, Pierre. *Masculine Domination.* Redwood City, CA: Stanford University Press, 2001.

———. *Outline of a Theory of Practice*. New York: Cambridge University Press, 1977.

Brash, Julian. *Bloomberg's New York: Class and Governance in the Luxury City*. Athens: University of Georgia Press, 2011.

———. "The Ghost in the Machine: The Neoliberal Urban Visions of Michael Bloomberg." *Journal of Cultural Geography* 29, no. 2 (June 1, 2012): 135–53.

Bridger, Jeffrey C., and David R. Maines. "Narrative Structures and the Catholic Church Closings in Detroit." *Qualitative Sociology* 21, no. 3 (September 1, 1998): 319–40.

Britton, Dana M. "Homophobia and Homosociality: An Analysis of Boundary Maintenance." *Sociological Quarterly* 31, no. 3 (1990): 423–39.

Brown, Karen McCarthy. *Mama Lola: A Vodou Priestess in Brooklyn*. Berkeley: University of California Press, 2001.

Brown, Kathleen. "'Strength of the Lion . . . Arms Like Polished Iron': Embodying Black Masculinity in an Age of Slavery and Propertied Manhood." In Foster, *New Men*, 172–94.

Brown, Mary Elizabeth. "The Making of Italian-American Catholics: Jesuit Work on the Lower East Side, New York, 1890's–1950's." *Catholic Historical Review* 73, no. 2 (1987): 195–210.

Brown, Peter. *The Cult of the Saints: Its Rise and Function in Latin Christianity*. Enlarged ed. Chicago: University of Chicago Press, 2014.

Browning, Barbara. *Infectious Rhythm: Metaphors of Contagion and the Spread of African Culture*. Abingdon: Routledge, 2013.

Brown-Saracino, Japonica. *The Gentrification Debates: A Reader*. London: Routledge, 2013.

Bruce, Tricia Colleen. *Parish and Place: Making Room for Diversity in the American Catholic Church*. New York: Oxford University Press, 2017.

Burke, Kevin. *Masculinities and Other Hopeless Causes at an All-Boys Catholic School*. New York: Peter Lang, 2011.

Burton, Richard D. E. *Holy Tears, Holy Blood: Women, Catholicism, and the Culture of Suffering in France, 1840–1970*. Ithaca, NY: Cornell University Press, 2004.

Butler, Alban. "The Lives of the Saints." *Bartleby* (1866). www.bartleby.com.

Butler, Anthea D. *Women in the Church of God in Christ: Making a Sanctified World*. Chapel Hill: University of North Carolina Press, 2007.

Butler, Judith. *Gender Trouble: Feminism and the Subversion of Identity*. Routledge, 2011.

———. "Performative Acts and Gender Constitution: An Essay in Phenomenology and Feminist Theory." *Theatre Journal* 40, no. 4 (1988): 519–31.

Bynum, Caroline Walker. *Christian Materiality: An Essay on Religion in Late Medieval Europe*. New York: Zone Books, 2011.

———. *Wonderful Blood: Theology and Practice in Late Medieval Northern Germany and Beyond*. Philadelphia: University of Pennsylvania Press, 2007.

Byrne, Julie. "Catholicism Doesn't Always Mean What You Think It Means." *Exchange* 48, no. 3 (July 19, 2019): 214–24.

———. *O God of Players: The Story of the Immaculata Mighty Macs*. New York: Columbia University Press, 2003.

Carnes, Mark C. *Secret Ritual and Manhood in Victorian America*. New Haven, CT: Yale University Press, 1991.

Caro, Robert A. *The Power Broker: Robert Moses and the Fall of New York*. New York: Vintage, 1975.

Carroll, Michael P. *American Catholics in the Protestant Imagination: Rethinking the Academic Study of Religion*. Baltimore: Johns Hopkins University Press, 2007.

Casavantes Bradford, Anita. "'Let the Cuban Community Aid Its Haitian Brothers': Monsignor Bryan Walsh, Miami's Immigrant Church, and the Making of a Multiethnic City, 1960–2000." *U.S. Catholic Historian* 34, no. 3 (2016): 99–126.

Casselberry, Judith. *The Labor of Faith: Gender and Power in Black Apostolic Pentecostalism*. Durham, NC: Duke University Press, 2017.

Castañeda-Liles, María Del Socorro. *Our Lady of Everyday Life: La Virgen de Guadalupe and the Catholic Imagination of Mexican Women in America*. New York: Oxford University Press, 2018.

Ceparano, Felice. "The *Gigli* of Nola during Rodia's Times." In *Sabato Rodia's Towers in Watts: Art, Migrations, Development*, edited by Luisa Del Giudice, 125–44. New York: Fordham University Press, 2014.

Chávez, Arturo. "Virgin of Guadalupe Tattoos: Embodied Symbols and the Construction of Racial and Gendered Identity among Mexican American Men." PhD dissertation, Iliff School of Theology and University of Denver, 2006.

Chesnut, R. Andrew. *Devoted to Death: Santa Muerte, the Skeleton Saint*. Oxford: Oxford University Press, 2018.

Chidester, David. "Haptics of the Heart: The Sense of Touch in American Religion and Culture." *Culture and Religion* 1, no. 1 (May 1, 2000): 61–84.

Chidester, David, and Edward Tabor Linenthal. *American Sacred Space*. Bloomington: Indiana University Press, 1995.

Chinnici, Joseph. "The Catholic Community at Prayer, 1926–1976." In O'Toole, *Habits of Devotion*, 9–87.

Christian, William A. *Local Religion in Sixteenth-Century Spain*. Princeton, NJ: Princeton University Press, 1989.

Christin, Pierre. *Robert Moses: The Master Builder of New York City*. London: Nobrow, 2018.

Cimino, Richard. "Neighborhoods, Niches, and Networks: The Religious Ecology of Gentrification." *City and Community* 10, no. 2 (June 1, 2011): 157–81.

Clites, Brian J. "Soul Murder: Sketches of Survivor Imaginaries." *Exchange* 48, no. 3 (July 19, 2019): 268–79.

Coe, Kathryn, Mary P. Harmon, Blair Verner, and Andrew Tonn. "Tattoos and Male Alliances." *Human Nature* 4, no. 2 (June 1, 1993): 199–204.

Collinson, David L. "'Engineering Humour': Masculinity, Joking and Conflict in Shop-Floor Relations." *Organization Studies* 9, no. 2 (1988): 181–99.

Connell, R. W. "Growing Up Masculine: Rethinking the Significance of Adolescence in the Making of Masculinities." *Irish Journal of Sociology* 14, no. 2 (2005): 11–28.

———. *Masculinities.* 2nd ed. Berkeley: University of California Press, 2005.

Connell, R. W., and James W. Messerschmidt. "Hegemonic Masculinity: Rethinking the Concept." *Gender and Society* 19, no. 6 (2005): 829–59.

Conquergood, Dwight. "Performing as a Moral Act: Ethical Dimensions of the Ethnography of Performance." *Literature in Performance* 5, no. 2 (April 1985): 1–13.

Conway, Daniel. "Faith versus Money: Conflicting Views of Stewardship and Fundraising in the Church." *New Directions for Philanthropic Fundraising* 1995, no. 7 (1995): 71–77.

Copsey, Richard. "Simon Stock and the Scapular Vision." *Journal of Ecclesiastical History* 50, no. 4 (October 1999): 652–83.

Cosentino, Donald. "Vernacular Miracles: Blood and Bones in Neapolitan Religion." *Material Religion* 10, no. 4 (December 1, 2014): 472–92.

Coster, Charles Henry. "Christianity and the Invasions: Two Sketches." *Classical Journal* 54, no. 4 (1959): 146–59.

Cressler, Matthew J. *Authentically Black and Truly Catholic: The Rise of Black Catholicism in the Great Migration.* New York: New York University Press, 2017.

Cummings, Kathleen Sprows. *New Women of the Old Faith: Gender and American Catholicism in the Progressive Era.* Chapel Hill: University of North Carolina Press, 2009.

Curran, Winifred. "'From the Frying Pan to the Oven': Gentrification and the Experience of Industrial Displacement in Williamsburg, Brooklyn." *Urban Studies* 44, no. 8 (July 1, 2007): 1427–40.

———. "Gentrification and the Nature of Work: Exploring the Links in Williamsburg, Brooklyn." *Environment and Planning A* 36, no. 7 (July 1, 2004): 1243–58.

———. "In Defense of Old Industrial Spaces: Manufacturing, Creativity and Innovation in Williamsburg, Brooklyn." *International Journal of Urban and Regional Research* 34, no. 4 (December 1, 2010): 871–85.

Curran, Winifred, and Susan Hanson. "Getting Globalized: Urban Policy and Industrial Displacement in Williamsburg, Brooklyn." *Urban Geography* 26, no. 6 (September 2005): 461–82.

D'Agostino, Peter R. "The Scalabrini Fathers, the Italian Emigrant Church, and Ethnic Nationalism in America." *Religion and American Culture* 7, no. 1 (1997): 121–59.

Davidson, Deborah, ed. *The Tattoo Project: Commemorative Tattoos, Visual Culture, and the Digital Archive.* Toronto: Canadian Scholars, 2016.

Davis, Cyprian. "Catholicism and Racism." *Review of Politics* 60, no. 1 (December 1, 1998): 186–89.

Davis, John A. *Naples and Napoleon: Southern Italy and the European Revolutions, 1780–1860.* New York: Oxford University Press, 2006.

Davis, Shannon N. "Sociology, Theory, and the Feminist Sociological Canon: Questioning the Use of 'Doing Gender' as a Sociological Theory." *SAGE Open* 7, no. 1 (January 1, 2017): 3.

de Certeau, Michel. *The Practice of Everyday Life*. Berkeley: University of California Press, 2011.

Delgado, Jessica L. *Laywomen and the Making of Colonial Catholicism in New Spain, 1630–1790*. Cambridge: Cambridge University Press, 2018.

DeMello, Margo. *Bodies of Inscription: A Cultural History of the Modern Tattoo Community*. Durham, NC: Duke University Press, 2000.

D'Emilio, John, and Estelle B. Freedman. *Intimate Matters: A History of Sexuality in America*. 3rd ed. Chicago: University of Chicago Press, 2012.

De Marco, William M. "Boston's Italian Enclave, 1880–1930." *Studi Emigrazione / Etudes Migrations* 17, no. 59 (1980): 331–59.

DeSena, Judith N. *Gentrification and Inequality in Brooklyn: The New Kids on the Block*. Lanham, MD: Lexington Books, 2009.

———. *Protecting One's Turf*. Lanham, MD: University Press of America, 2005.

DeSena, Judith, and Jerome Krase. "Brooklyn Revisited: An Illustrated View from the Street 1970 to the Present." *Urbanities—Journal of Urban Ethnography* 5, no. 2 (2015): 3–19.

DeSena, Judith, and Timothy Shortell. *The World in Brooklyn: Gentrification, Immigration, and Ethnic Politics in a Global City*. Lanham, MD: Lexington Books, 2012.

Diefendorf, Sarah. "After the Wedding Night Sexual Abstinence and Masculinities over the Life Course." *Gender and Society* 29, no. 5 (October 1, 2015): 647–69.

Dolan, Jay P. *The American Catholic Experience*. New York: Crown, 2011.

———. *In Search of an American Catholicism: A History of Religion and Culture in Tension*. New York: Oxford University Press, 2003.

Downey, Greg, Monica Dalidowicz, and Paul H. Mason. "Apprenticeship as Method: Embodied Learning in Ethnographic Practice." *Qualitative Research* 15, no. 2 (April 1, 2015): 183–200.

Driessen, Henk. "Male Sociability and Rituals of Masculinity in Rural Andalusia." *Anthropological Quarterly* 56, no. 3 (1983): 125–33.

Driessen, Henk, and Willy Jansen. "Staging Hyper-Masculinity on Maundy Thursday: Christ of the Good Death, the Legion and Changing Gender Practices in Spain." *Exchange* 42, no. 1 (January 1, 2013): 86–106.

Dugan, Katherine. *Millennial Missionaries: How a Group of Young Catholics Is Trying to Make Catholicism Cool*. New York: Oxford University Press, 2019.

———. "'St. Gemma Is My Girl!' Devotional Practices among Millennial Catholics and the Making of Contemporary Catholic Saints." *American Catholic Studies* 127, no. 4 (2016): 1–21.

Durkheim, Émile. *The Elementary Forms of the Religious Life*. Mineola, NY: Courier Dover, 2012.

Dwyer-McNulty, Sally. *Common Threads: A Cultural History of Clothing in American Catholicism*. Chapel Hill: University of North Carolina Press, 2014.

Easterday, Lois, Diana Papademas, Laura Schorr, and Catherine Valentine. "The Making of a Female Researcher: Role Problems in Field Work." *Journal of Contemporary Ethnography* 6, no. 3 (October 1, 1977): 333–48.

Edward Bloustein School of Planning and Public Policy. "Gentrification and Rezoning in Williamsburg-Greenpoint." New Brunswick, NJ: Rutgers University, Edward Bloustein School of Planning and Public Policy, 2007.

Erzen, Tanya. *Straight to Jesus: Sexual and Christian Conversions in the Ex-Gay Movement.* Berkeley: University of California Press, 2006.

Escalante, Alejandro. "Playful Masculinity: Drag Performance in La Fiesta de Santiago and Religious Belonging." Paper presented at the American Academy of Religion, San Diego, November 2019.

Eula, Michael J. "Cultural Continuity and Cultural Hegemony: Italian Catholics in New Jersey and New York, 1880–1940." *Religion* 22, no. 4 (October 1, 1992): 327–48.

Evans, Curtis J. *The Burden of Black Religion.* Oxford: Oxford University Press, 2008.

Fader, Ayala. *Mitzvah Girls: Bringing Up the Next Generation of Hasidic Jews in Brooklyn.* Princeton, NJ: Princeton University Press, 2009.

Femminella, Francis X. "The Impact of Italian Migration and American Catholicism." *American Catholic Sociological Review* 22, no. 3 (1961): 233–41.

Ferraiuolo, Augusto. "Boston's North End: Negotiating Identity in an Italian American Neighborhood." *Western Folklore* 65, no. 3 (2006): 263–302.

———. *Religious Festive Practices in Boston's North End: Ephemeral Identities in an Italian American Community.* Albany: State University of New York Press, 2012.

Ferraro, Thomas J. *Feeling Italian: The Art of Ethnicity in America.* New York: New York University Press, 2005.

Finch, Martha L. "Rehabilitating Materiality: Bodies, Gods, and Religion." *Religion* 42, no. 4 (2012): 625–31.

Fine, Gary Alan. "One of the Boys: Women in Male-Dominated Settings." In *Changing Men: New Directions in Research on Men and Masculinity,* ed. Michael S. Kimmel, 131–47. Thousand Oaks, CA: SAGE, 1987.

Fine, Gary Alan, and Michaela de Soucey. "Joking Cultures: Humor Themes as Social Regulation in Group Life." *Humor—International Journal of Humor Research* 18, no. 1 (January 20, 2005): 1–22.

Fine, Michelle, Lois Weis, Judi Addelston, and Julia Marusza. "(In)secure Times: Constructing White Working-Class Masculinities in the Late 20th Century." *Gender and Society* 11, no. 1 (1997): 52–68.

Fisher, James T. *Communion of Immigrants: A History of Catholics in America.* New York: Oxford University Press, 2002.

Flood, Michael. "Men, Sex, and Homosociality: How Bonds between Men Shape Their Sexual Relations with Women." *Men and Masculinities* 10, no. 3 (April 1, 2008): 339–59.

Fogarty, Gerald P., Robert F. Sanchez, Howard J. Hubbard, and W. Thomas Larkin. "The Parish and Community in American Catholic History." *U.S. Catholic Historian* 4, nos. 3/4 (1985): 233–69.

Fortier, Anne-Marie. "Re-membering Places and the Performance of Belonging(s)." *Theory, Culture and Society* 16, no. 2 (1999): 41–64.

Foster, Thomas A., ed. *New Men: Manliness in Early America*. New York: New York University Press, 2011.

Foucault, Michel. *The History of Sexuality*. New York: Vintage, 1988.

Fouron, Georges E. "Race, Blood, Disease and Citizenship: The Making of the Haitian-Americans and the Haitian Immigrants into 'the Others' during the 1980s–1990s AIDS Crisis." *Identities* 20, no. 6 (December 1, 2013): 705–19.

Franchot, Jenny. *Roads to Rome: The Antebellum Protestant Encounter with Catholicism*. Berkeley: University of California Press, 1994.

Franco, Philip Anthony. "Educating toward Communion: The Traditional Italian Festa as a Means of Christian Religious Education." *Religious Education* 102, no. 1 (April 1, 2007): 25–43.

———. "The Traditional Italian Festa: Toward a Theology of Communion and Catechesis." PhD dissertation, Fordham University, 2006.

Franz, Yvonne. *Gentrification in Neighbourhood Development: Case Studies from New York City, Berlin and Vienna*. Göttingen: V&R Unipress, 2015.

Frederick, Marla. *Between Sundays: Black Women and Everyday Struggles of Faith*. Berkeley: University of California Press, 2003.

Freedberg, David. *The Power of Images: Studies in the History and Theory of Response*. Chicago: University of Chicago Press, 1989.

Freeman, Robert C. "The Development and Maintenance of New York City's Italian-American Neighborhoods." *Center for Migration Studies Special Issues* 6, no. 4 (July 1, 1988): 223–38.

Furey, Constance M. "Body, Society, and Subjectivity in Religious Studies." *Journal of the American Academy of Religion* 80, no. 1 (March 1, 2012): 7–33.

Galvez, Alyshia. *Guadalupe in New York: Devotion and the Struggle for Citizenship Rights*. New York: New York University Press, 2010.

Gamm, Gerald. *Urban Exodus: Why the Jews Left Boston and the Catholics Stayed*. Cambridge, MA: Harvard University Press, 2009.

Gans, Herbert J. "The Coming Darkness of Late-Generation European American Ethnicity." *Ethnic and Racial Studies* 37, no. 5 (April 16, 2014): 757–65.

———. "Symbolic Ethnicity: The Future of Ethnic Groups and Cultures in America." *Ethnic and Racial Studies* 2 (1979): 1–20.

———. "Symbolic Ethnicity and Symbolic Religiosity: Towards a Comparison of Ethnic and Religious Acculturation." *Ethnic and Racial Studies* 17, no. 4 (October 1, 1994): 577–92.

———. *Urban Villagers*. Rev. ed. New York: Simon & Schuster, 1982.

Garces-Foley, Kathleen. "From the Melting Pot to the Multicultural Table: Filipino Catholics in Los Angeles." *American Catholic Studies* 120, no. 1 (2009): 27–53.

Gelfer, Joseph. "Identifying the Catholic Men's Movement." *Journal of Men's Studies* 16, no. 1 (Winter 2008): 41–56.

Gerber, Lynne. "Grit, Guts, and Vanilla Beans Godly Masculinity in the Ex-Gay Movement." *Gender and Society* 29, no. 1 (February 1, 2015): 26–50.

Gibino, Joseph Raymond. "Facciamo Una Festa: Politics and Ritual in an Italo-American Folk Festival." PhD dissertation, University of Rochester, 1990.

Gill, Rosalind, Karen Henwood, and Carl McLean. "Body Projects and the Regulation of Normative Masculinity." *Body and Society* 11, no. 1 (March 1, 2005): 37–62.

Gleason, Arthur. "Going after Souls on a Business Basis." *Collier's* 48, no. 14 (December 1911): 13.

Goetz, Hermann. "Oriental Types and Scenes in Renaissance and Baroque Painting-I." *Burlington Magazine for Connoisseurs* 73, no. 425 (1938): 56.

Goffman, Erving. *The Presentation of Self in Everyday Life*. New York: Doubleday, 1959.

Goldin, Greg, and Sam Lubell. *Never Built New York*. New York: Metropolis Books, 2016.

Goldschmidt, Henry. *Race and Religion among the Chosen People of Crown Heights*. New Brunswick, NJ: Rutgers University Press, 2006.

Gooch, Brad. "The New Bohemia: Portrait of an Artists' Colony." *New York Magazine*, June 22, 1992, 24–31.

Gordon, Michelle Y. "'Midnight Scenes and Orgies': Public Narratives of Voodoo in New Orleans and Nineteenth-Century Discourses of White Supremacy." *American Quarterly* 64, no. 4 (December 30, 2012): 767–86.

Gratz, Roberta Brandes. *The Battle for Gotham: New York in the Shadow of Robert Moses and Jane*. New York: PublicAffairs, 2010.

Gravot, Dana David. "Re-membering Community: Ritual Exchange in Williamsburg's Questua." *Folk Life* 55, no. 2 (July 3, 2017): 88–111.

Grazian, David. "The Girl Hunt: Urban Nightlife and the Performance of Masculinity as Collective Activity." *Symbolic Interaction* 30, no. 2 (April 1, 2007): 221–43.

Graziano, Frank. *Cultures of Devotion: Folk Saints of Spanish America*. New York: Oxford University Press, 2006.

Greeley, Andrew. *The Catholic Imagination*. Berkeley: University of California Press, 2000.

Greer, Allan. *Mohawk Saint: Catherine Tekakwitha and the Jesuits*. New York: Oxford University Press, 2005.

Griffith, R. Marie. "Apostles of Abstinence: Fasting and Masculinity during the Progressive Era." *American Quarterly* 52, no. 4 (2000): 599–638.

———. *Born Again Bodies: Flesh and Spirit in American Christianity*. Berkeley: University of California Press, 2004.

———. *God's Daughters: Evangelical Women and the Power of Submission*. Berkeley: University of California Press, 2000.

Griswold, Robert L., and E. Anthony Rotundo. "American Manhood: Transformations in Masculinity from the Revolution to the Modern Era." *Contemporary Sociology* 23, no. 1 (January 1994): 103–4.

Guglielmo, Thomas A. *White on Arrival: Italians, Race, Color, and Power in Chicago, 1890–1945*. New York: Oxford University Press, 2004.

Gupta, Akhil, and James Ferguson. *Anthropological Locations: Boundaries and Grounds of a Field Science*. Berkeley: University of California Press, 1997.

Gurney, Joan Neff. "Not One of the Guys: The Female Researcher in a Male-Dominated Setting." *Qualitative Sociology* 8, no. 1 (1985): 42–62.

Gustav-Wrathall, John Donald. *Take the Young Stranger by the Hand: Same-Sex Relations and the YMCA*. Chicago: University of Chicago Press, 2000.

Gutmann, Matthew C. *The Meanings of Macho: Being a Man in Mexico City*. Berkeley: University of California Press, 2006.

Haas, Katherine. "The Fabric of Religion: Vestments and Devotional Catholicism in Nineteenth-Century America." *Material Religion* 3, no. 2 (July 1, 2007): 190–217.

Hackett, Rosalind I. J. "Field Envy: Or, the Perils and Pleasures of Doing Fieldwork." *Method and Theory in the Study of Religion* 13, no. 1 (2001): 98–109.

Hackworth, Jason, and Erin Gullikson. "Giving New Meaning to Religious Conversion: Churches, Redevelopment, and Secularization in Toronto." *Canadian Geographer / Le Géographe Canadien* 57, no. 1 (2013): 72–89.

Hackworth, Jason, and Neil Smith. "The Changing State of Gentrification." *Tijdschrift Voor Economische En Sociale Geografie* 92, no. 4 (November 1, 2001): 464–77.

Hadley, Herbert. "Religious Conditions in Italy." *America*, October 31, 1914.

Hall, David D., ed. *Lived Religion in America: Toward A History of Practice*. Princeton, NJ: Princeton University Press, 1997.

Halperin, David M. "Forgetting Foucault: Acts, Identities, and the History of Sexuality." *Representations*, no. 63 (July 1, 1998): 93–120.

Hammarén, Nils, and Thomas Johansson. "Homosociality." *SAGE Open* 4, no. 1 (January 1, 2014): 1–11.

Hammond, Phillip E., and Kee Warner. "Religion and Ethnicity in Late-Twentieth-Century America." *Annals of the American Academy of Political and Social Science* 527 (May 1, 1993): 55–66.

Harper, James G. *The Turk and Islam in the Western Eye, 1450–1750: Visual Imagery before Orientalism*. Farnham, UK: Ashgate, 2011.

Hartman, Saidiya. *Wayward Lives, Beautiful Experiments: Intimate Histories of Social Upheaval*. New York: Norton, 2019.

Harvey, David. "From Managerialism to Entrepreneurialism: The Transformation in Urban Governance in Late Capitalism." *Geografiska Annaler: Series B, Human Geography* 71, no. 1 (April 1, 1989): 3–17.

———. "Neo-liberalism as Creative Destruction." *Geografiska Annaler: Series B, Human Geography* 88, no. 2 (2006): 145–58.

Hasinoff, Erin L. *Faith in Objects: American Missionary Expositions in the Early Twentieth Century*. New York: Palgrave Macmillan, 2011.

Hastrup, Kirsten. "The Ethnographic Present: A Reinvention." *Cultural Anthropology* 5, no. 1 (1990): 45–61.

Hayden, Dolores. *The Power of Place: Urban Landscapes as Public History.* Cambridge, MA: MIT Press, 1997.

Hazard, Sonia. "The Material Turn in the Study of Religion." *Religion and Society: Advances in Research* 4, no. 1 (December 1, 2013): 58–78.

Heatherington, Tracey. "Street Tactics: Catholic Ritual and the Senses of the Past in Central Sardinia." *Ethnology* 38, no. 4 (1999): 315–34.

Hebblethwaite, Benjamin. "The Scapegoating of Haitian Vodou Religion." *Journal of Black Studies* 46, no. 1 (October 29, 2014): 3–22.

Hoover, Brett C. *The Shared Parish: Latinos, Anglos, and the Future of U.S. Catholicism.* New York: New York University Press, 2014.

Horn, Rebecca. "Not 'One of the Boys': Women Researching the Police." *Journal of Gender Studies* 6, no. 3 (November 1, 1997): 297–308.

Houtman, Dick, and Birgit Meyer, eds. *Things: Religion and the Question of Materiality.* New York: Fordham University Press, 2012.

Hufford, David J. "Ste. Anne de Beaupré: Roman Catholic Pilgrimage and Healing." *Western Folklore* 44, no. 3 (1985): 194–207.

Hughes, Jennifer Scheper. *Biography of a Mexican Crucifix: Lived Religion and Local Faith from the Conquest to the Present.* New York: Oxford University Press, 2010.

———. "Cradling the Sacred: Image, Ritual, and Affect in Mexican and Mesoamerican Material Religion." *History of Religions* 56, no. 1 (July 25, 2016): 55–107.

———. "God-Bearers on Pilgrimage to Tepeyac: A Scholar of Religion Encounters the Material Dimension of Marian Devotion in Mexico." *Religion and the Arts* 18, nos. 1–2 (2014): 156–83.

———. "Mysterium Materiae: Vital Matter and the Object as Evidence in the Study of Religion." *Bulletin for the Study of Religion* 41, no. 4 (November 2012): 16–24.

———. "The Niño Jesús Doctor: Novelty and Innovation in Mexican Religion." *Nova Religio* 16, no. 2 (2012): 4–28.

Hughey, Matthew W. "Backstage Discourse and the Reproduction of White Masculinities." *Sociological Quarterly* 52, no. 1 (January 1, 2011): 132–53.

Hunt, Jennifer. "The Development of Rapport through the Negotiation of Gender in Field Work among Police." *Human Organization* 43, no. 4 (Winter 1984): 283–96.

Huyssen, Andreas. *Present Pasts: Urban Palimpsests and the Politics of Memory.* Redwood City, CA: Stanford University Press, 2003.

Hymowitz, Kay S. *The New Brooklyn: What It Takes to Bring a City Back.* Lanham, MD: Rowman & Littlefield, 2017.

Iacuone, David. "'Real Men Are Tough Guys': Hegemonic Masculinity and Safety in the Construction Industry." *Journal of Men's Studies* 13, no. 2 (Winter 2005): 247–66.

Ibson, John. *Picturing Men: A Century of Male Relationships in Everyday American Photography.* Chicago: University of Chicago Press, 2006.

Imhoff, Sarah. "Manly Missions: Jews, Christians, and American Religious Masculinity, 1900–1920." *American Jewish History* 97, no. 2 (May 1, 2013): 139–58.

————. *Masculinity and the Making of American Judaism*. Bloomington: Indiana University Press, 2017.

Jackson, Regine O. "After the Exodus: The New Catholics in Boston's Old Ethnic Neighborhoods." *Religion and American Culture* 17, no. 2 (2007): 191–212.

Jacobs, Jane. *The Death and Life of Great American Cities*. New York: Random House, 1961.

Jacobson, Matthew Frye. *Whiteness of a Different Color*. Cambridge, MA: Harvard University Press, 1999.

Jasienski, Adam. "A Savage Magnificence: Ottomanizing Fashion and the Politics of Display in Early Modern East-Central Europe." *Muqarnas* 31 (2014): 173–205.

Jensen, Lori, Richard W. Flory, and Donald E. Miller. "Marked for Jesus: Sacred Tattooing among Evangelical GenXers." In *GenX Religion*, edited by Richard W. Flory and Donald E. Miller, 15–30. Abingdon: Routledge, 2013.

Jezernik, Božidar. *Imagining "the Turk."* Cambridge: Cambridge Scholars, 2009.

Jirousek, Charlotte A. *Ottoman Dress and Design in the West: A Visual History of Cultural Exchange*. Bloomington: Indiana University Press, 2019.

————. "Ottoman Influences in Western Dress." www.char.txa.cornell.edu.

Johnson, Christopher H., Bernhard Jussen, David Warren Sabean, and Simon Teuscher, eds. *Blood and Kinship: Matter for Metaphor from Ancient Rome to the Present*. New York: Berghahn Books, 2013.

Joosse, Paul. "The Presentation of the Charismatic Self in Everyday Life: Reflections on a Canadian New Religious Movement." *Sociology of Religion* 73, no. 2 (June 1, 2012): 174–99.

Juliani, Richard N. *Priest, Parish, and People: Saving the Faith in Philadelphia's "Little Italy."* South Bend, IN: University of Notre Dame Press, 2007.

Kaell, Hillary, ed. *Everyday Sacred: Religion in Contemporary Quebec*. Montreal: McGill-Queen's Press, 2017.

————. "Place Making and People Gathering at Rural Wayside Crosses." In Kaell, *Everyday Sacred*, 129–55.

Kane, Paula M. "Marian Devotion since 1940: Continuity or Casualty?" In O'Toole, *Habits of Devotion*, 89–129.

————. *Separatism and Subculture: Boston Catholicism, 1900–1920*. Chapel Hill: University of North Carolina Press, 2001.

————. "'She Offered Herself Up': The Victim Soul and Victim Spirituality in Catholicism." *Church History* 71, no. 1 (2002): 80–119.

————. *Sister Thorn and Catholic Mysticism in Modern America*. Chapel Hill: University of North Carolina Press, 2013.

Kanter, Deborah. "Making Mexican Parishes: Ethnic Succession in Chicago Churches, 1947–1977." *U.S. Catholic Historian* 30, no. 1 (2012): 35–58.

Kauffman, Christopher J. *Faith and Fraternalism: The History of the Knights of Columbus, 1882–1982*. New York: Harper & Row, 1982.

————. "The Knights of Columbus: Lay Activism from the Origins through the Great Depression." *U.S. Catholic Historian* 9, no. 3 (July 1, 1990): 261–74.

Kelleher, Patricia. "Class and Catholic Irish Masculinity in Antebellum America: Young Men on the Make in Chicago." *Journal of American Ethnic History* 28, no. 4 (July 1, 2009): 7–42.

Kelly, Timothy. "Pittsburgh Catholicism." *U.S. Catholic Historian* 18, no. 4 (October 1, 2000): 64–75.

———. "Suburbanization and the Decline of Catholic Public Ritual in Pittsburgh." *Journal of Social History* 28, no. 2 (December 1, 1994): 311–30.

———. *The Transformation of American Catholicism: The Pittsburgh Laity and the Second Vatican Council, 1950–1972.* South Bend, IN: University of Notre Dame, 2009.

Kelly, Timothy, and Joseph Kelly. "Our Lady of Perpetual Help, Gender Roles, and the Decline of Devotional Catholicism." *Journal of Social History* 32, no. 1 (October 1, 1998): 5–26.

Kendall, Laurel. "Things Fall Apart: Material Religion and the Problem of Decay." *Journal of Asian Studies* 76, no. 4 (November 2017): 861–86.

———. "Three Goddesses in and out of Their Shrine." *Asian Ethnology* 67, no. 2 (2008): 219–36.

Kendall, Laurel, Vũ Thị Hà, Vũ Thị Thanh Tâm, Nguyễn Văn Huy, and Nguyễn Thị Hiền. "Is It a Sin to Sell a Statue? Catholic Statues and the Traffic in Antiquities in Vietnam." *Museum Anthropology* 36, no. 1 (April 1, 2013): 66–82.

Kendall, Laurel, Vũ Thị Thanh Tâm, and Nguyễn Thị Thu Hu'o'ng. "Beautiful and Efficacious Statues: Magic, Commodities, Agency and the Production of Sacred Objects in Popular Religion in Vietnam." *Material Religion* 6, no. 1 (March 1, 2010): 60–85.

Kiesling, Scott Fabius. "Homosocial Desire in Men's Talk: Balancing and Re-creating Cultural Discourses of Masculinity." *Language in Society* 34, no. 5 (November 2005): 695–726.

Kimmel, Michael. *Angry White Men: American Masculinity at the End of an Era.* New York: PublicAffairs, 2017.

———. *Manhood in America: A Cultural History.* 4th ed. New York: Oxford University Press, 2018.

———. *Misframing Men: The Politics of Contemporary Masculinities.* Piscataway, NJ: Rutgers University Press, 2010.

Knott, Kim. "Spatial Theory and the Study of Religion." *Religion Compass* 2 (2008): 1102–16.

Koch, Jerome, and Alden E. Roberts. "The Protestant Ethic and the Religious Tattoo." *Social Science Journal* 49, no. 2 (June 1, 2012): 210–13.

Koehlinger, Amy L. "Blood and Adrenaline: Introduction to the Review Roundtable on Manuel Vásquez's More Than Belief: A Materialist Theory of Religion." *Method and Theory in the Study of Religion* 24, nos. 4–5 (January 1, 2012): 424–29.

———. "'Let Us Live for Those Who Love Us': Faith, Family, and the Contours of Manhood among the Knights of Columbus in Late Nineteenth-Century Connecticut." *Journal of Social History* 38, no. 2 (December 1, 2004): 455–69.

Kosut, Mary. "The Artification of Tattoo: Transformations within a Cultural Field." *Cultural Sociology* 8, no. 2 (June 1, 2014): 142–58.

———. "Tattoo Narratives: The Intersection of the Body, Self-identity and Society." *Visual Sociology* 15, no. 1 (January 1, 2000): 79–100.

Krase, Jerome. "Italian American Urban Landscapes: Images of Social and Cultural Capital." *Italian Americana* 22, no. 1 (2004): 17–44.

———. "Seeing Ethnic Succession in Little Italy: Change Despite Resistance." *Modern Italy* 11, no. 1 (2006): 79–95.

Krase, Jerome, and Judith DeSena. *Race, Class, and Gentrification in Brooklyn: A View from the Street*. Lanham, MD: Lexington Books, 2016.

Kriegel, Leonard. *On Men and Manhood*. New York: Hawthorn Books, 1979.

Kuran-Burçoğlu, Nedret. "The Image of the Turk in Europe from 11th to 20th Century as Represented in Literary and Visual Sources." *Marmara Üniversitesi Avrupa Topluluğu Enstitüsü Avrupa Araştırmaları Dergisi* 7, nos. 1–2 (1999): 187–201.

Laguerre, Michel. "Haïtian Pilgrimage to O.L. of Saut d'Eau: A Sociological Analysis." *Social Compass* 33, no. 1 (February 1, 1986): 5–21.

Lahiri, Shompa. "Remembering the City: Translocality and the Senses." *Social and Cultural Geography* 12, no. 8 (December 1, 2011): 855–69.

Lande, Brian. "Breathing like a Soldier: Culture Incarnate." *Sociological Review* 55, no. s1 (2007): 95–108.

Larson, Scott. *Building Like Moses with Jacobs in Mind: Contemporary Planning in New York City, Urban Life, Landscape, and Policy*. Philadelphia: Temple University Press, 2013.

Latour, Bruno. *On the Modern Cult of the Factish Gods*. Durham, NC: Duke University Press, 2010.

———. *Reassembling the Social: An Introduction to Actor-Network-Theory*. Oxford: Oxford University Press, 2005.

Laurence, Peter L. *Becoming Jane Jacobs*. Philadelphia: University of Pennsylvania Press, 2016.

Lawrence, Denise L., and Setha M. Low. "The Built Environment and Spatial Form." *Annual Review of Anthropology* 19 (January 1, 1990): 453–505.

Laycock, Joseph P. *The Seer of Bayside: Veronica Lueken and the Struggle to Define Catholicism*. New York: Oxford University Press, 2014.

Lees, Loretta, Tom Slater, and Elvin Wyly. *Gentrification*. London: Routledge, 2013.

Lefebvre, Henri. *The Production of Space*. Hoboken, NJ: Wiley, 1992.

Ley, David, and R. Bruce Martin. "Gentrification as Secularization: The Status of Religious Belief in the Post-industrial City." *Social Compass*, August 18, 2016.

Lindman, Janet Moore. *Bodies of Belief: Baptist Community in Early America*. Philadelphia: University of Pennsylvania Press, 2011.

Linkon, Sherry Lee. "Men without Work: White Working-Class Masculinity in Deindustrialization Fiction." *Contemporary Literature* 55, no. 1 (May 21, 2014): 148–67.

Lipman-Blumen, Jean. "Toward a Homosocial Theory of Sex Roles: An Explanation of the Sex Segregation of Social Institutions." *Signs* 1, no. 3 (April 1, 1976): 15–31.

Longhurst, Robyn, Elsie Ho, and Lynda Johnston. "Using 'the Body' as an 'Instrument of Research': Kimch'i and Pavlova." *Area* 40, no. 2 (2008): 208–17.

Loveland, Matthew T., and Margret Ksander. "Shepherds and Sheep: Parish Reconfiguration, Authority, and Activism in a Catholic Diocese." *Review of Religious Research* 56, no. 3 (September 1, 2014): 443–65.

Luhrmann, Tanya M. *When God Talks Back: Understanding the American Evangelical Relationship with God.* New York: Vintage, 2012.

Lumsden, Karen. "'Don't Ask a Woman to Do Another Woman's Job': Gendered Interactions and the Emotional Ethnographer." *Sociology* 43, no. 3 (2009): 497–513.

Lupkin, Paula. *Manhood Factories: YMCA Architecture and the Making of Modern Urban Culture.* Minneapolis: University of Minnesota Press, 2010.

Luzzatto, Sergio. *Padre Pio: Miracles and Politics in a Secular Age.* New York: Henry Holt, 2010.

Machado, Daisy L. "Santa Muerte: A Transgressing Saint Transgresses Borders." In *Borderland Religion*, edited by Daisy L. Machado, Bryan S. Turner, and Trygve Eiliv Wyller, 77–85. London: Routledge, 2018.

Madison, D. Soyini. "Co-performative Witnessing." *Cultural Studies* 21, no. 6 (November 1, 2007): 826–31.

Maffly-Kipp, Laurie F., Leigh E. Schmidt, and Mark Valeri, *Practicing Protestants Histories of Christian Life in America, 1630–1965.* Baltimore: Johns Hopkins University Press, 2006.

Maldonado-Estrada, Alyssa. "Catholic Devotion in the Americas." *Religion Compass* 13, no. 1 (January 2019): e12292.

———. "Loving Saint Paulinus: Patron Saint of Williamsburg, Brooklyn." *Global Catholic Review*, June 17, 2019.

———. "Tattoos as Sacramentals." *American Religion*, September 2019. www.americanreligion.org.

Mangano, Antonio. "Italian Tent Work in Brooklyn." *Baptist Home Mission Monthly* 27–28 (1905): 370–71.

Marinaccio, Rocco. "'Tea and Cookies. Diavolo!' Italian American Masculinity in John Fante's 'Wait until Spring, Bandini.'" *MELUS* 34, no. 3 (October 1, 2009): 43–69.

Martínez, María Elena. *Genealogical Fictions: Limpieza de Sangre, Religion, and Gender in Colonial Mexico.* Redwood City, CA: Stanford University Press, 2008.

Marwell, Nicole P. *Bargaining for Brooklyn: Community Organizations in the Entrepreneurial City.* Chicago: University of Chicago Press, 2009.

Mason, Michael Atwood. "'I Bow My Head to the Ground': The Creation of Bodily Experience in a Cuban American Santería Initiation." *Journal of American Folklore* 107, no. 423 (1994): 23–39.

———. *Living Santería: Rituals and Experiences in an Afro-Cuban Religion.* Washington, DC: Smithsonian Institution Press, 2002.

Matovina, Timothy M. *Guadalupe and Her Faithful: Latino Catholics in San Antonio, from Colonial Origins to the Present.* Baltimore: Johns Hopkins University Press, 2005.

———. "The National Parish and Americanization." *U.S. Catholic Historian* 17, no. 1 (1999): 45–58.

Mauss, Marcel. "Techniques of the Body." *Economy and Society* 2, no. 1 (February 1, 1973): 70–88.

Mayblin, Maya. *Gender, Catholicism, and Morality in Brazil: Virtuous Husbands, Powerful Wives*. New York: Springer, 2010.

Mazzei, Julie, and Erin E. O'Brien. "You Got It, So When Do You Flaunt It? Building Rapport, Intersectionality, and the Strategic Deployment of Gender in the Field." *Journal of Contemporary Ethnography* 38, no. 3 (June 1, 2009): 358–83.

McAlister, Elizabeth. "From Slave Revolt to a Blood Pact with Satan." In *The Idea of Haiti*, edited by Millery Polyné, 203–42. Minneapolis: University of Minnesota Press, 2013.

———. "The Madonna of 115th Street Revisited: Vodou and Haitian Catholicism in the Age of Transnationalism." In *Gatherings in Diaspora*, edited by R. Stephen Warner and Judith G. Wittner, 123–60. Philadelphia: Temple University Press, 1998.

———. *Rara! Vodou, Power, and Performance in Haiti and Its Diaspora*. Berkeley: University of California Press, 2002.

McCartin, James P. "Engendering Faith: American Catholics and Gender History." *American Quarterly* 62, no. 4 (2010): 977–88.

———. "The Sacred Heart of Jesus, Thérèse of Lisieux, and the Transformation of U.S. Catholic Piety, 1865–1940." *U.S. Catholic Historian* 25, no. 2 (April 1, 2007): 53–67.

McCowin, David J. "'For Faith and for Freedom': American Catholic Manhood and the Holy Name Society in Boston, 1870–1960." PhD dissertation, Boston College, 2011.

McDannell, Colleen. *Catholics in the Movies*. New York: Oxford University Press, 2008.

———. *The Christian Home in Victorian America, 1840–900*. Bloomington: Indiana University Press, 1994.

———. "Interpreting Things: Material Culture Studies and American Religion." *Religion* 21, no. 4 (October 1, 1991): 371–87.

———. *Material Christianity: Religion and Popular Culture in America*. New Haven, CT: Yale University Press, 1998.

———. *The Spirit of Vatican II: A History of Catholic Reform in America*. New York: Basic Books, 2011.

———. "'True Men as We Need Them': Catholicism and the Irish-American Male." *American Studies* 27, no. 2 (October 1, 1986): 19–36.

McGee, Adam M. "Haitian Vodou and Voodoo: Imagined Religion and Popular Culture." *Studies in Religion / Sciences Religieuses* 41, no. 2 (June 1, 2012): 231–56.

———. "Imagined Voodoo: Terror, Sex, and Racism in American Popular Culture." PhD dissertation, Harvard University, June 6, 2014.

McGreevy, John T. *Parish Boundaries: The Catholic Encounter with Race in the Twentieth-Century Urban North*. Chicago: University of Chicago Press, 1998.

McGuire, Meredith B. *Lived Religion: Faith and Practice in Everyday Life*. New York: Oxford University Press, 2008.

McMahon, Eileen M. *What Parish Are You From? A Chicago Irish Community and Race Relations.* Lexington: University Press of Kentucky, 1995.

Mears, Ashley. "Ethnography as Precarious Work." *Sociological Quarterly* 54, no. 1 (February 1, 2013): 20–34.

Merrills, Andrew, and Richard Miles. *The Vandals.* Hoboken, NJ: Wiley, 2009.

Messner, Michael A. *Politics of Masculinities: Men in Movements.* Thousand Oaks, CA: SAGE, 1997.

Meyer, Birgit. "How Pictures Matter: Religious Objects and the Imagination in Ghana." In *Objects and Imagination: Perspectives on Materialization and Meaning,* edited by Oivind Fuglerud and Leon Wainwright, 160–83. New York: Berghahn Books, 2015.

Mian, Nadia A. "'Prophets-for-Profits': Redevelopment and the Altering Urban Religious Landscape." *Urban Studies* 45, no. 10 (September 1, 2008): 2143–61.

Mitchell, Jon P. "A Catholic Body? Miracles, Secularity, and the Porous Self in Malta." In Norget, Napolitano, and Mayblin, *Anthropology of Catholicism,* 211–26.

———. "Performances of Masculinity in a Maltese 'Festa.'" In *Recasting Ritual: Performance Media Identity,* edited by Felicia Hughes-Freeland and Mary M. Crain, 68–92. London: Routledge, 1998.

———. "Ritual Structure and Ritual Agency. 'Rebounding Violence' and Maltese Festa." *Social Anthropology* 12, no. 1 (February 2004): 57–75.

Moore, Brenna. "Friendship and the Cultivation of Religious Sensibilities." *Journal of the American Academy of Religion* 83, no. 2 (June 1, 2015): 437–63.

Moore, Deborah Dash. *Urban Origins of American Judaism.* Athens: University of Georgia Press, 2014.

Morgan, David. *Images at Work: The Material Culture of Enchantment.* New York: Oxford University Press, 2018.

———. *Religion and Material Culture: The Matter of Belief.* London: Routledge, 2010.

———. "Rhetoric of the Heart: Figuring the Body in Devotion to the Sacred Heart of Jesus." In Houtman and Meyer, *Things,* 90–126.

———. *Visual Piety: A History and Theory of Popular Religious Images.* Berkeley: University of California Press, 1998.

Morgan, David, and Sally M. Promey. *The Visual Culture of American Religions.* Berkeley: University of California Press, 2001.

Moss, Jeremiah. *Vanishing New York: How a Great City Lost Its Soul.* New York: HarperCollins, 2017.

Muhammad, Khalil Gibran. *The Condemnation of Blackness: Race, Crime, and the Making of Modern Urban America.* Cambridge, MA: Harvard University Press, 2010.

Mumford, Lewis, and Robert Wojtowicz. *Sidewalk Critic: Lewis Mumford's Writings on New York.* Princeton, NJ: Princeton Architectural Press, 1998.

Mundey, Peter, Hilary Davidson, and Patricia Snell Herzog. "Making Money Sacred: How Two Church Cultures Translate Mundane Money into Distinct Sacralized Frames of Giving." *Sociology of Religion* 72, no. 3 (2011): 303–26.

Nabhan-Warren, Kristy. "Embodied Research and Writing: A Case for Phenomenolog-
ically Oriented Religious Studies Ethnographies." *Journal of the American Academy
of Religion* 79, no. 2 (June 1, 2011): 378–407.
———. *The Virgin of El Barrio: Marian Apparitions, Catholic Evangelizing, and Mexican
American Activism.* New York: New York University Press, 2005.
———. "Working toward an Inclusive Narrative: A Call for Interdisciplinarity and Eth-
nographic Reflexivity in Catholic Studies." In *The Catholic Studies Reader,* edited
by James T. Fisher and Margaret M. McGuinness, 309–28. New York: Fordham
University Press, 2011.
Neary, Timothy B. "Black-Belt Catholic Space: African-American Parishes in Interwar
Chicago." *U.S. Catholic Historian* 18, no. 4 (2000): 76–91.
———. *Crossing Parish Boundaries: Race, Sports, and Catholic Youth in Chicago, 1914–
1954.* Chicago: University of Chicago Press, 2016.
Nelson, Louis. *Beauty of Holiness: Anglicanism and Architecture in Colonial South
Carolina: Anglicanism and Architecture in Colonial South Carolina.* Chapel Hill:
University of North Carolina Press, 2009.
Nesvig, Martin Austin, ed. *Local Religion in Colonial Mexico.* Albuquerque: University
of New Mexico Press, 2006.
Norget, Kristin, Valentina Napolitano, and Maya Mayblin, eds. *The Anthropology of
Catholicism: A Reader.* Berkeley: University of California Press, 2017.
Noyes, Dorothy. *Fire in the Plaça: Catalan Festival Politics after Franco.* Philadelphia:
University of Pennsylvania Press, 2012.
O'Neill, Kevin Lewis. "Beyond Broken: Affective Spaces and the Study of American
Religion." *Journal of the American Academy of Religion* 81, no. 4 (December 1, 2013):
1093–116.
Orsi, Robert A. "Abundant History: Marian Apparitions as Alternative Modernity."
Historically Speaking 9, no. 7 (2008): 12–16.
———. *Between Heaven and Earth: The Religious Worlds People Make and the Scholars
Who Study Them.* Princeton, NJ: Princeton University Press, 2005.
———, ed. *Gods of the City: Religion and the American Urban Landscape.* Bloomington:
Indiana University Press, 1999.
———. *History and Presence.* Cambridge, MA: Harvard University Press, 2016.
———. "I'm Starting to Think This Is Not about Catholics." *Fides et Historia* 44, no. 2
(Summer 2012): 80–83.
———. "'The Infant of Prague's Nightie': The Devotional Origins of Contemporary
Catholic Memory." *U.S. Catholic Historian* 21, no. 2 (2003): 1–18.
———. *The Madonna of 115th Street: Faith and Community in Italian Harlem, 1880–
1950.* New Haven, CT: Yale University Press, 2002.
———. "The Religious Boundaries of an Inbetween People: Street Feste and the Prob-
lem of the Dark-Skinned Other in Italian Harlem, 1920–1990." *American Quarterly*
44, no. 3 (September 1, 1992): 313–47.
———. "Roundtable on Ethnography and Religion: Doing Religious Studies with Your
Whole Body." *Practical Matters,* no. 2 (Spring 2013): 1–6.

———. *Thank You, St. Jude: Women's Devotion to the Patron Saint of Hopeless Causes.* New Haven, CT: Yale University Press, 1996.

———. "What Did Women Think They Were Doing When They Prayed to Saint Jude?" *U.S. Catholic Historian* 8, nos. 1/2 (1989): 67–79.

Osman, Suleiman. *The Invention of Brownstone Brooklyn: Gentrification and the Search for Authenticity in Postwar New York.* New York: Oxford University Press, 2011.

O'Toole, James M., ed. *Habits of Devotion: Catholic Religious Practice in Twentieth-Century America.* Ithaca, NY: Cornell University Press, 2005.

Pascoe, C. J. *Dude, You're a Fag: Masculinity and Sexuality in High School.* Berkeley: University of California Press, 2011.

Pasquier, Michael. *Fathers on the Frontier: French Missionaries and the Roman Catholic Priesthood in the United States, 1789–1870.* New York: Oxford University Press, 2010.

Patch, Jason. "The Embedded Landscape of Gentrification." *Visual Studies* 19 (October 2004): 169–87.

Peacock, James. "Those the Dead Left Behind: Gentrification and Haunting in Contemporary Brooklyn Fictions." *Studies in American Fiction* 46, no. 1 (July 18, 2019): 131–56.

Peña, Elaine A. *Performing Piety: Making Space Sacred with the Virgin of Guadalupe.* Berkeley: University of California Press, 2011.

Pérez, Elizabeth. "Cooking for the Gods: Sensuous Ethnography, Sensory Knowledge, and the Kitchen in Lucumí Tradition." *Religion* 41, no. 4 (December 1, 2011): 665–83.

———. *Religion in the Kitchen: Cooking, Talking, and the Making of Black Atlantic Traditions.* New York: New York University Press, 2016.

Perez, Gina. *The Near Northwest Side Story: Migration, Displacement, and Puerto Rican Families.* Berkeley: University of California Press, 2004.

Perrone, Dina. "Gender and Sexuality in the Field: A Female Ethnographer's Experience Researching Drug Use in Dance Clubs." *Substance Use and Misuse* 45, no. 5 (April 2010): 717–35.

Pierce, Jennifer L. "Lawyers, Lethal Weapons, and Ethnographic Authority: Reflections on Fieldwork for Gender Trials." In *The Researcher Experience in Qualitative Research*, edited by Susan Diemert Moch and Marie F. Gates, 146–62. Thousand Oaks, CA: SAGE, 2000.

Plester, Barbara. "'Take It Like a Man!' Performing Hegemonic Masculinity through Organizational Humour." *Ephemera* 15, no. 3 (2015): 539.

Posen, I. Sheldon. "Storing Contexts: The Brooklyn Giglio as Folk Art." In *Folk Art and Worlds*, edited by J. M. Vlach and S. J. Bronner, 171–91. Ann Arbor: UMI Research Press, 1986.

Posen, I. Sheldon, Joseph Sciorra, and Martha Cooper. "Brooklyn's Dancing Tower." *Natural History* 92, no. 6 (1983): 30–37.

Primeggia, Salvatore, and Pamela Primeggia. "Every Year, the Feast." *Italian Americana* 7, no. 2 (1983): 4–12.

Primeggia, Salvatore, and Joseph A. Varacalli. "The Sacred and Profane among Italian American Catholics: The Giglio Feast." *International Journal of Politics, Culture, and Society* 9, no. 3 (1996): 423–49.

Primiano, Leonard Norman. "Vernacular Religion and the Search for Method in Religious Folklife." *Western Folklore* 54, no. 1 (January 1995): 37–56.

Promey, Sally M. "Chalkware, Plaster, Plaster of Paris." *MAVCOR*, November 11, 2013. www.mavcor.yale.edu.

———. *Sensational Religion*. New Haven, CT: Yale University Press, 2014.

Puar, Jasbir K. *Terrorist Assemblages: Homonationalism in Queer Times*. Durham, NC: Duke University Press, 2018.

Putney, Clifford. *Muscular Christianity: Manhood and Sports in Protestant America, 1880–1920*. Cambridge, MA: Harvard University Press, 2001.

Ramirez, Hernan. "Masculinity in the Workplace: The Case of Mexican Immigrant Gardeners." *Men and Masculinities* 14, no. 1 (2011): 97–116.

Rauscher, Raymond Charles, and Salim Momtaz. *Brooklyn's Bushwick—Urban Renewal in New York, USA: Community, Planning and Sustainable Environments*. New York: Springer, 2014.

Rey, Terry. "Marian Devotion at a Haitian Catholic Parish in Miami: The Feast of Our Lady of Perpetual Help." *Journal of Contemporary Religion* 19, no. 3 (October 1, 2004): 353–74.

Rey, Terry, and Alex Stepick. *Crossing the Water and Keeping the Faith: Haitian Religion in Miami*. New York: New York University Press, 2013.

Richman, Karen E. *Migration and Vodou*. Gainesville: University Press of Florida, 2005.

Richter, Philip. "From Backstage to Front: The Role of the Vestry in Managing Clergy Self-Presentation." In *Seeing Religion: Toward a Visual Sociology of Religion*, edited by Roman R. Williams, 103–21. London: Routledge, 2015.

Ridgely, Susan B. *When I Was a Child: Children's Interpretations of First Communion*. Chapel Hill: University of North Carolina Press, 2006.

Rieder, Jonathan. *Canarsie: The Jews and Italians of Brooklyn Against Liberalism*. Cambridge, MA: Harvard University Press, 1987.

Risman, Barbara J. "From Doing to Undoing: Gender as We Know It." *Gender and Society* 23, no. 1 (2009): 81–84.

Roediger, David R. *Working toward Whiteness: How America's Immigrants Became White: The Strange Journey from Ellis Island to the Suburbs*. New York: Basic Books, 2006.

Rotella, Carlo. *October Cities: The Redevelopment of Urban Literature*. Berkeley: University of California Press, 1998.

Rotundo, E. Anthony. *American Manhood Transformations in Masculinity from the Revolution to the Modern Era*. New York: Basic Books, 1993.

Sabean, David Warren. "Descent and Alliance: Cultural Meanings of Blood in the Baroque." In Johnson et al., *Blood and Kinship*, 144–74.

Sabean, David Warren, and Simon Teuscher. "Introduction." In Johnson et al., *Blood and Kinship*, 1–17.

Said, Edward W. *Orientalism*. New York: Vintage, 1979.

Sallee, Margaret W., and Frank Harris. "Gender Performance in Qualitative Studies of Masculinities." *Qualitative Research* 11, no. 4 (August 1, 2011): 409–29.

Samudra, Jaida Kim. "Memory in Our Body: Thick Participation and the Translation of Kinesthetic Experience." *American Ethnologist* 35, no. 4 (November 1, 2008): 665–81.

Sanders, Joel, ed. *Stud: Architectures of Masculinity*. New York: Princeton Architectural Press, 1996.

Sanjek, Roger. "The Ethnographic Present." *Man* 26, no. 4 (1991): 609–28.

Savastano, Peter. "Changing St. Gerard's Clothes: An Exercise in Italian-American Catholic Devotion and Material Culture." In *Italian Folk: Vernacular Culture in Italian-American Lives*, edited by Joseph Sciorra, 171–87. New York: Fordham University Press, 2010.

Schildkrout, Enid. "Inscribing the Body." *Annual Review of Anthropology* 33 (January 1, 2004): 319–44.

Schiller, Nina Glick, and Georges Eugene Fouron. *Georges Woke Up Laughing: Long-Distance Nationalism and the Search for Home*. Durham, NC: Duke University Press, 2001.

Schneider, Cathy Lisa. *Police Power and Race Riots: Urban Unrest in Paris and New York*. Philadelphia: University of Pennsylvania Press, 2014.

Schrock, Douglas, and Michael Schwalbe. "Men, Masculinity, and Manhood Acts." *Annual Review of Sociology* 35 (2009): 277–95.

Schwartz, Joel. *The New York Approach: Robert Moses, Urban Liberals, and Redevelopment of the Inner City*. Columbus: Ohio State University Press, 1993.

Sciorra, Joseph. *Built with Faith: Italian American Imagination and Catholic Material Culture in New York City*. Knoxville: University of Tennessee Press, 2015.

———. "'O' Giglio e Paradiso': Celebration and Identity in an Urban Ethnic Community." *Urban Resources* 5, no. 43 (Spring 1989): 15–20, 44–45.

———. "Religious Processions in Italian Williamsburg." *Drama Review* 29, no. 3 (1985): 65–81.

———. "We Go Where the Italians Live: Religious Processions as Ethnic and Territorial Markers in a Multi-ethnic Brooklyn Neighborhood." In Orsi, *Gods of the City*, 310–40.

Scales, Chad F. *The Secular Spectacle: Performing Religion in a Southern Town*. New York: Oxford University Press, 2013.

Sedgwick, Eve Kosofsky. *Between Men: English Literature and Male Homosocial Desire*. New York: Columbia University Press, 1985.

Seitz, John C. "The Lives of Priests." *American Catholic Studies* 127, no. 2 (August 7, 2016): 18–23.

———. *No Closure: Catholic Practice and Boston's Parish Shutdowns*. Cambridge, MA: Harvard University Press, 2011.

Shkuda, Aaron. *The Lofts of SoHo: Gentrification, Art, and Industry in New York, 1950–1980*. Chicago: University of Chicago Press, 2016.

Sigmon, Casey. "The Gospel According to Her: A Qualitative Study of Christian Women and Tattoo Culture." Paper presented at the Harvard Divinity School Ways of Knowing Conference, October 24, 2014.

Simmel, Georg. "Adornment." In *The Sociology of Georg Simmel*, edited by Kurt H. Wolff, 338–44. Glencoe, IL: Free Press, 1950.

Skinner, Jonathan. "Leading Questions and Body Memories: A Case of Phenomenology and Physical Ethnography in the Dance Interview." In *The Ethnographic Self as Resource: Writing Memory and Experience into Ethnography*, edited by Peter Collins and Anselma Gallinat, 11–28. New York: Berghahn Books, 2010.

Sklar, Deidre. *Dancing with the Virgin: Body and Faith in the Fiesta of Tortugas, New Mexico*. Berkeley: University of California Press, 2001.

Smith, Christian, Michael O. Emerson, and Patricia Snell. *Passing the Plate: Why American Christians Don't Give Away More Money*. New York: Oxford University Press, 2008.

Smith, Neil. *The New Urban Frontier: Gentrification and the Revanchist City*. London: Routledge, 2005.

Snooks, Gina. "Enshrined in Flesh: Tattoos and Contemporary Women's Spirituality." In Davidson, *Tattoo Project*, 129–32.

Snyder, Jon. "Bodies of Water: The Mediterranean in Italian Baroque Theater." *California Italian Studies* 1, no. 1 (2010): 1–23.

Soyer, Michaela. "Off the Corner and into the Kitchen: Entering a Male-Dominated Research Setting as a Woman." *Qualitative Research* 14, no. 4 (August 1, 2014): 459–72.

Spickard, James V., Shawn Landres, and Meredith B. McGuire. *Personal Knowledge and Beyond: Reshaping the Ethnography of Religion*. New York: New York University Press, 2002.

Sponsler, Claire. *Ritual Imports: Performing Medieval Drama in America*. Ithaca, NY: Cornell University Press, 2004.

Stabrowski, Filip. "New-Build Gentrification and the Everyday Displacement of Polish Immigrant Tenants in Greenpoint, Brooklyn." *Antipode* 46, no. 3 (June 1, 2014): 794–815.

Stoller, Paul. *Sensuous Scholarship*. Philadelphia: University of Pennsylvania Press, 1997.

———. *The Taste of Ethnographic Things: The Senses in Anthropology*. Philadelphia: University of Pennsylvania Press, 1989.

Sussman, Herbert L. *Masculine Identities: The History and Meanings of Manliness*. Santa Barbara: Praeger, 2012.

Swift, Christopher. "Robot Saints." *Preternature* 4, no. 1 (2015): 52–77.

Taves, Ann. *The Household of Faith: Roman Catholic Devotions in Mid-Nineteenth Century America*. South Bend, IN: University of Notre Dame, 1986.

Tentler, Leslie Woodcock. "Evidence and Historical Confidence." *American Catholic Studies* 127, no. 2 (August 7, 2016): 10–13.

———. "On the Margins: The State of American Catholic History." *American Quarterly* 45, no. 1 (1993): 104–27.

Thornton, Brendan Jamal. *Negotiating Respect: Pentecostalism, Masculinity, and the Politics of Spiritual Authority in the Dominican Republic.* Gainesville: University Press of Florida, 2016.

Thurnell-Read, Thomas. "What Happens on Tour: The Premarital Stag Tour, Homosocial Bonding, and Male Friendship." *Men and Masculinities* 15, no. 3 (August 1, 2012): 249–70.

Tolino, John V. "Solving the Italian Problem." *Ecclesiastical Review* 99 (September 1938).

Tomasi, Silvano M. *Piety and Power: The Role of the Italian Parishes in the New York Metropolitan Area, 1880–1930.* New York: Center for Migration Studies, 1975.

Treviño, Roberto R. *The Church in the Barrio: Mexican American Ethno-Catholicism in Houston.* Chapel Hill: University of North Carolina Press, 2006.

Trout, Dennis. "Christianizing the Nolan Countryside: Animal Sacrifice at the Tomb of St. Felix." *Journal of Early Christian Studies* 3, no. 3 (1995): 281–98.

———. *Paulinus of Nola: Life, Letters, and Poems.* Berkeley: University of California Press, 1999.

Trudeau, Stephanie. "Born to Giglio." *Voices* 31, nos. 1/2 (Spring 2005): 20–21.

Tweed, Thomas. *Crossing and Dwelling: A Theory of Religion.* Cambridge, MA: Harvard University Press, 2009.

———. "On Moving Across: Translocative Religion and the Interpreter's Position." *Journal of the American Academy of Religion* 70, no. 2 (2002): 253–77.

———. *Our Lady of the Exile: Diasporic Religion at a Cuban Catholic Shrine in Miami.* New York: Oxford University Press, 2002.

van den Hoek, Annewies, and John J. Herrmann. "Paulinus of Nola, Courtyards, and Canthari." *Harvard Theological Review* 93, no. 3 (2000): 173–219.

Van Osselaer, Tine. "Christening Masculinity? Catholic Action and Men in Interwar Belgium." *Gender and History* 21, no. 2 (August 1, 2009): 380–401.

———. "'Heroes of the Heart': Ideal Men in the Sacred Heart Devotion." *Journal of Men, Masculinities and Spirituality* 3, no. 1 (January 2009): 22–40.

Varacalli, Joseph A., Salvatore Primeggia, Salvatore J. LaGumina, and Donald J. D'Elia. *The Saints in the Lives of Italian-Americans.* Stony Brook, NY: Forum Italicum, 1999.

Vásquez, Manuel A. *More Than Belief: A Materialist Theory of Religion.* New York: Oxford University Press, 2011.

Vecoli, Rudolph J. *Cult and Occult in Italian-American Culture: The Persistence of a Religious Heritage.* Saint Paul: University of Minnesota Press, 1977.

———. "Prelates and Peasants: Italian Immigrants and the Catholic Church." *Journal of Social History* 2, no. 3 (1969): 217–68.

Wacquant, Loïc. *Body and Soul: Notebooks of an Apprentice Boxer*. New York: Oxford University Press, 2006.

———. "Carnal Connections: On Embodiment, Apprenticeship, and Membership." *Qualitative Sociology* 28, no. 4 (2005): 445–74.

———. "Habitus as Topic and Tool: Reflections on Becoming a Prizefighter." *Qualitative Research in Psychology* 8, no. 1 (January 2011): 81–92.

Walkerdine, Valerie, and Luis Jimenez, *Gender, Work and Community After Deindustrialisation: A Psychosocial Approach to Affect*. New York: Springer, 2012.

Wallock, Leonard. "The Myth of the Master Builder: Robert Moses, New York, and the Dynamics of Metropolitan Development since World War II." *Journal of Urban History* 17, no. 4 (August 1, 1991): 339–62.

Weiner, Isaac. *Religion Out Loud: Religious Sound, Public Space, and American Pluralism*. New York: New York University Press, 2013.

Weisenfeld, Judith. *New World A-Coming: Black Religion and Racial Identity during the Great Migration*. New York: New York University Press, 2017.

Wenger, Beth S. "Federation Men: The Masculine World of New York Jewish Philanthropy, 1880–1945." *American Jewish History* 101, no. 3 (August 2, 2017): 377–99.

West, Candace, and Don H. Zimmerman. "Accounting for Doing Gender." *Gender and Society* 23, no. 1 (2009): 112–22.

———. "Doing Gender." *Gender and Society* 1, no. 2 (1987): 125–51.

White, Deborah Gray. *Lost in the USA: American Identity from the Promise Keepers to the Million Mom March*. Champaign: University of Illinois Press, 2017.

Whitehead, Amy. *Religious Statues and Personhood: Testing the Role of Materiality*. London: Bloomsbury, 2013.

Whyte, William Foote. *Street Corner Society: The Social Structure of an Italian Slum*. Chicago: University of Chicago Press, 2012.

Wimmer, Andreas. *Ethnic Boundary Making: Institutions, Power, Networks*. New York: Oxford University Press, 2013.

Winchester, Daniel. "Embodying the Faith: Religious Practice and the Making of a Muslim Moral Habitus." *Social Forces* 86, no. 4 (July 20, 2008): 1753–80.

Wise, Sheila J. "Redefining Black Masculinity and Manhood: Successful Black Gay Men Speak Out." *Journal of African American Studies* 5, no. 4 (2001): 3–22.

Woodstock, Louise. "Tattoo Therapy: Storying the Self on Reality TV in Neoliberal Times." *Journal of Popular Culture* 47, no. 4 (August 1, 2014): 780–99.

Woodward, Kath. "Hanging Out and Hanging About: Insider/Outsider Research in the Sport of Boxing." *Ethnography* 9, no. 4 (December 1, 2008): 536–60.

Wuthnow, Robert J. "Taking Talk Seriously: Religious Discourse as Social Practice." *Journal for the Scientific Study of Religion* 50, no. 1 (March 1, 2011): 1–21.

Zelizer, Viviana A. Rotman. *The Social Meaning of Money*. Princeton, NJ: Princeton University Press, 1997.

Zubrzycki, Geneviève. "Aesthetic Revolt and the Remaking of National Identity in Québec, 1960–1969." *Theory and Society* 42, no. 5 (July 25, 2013): 423–75.

Zukin, Sharon. "Changing Landscapes of Power: Opulence and the Urge for Authenticity." *International Journal of Urban and Regional Research* 33, no. 2 (2009): 543–53.

———. "Consuming Authenticity." *Cultural Studies* 22, no. 5 (September 1, 2008): 724–48.

———. *Naked City: The Death and Life of Authentic Urban Places.* New York: Oxford University Press, 2009.

Zukin, Sharon, Valerie Trujillo, Peter Frase, Danielle Jackson, Tim Recuber, and Abraham Walker. "New Retail Capital and Neighborhood Change: Boutiques and Gentrification in New York City." *City and Community* 8, no. 1 (2009): 47–64.

INDEX

joking, 99, 103–4, 135–36; in basement, 78, 79; in creativity and dedication, 89; about money, 217–18; about presence, 93; in Questua, 148–49. *See also* homosociality, ethnography, and joking
Joseph (saint), 90, 176

Kimmel, Michael, 144–45
kinesthetics, 20, 21; belonging and, 19; competence and, 62, 65; darkness and, 26; as devotion, 65, 67; ethnographic access/practice and, 65; of lifters, 19
Knights of Columbus, 35
Krase, Jerome, 203

labor, 76, 80, 121–22; artistic, 89–90, 98, 120; flea market, 114–15, 132; logistic, 21, 28, 106, 115–16, 123; ride tickets, 133–34. *See also* basement; money
Lahiri, Shompa, 234n43
landscapes, 230n55
languages, 64, 67, 176–77
Latour, Bruno, 77
laughter, 101
Lázaro (saint), 75
lieutenants, 36, 50, 85, 223; in public masculinity, 140–42
lifeblood: feast and, 211; generations and, 111, 112; identity and, 211; insularity and, 211
lifters (*paranza*), 5, 24, 35–36, 37, 42–45, 46, 47, 64–66, 84, 110, 123, 219; capability of, 221; Cavemen as, 44; in childhood, 14, 31, 36–37, 44; in children's giglio, 68, 71, 73, 169; clothing of, 26, 140; devotion of, 65–66; generations of, 44, 47; in hierarchy, 36; kinesthetics of, 19; at planning meeting, 123; in song, 155–56; Turk related to, 61
Line of the March, 72, 73, 161–62; apprentice capo in, 157–58; community in, 157; decorations in, 157; description of, 138–39, 157; loss in, 158–60; men of

steel in, 155–56; prayer in, 158; sexuality in, 138–39; women in, 158–60
Lipman-Blumen, Jean, 162, 238n20
logistic labor, 21, 28, 106, 115–16, 123
Lucumí, 234n2
Lumsden, Karen, 236n28
Lupkin, Paula, 237n1
Lynch, Bernard, 241n36
Lynch, Thomas, 241n36

Madonna. *See* Our Lady of Mount Carmel
The Madonna of 115th Street (Orsi), 9
male lineage, 168
Manhattan, 201–2, 206
Manhattan Avenue, 152–54
manhood, 11, 139, 144; route to, 221–22
manhood and masculinity: capos and, 143; comparison of, 144–45; fatherhood in, 143–44; performance in, 144–45; race in, 145; varieties of, 143
Manhood Factories (Lupkin), 237n1
manual labor. *See* basement
marital relationships, 102–3
Marwell, Nicole, 197, 241n22, 244n39
Mary. *See* Our Lady of Mount Carmel
masculine capital, 7–18, 20–21
masculinity, 6, 12–13, 19, 139–40, 143–45; dressing up as Turk and, 53–54; Williamsburg related to, 23. *See also* public masculinity
masculinity and Church work: business man in, 124–25; Century Board in, 117–18; competition in, 114; executive labor in, 121–22; feminization in, 114–15, 120–21; Jewish philanthropy and, 120; M&RFM in, 118–20; recognition in, 115–16; solicitations in, 123–24; suburbanization in, 122; success as money in, 122–23
masculinization, 12, 114, 119
Master in Business Administration (MBA), 124–25, 126
material culture, 28, 36, 98

ABOUT THE AUTHOR

Alyssa Maldonado-Estrada is Assistant Professor in the Department of Religion at Kalamazoo College. She received her PhD in religion from Princeton University and hails from New York City's Lower East Side.

Lightning Source UK Ltd.
Milton Keynes UK
UKHW012059081120
372905UK00014B/213